LANCASHIRE'S
SACRED LANDSCAPE

LANCASHIRE'S SACRED LANDSCAPE

EDITED BY LINDA SEVER

The
History
Press

This second printing is dedicated to all those who for generations have walked and appreciated the beauty of the landscape of Lancashire and especially for those who are committed to protecting and saving the land from fracking. This includes:

Frack Free Lancashire:
https://www.facebook.com/FrackFreeLancashire/?fref=ts

Frack Free Chorley and South Ribble:
http://www.frackfreechorley.com/
https://www.facebook.com/FrackfreeChorley/?fref=ts

Bolton Against Fracking:
https://www.facebook.com/groups/186187894906295/?fref=ts

Cover image: Phil Davies

First published 2010

The History Press
The Mill, Brimscombe Port
Stroud, Gloucestershire, GL5 2QG
www.thehistorypress.co.uk

Reprinted 2015

2010 © Linda Sever for selection, Introduction and Chapter 5;
individual chapters © the contributors

British Library Cataloguing in Publication Data.
A catalogue record for this book is available from the British Library.

ISBN 978 0 7524 5587 7

Typesetting and origination by The History Press
Printed in Great Britain

CONTENTS

ACKNOWLEDGEMENTS

There are so many people to thank for bringing this book to print. Firstly, all the contributors for their enthusiasm and prompt submission of chapters, with particular thanks to Sara Vernon for the conversations which led to the submission of the book proposal. Secondly, thanks to the photographers and especially to Karen Lawrinson who spent such a good deal of time driving to the sites to take photographs for chapters 3, 4, 5 and 8.

To my mother and friends (and cats!), especially Jenny B, Jen P, Sarah (who sadly passed away before the completion of this book), Kate, Tina and, of course, Chris, whose humour and encouragement kept me going even when technology didn't. Also, thank you to Peter Wobser, who rescued the chapters that got lost somewhere in the ether when the flash drive failed!

Finally, a very special thanks to Mick who has visited and revisited many of the sites with me. Thank you for joining me on the journey.

FOREWORD

When we hear the words 'sacred landscape', Lancashire is not the first area of Britain that comes to mind. This book will come as a surprise to many. Nevertheless, 'sacred landscapes' of Lancashire there indeed are, and of many kinds.

But what is a sacred landscape? The concept of 'sacredness' is treated very differently within the various religions or spiritualities that make up the spiritual scene of Britain and it may be worth recollecting that people who profess 'no religion', humanism or atheism, may have been powerfully touched by beauty within landscape, by richness of biodiversity, or by a personal, family or historical connection that somehow matters, that strikes a chord, that means the relationship they form with that place becomes part of who they are, a piece of their identity.

Some religious traditions hold that it is we, humanity, or at least some of us (those particularly close to the divine, or those holding particular positions), who confer 'sacredness' on a particular place. The act of consecrating a church comes to mind. A place so consecrated can be deconsecrated. Hubert (1994) has pointed to the differences between many indigenous spiritual traditions around the world and the Christian concept of consecration. If sacredness is a property of the landscape, not conferred by human people, it cannot be taken away. Are there sacred sites in the midst of our cities, where huge constructions of steel, glass and concrete now stand? Are our own houses and workplaces built on once-sacred places and, if so, does that sacredness persist, though unrecognised? Implicit in this discussion is the concept of people as only one of many species, or 'kinds of people' who may relate to the landscape. For instance, Harvey's discussions of 'New Animism' (2005) may have a bearing on sacredness and how it is experienced.

As an example, several years ago I was in Iceland at the winter solstice and interviewed Jörmundur Ingi Hansen, then head of the Ásatrúarmenn, a group recognised by the Icelandic Government as reconstituting the 'old way' of Icelandic spirituality or religion. We talked about landwights or *Vættur*, beings (*wight* is from Old English *wiht*, a being, implying sentience) well established in folklore of Iceland and Scandinavia. What was a landwight, I asked, and he gave me an explanation from a friend: a being that has earth, rock, or mountains for a body. A difficult concept for a twenty-first-century Briton to understand, and one that is not definitive, as there are many differing understandings of this folkloric – or spiritual – concept. And how did one know where a landwight had its being?

> … this is usually the idea in Iceland, that the landwights are tied to a spot in the landscape, to a huge rock, to a mountain, or to a specially beautiful place. A friend of mine has given a definition of how you can know where there is a landwight, or at least a particularly strong one … you will know where it is because there things are a little better. The grass is a little greener, all the colours of the flowers are a little bit, ah, brighter, and the bird song is more lilting and beautiful, than just a few yards away.

> Interview 1998, discussed in Blain & Wallis 2002

Is this a form of sacredness of place? If so, how do we – or how have we through history and prehistory – marked or recorded that intensification of landscape and meaning? Perhaps with our meeting-places, stone circles, churches and other monuments, or perhaps when our poetry, songs and stories beome legend? And if so, what happens when this place becomes part of a city, built up, concreted over, or neglected? Or what happens when this place has been forgotten or ignored for years, but then begins to attract attention once again, when people come to it to pay their respects, or to plant trees or bulbs, give honour to the place, see it as part of a complex network of associated places or sites, and birdsong begins to return? And what of the claim that all land, all landscape, is sacred? This, too, is part of many indigenous and pre-Christian traditions and understandings. I can see the potential here for a theology of place and sacredness that goes beyond the scope of this book, but to which this book will make an important contribution.

In discussing (theorising, rejoicing in) landscape, let us not forget the issues that surround many landscapes today. Sacred landscapes are not only, or necessarily, pretty places where we admire views, ancestors and meanings interpreted for us by friendly heritage management. Landscape is contested, and has been for a very long time – fought over, by battle and in the courts of law. There are winners and losers in every period of history, relating not only to ownership or mineral rights, but to how landscape is regarded and how we appropriate, listen to, steward or guard areas of the land, forests, trees, rivers and the 'built environment' that goes back far beyond our day, holding its own traces of sacredness. In stating the sacredness of place we enter the dimensions of legal as well as spiritual politics, and tensions between archaeology, spirituality, environmental campaigns and various forms of 'use' of the land, appropriations and exclusions (Bender & Winer 2001; Blain & Wallis 2007). How is sacredness attested and celebrated, and how are both celebration and sacredness negotiated?

This book is wide-ranging in its scope. The reader will meet many conceptualisations of 'sacredness' and indeed of 'landscape', and tracings of spirit and divinity through place names, archaeology, history and personal understanding. The focus on Lancashire meets a need, alerting people to what is here, to what is around them: places, traditions, folklores and heritage. For my own part, I can regard it in part as a gazetteer and guide to where I should look, as well as a contribution to those dialogues on sacredness and heritage that we need to explore today. I do not live in Lancashire, but over the Pennines in Sheffield, and my own ancestry and relationships with landscape lie, for the most part, rather further north. But I recall the family stories of one John Pendlebury, a handloom weaver by trade and an ex-soldier who, we were told, had walked from Wigan to Paisley for work. What were the landscapes he knew and for how long did the stories he knew (and which I do not) lie in the folklores of the industrialising areas of Bolton, Hindley and Wigan – from the boggarts and fairies of legend and their continuing presence within a Christian society, the divisions in that society and religious strife, further back to Viking settlements, Saxon influences, to the Roman presence and before to the mists of prehistory? Readers of this book will find suggestions, speculations, guidance, material to stimulate them to find out more about the sacred landscape of Lancashire and the many interpretations it may hold.

Jenny Blain
Sheffield Hallam University

ABOUT THE AUTHORS

Derek Berryman is a former head teacher who after retirement took an MA degree in Anglo-Saxon studies at the University of Manchester. At the same time he learned archaeology with the Extra-Mural department. Derek's other interests are geology and mountain walking. He has ascended Kilimanjaro, travelled extensively in Africa and visited Tibet, Kamchatka (eastern Russia) and North America.

Jenny Blain was a senior lecturer in the School of Social Science and Law at Sheffield Hallam University where she led the MA in social science research methods. Much of her teaching was on qualitative methods, discourse and critical ethnography. Research interests include constructions of identity within Western paganisms and neo-Shamanisms, gender and sexuality, spirituality, sacred sites and marginalised groups. She is the author of a number of books, and co-author of *Sacred Sites: Contested Rights/Rites* (Sussex University Press, 2007) with Robert J. Wallis. She has now retired from teaching.

Felicity H. Clarke was born and brought up in Lancaster and has a keen interest in local history. She is completing a PhD on the Anglo-Saxon Kingdom of Northumbria at Queen's College, Oxford. Her interests focus upon the concept of the frontier and upon the early Christian sites of Northumbria in the period *c.* AD 500 to *c.* AD 850.

Nick Ford spent most of his childhood and early adulthood in Lancashire and studied Roman archaeology at the University of Southampton. He practises a spirituality based on Romano-British concepts.

John Lamb gained a BSc in Environmental Biology from Liverpool University in 1986 and an MSc in Landscape Ecology, Design & Maintenance from Wye College, University of London in 1988. He is a full member of the Institute of Ecology and Environmental Management and has been employed as a Conservation Officer with the Lancashire Wildlife Trust since 1998. His interests cover such broad fields as ecology, nature conservation and prehistoric archaeology.

Heather Rawlin-Cushing studied History of Art at the Courtauld Institute of Art in London. She continued at the Institute as a postgraduate and, undertaking an MA in Greek and Roman Art focusing on funerary sculpture, has been engaged in a course of postgraduate research looking at monumental sculpture and the commemoration of the dead in Anglo-Saxon Northumbria.

Linda Sever is senior lecturer in the Faculty of Arts, Humanities and Social Sciences at the University of Central Lancashire. She is also currently attached as a postgraduate researcher to a medieval textiles project at the University of Manchester (*The Lexis of Cloth and Clothing in Britain c. 700–1450: Origins, Identification, Contexts and Change*). Formerly, she worked as a documentary maker for the BBC, primarily with the History and Archaeology Unit. Research interests include pre-Christian religious traditions and shamanic practices, folklore, Anglo-Saxon and early medieval art.

Bob Trubshaw has written numerous books, booklets and articles, as well as several books on folklore and mythology, including *Sacred Places: Prehistory and Popular Imagination* (2005). He founded Heart of Albion Press eighteen years ago and in 1996 founded *At the Edge* magazine.

Aidan Turner-Bishop has many interests which include local history and folklore, twentieth-century architecture and environmental and transport campaigning. As a boy he enjoyed walking with his father, trying to trace the courses of lost rivers and streams in Manchester, his home city. He learnt then that truly 'the fields lie sleeping beneath' our cities. After more than thirty years working in academic libraries, he is now retired.

Sara Vernon is Chairperson of two societies, Bolton Archaeology and Egyptology Society, and Friends of Seven Acres, and is on the committee of several other societies. She is currently researching the place- and field-names of Bolton-le-Moors and has just published her first book with The History Press entitled *Bolton Street Names – their meanings and origins*. Sara works as landscape archaeologist and historian, and took part in the *Time Team* Big Dig.

Karen Lawrinson (who contributed many of the photographs for this book) is a keen photographer interested in landscape and pre-Christian monuments. Other interests include motorcycling, folk music and reading. She is also a town councillor with interests in road safety and the environment.

PREFACE

THE INVENTION
OF SACRED PLACES

BOB TRUBSHAW

Places are not simply physical. They have a meaning and significance, which are conveyed in myths and legends, and possibly in ritual activities. Certain places gain importance from rituals performed there, so that in future they are increasingly appropriate for ritual activities – whether celebrating New Year at Trafalgar Square, or for 'rites of passage' at a church or prehistoric stone circle. Some of these rituals – such as marriages and handfastings – involve making promises whose solemnity 'borrow' from the sanctity of the location.

Places mean different things to different people, and often different things at different times. Places are the venues where we live out our lives, and as such, places range from entirely secular to entirely sacred, with plenty of variation in between. We live our lives in such places as houses, shops, pubs, parks, fields, woods, prehistoric sites and churches. Specific examples of each of these types of places may have more significance than others, and each type of place – and each specific place – can change in significance over time.

Modern sense of place has been greatly diluted by people spending so much time in dehumanised places – what might be termed 'architectural spaces' – such as supermarkets, shopping malls, office blocks, hotels, railway and tube stations, airports and motorways. While these are places, they do not have the depth of meaning that is typically associated with traditional notions of place, and have only rather negatively-valued meanings. (Douglas Adams wittily noted, '*It is no coincidence that in no known language does the phrase "As pretty as an airport" appear.*') Even our own homes are becoming less like specific places as we spend more time watching TV or in front of a computer – physically 'at home', but mentally elsewhere.

Places have significance to us because they have meaning. That meaning needs to be, in some way, retained and remembered. Simon Schama's study of place and memory looked in depth at the complexities of how cultures create and remember meanings for significant places (Schama 1995). However, such 'remembering' also takes place at quite mundane and everyday levels too. For example, the meaning of a place is often summarised in the name we give to the place. The study of place-names is far more than unravelling the complex changes to spelling and derivation of the original terminology. It is also more than relating places to the topography, even though a great number of British place-names incorporate subtle descriptions of the terrain. No place acquires its name arbitrarily. No matter how little of the original meaning has been remembered, all names link into a society's associations, people and stories.

Sometimes places are given additional significance by being linked with legends or myths. In northern Europe, stories giving significance to sacred places rarely emphasise a transcendental presence, a 'spirit of place' or *genius loci*, although these are common in Classical Mediterranean cultures. Even if these legends are *post hoc* explanations (as, for example, when prehistoric or Anglo-Saxon ditches become called the 'Devil's Dyke'), they add to the associations of a specific place. By adding a vivid narrative, place-related memories materialise as myths.

Our sense of places exists in the interplay between physical topography and 'mind scapes' conveyed in legends and myths. The meaning of a place needs to be passed on in the form of story or narrative, even if this has become 'fossilised' or shrunken to merely the name of the place whose original significance is lost or largely unknown. Places, like all other aspects of culture, only have significance when we ascribe to them 'narratives of meaning'. The meanings we give to a place may help to create the sense of belonging for a society and, intentionally or otherwise, exclude others from belonging there. People who do not belong – such as Gypsies and other travellers – have for centuries been despised by those who feel they do belong somewhere. So the significance of a place has less to do with the physical landscape than with the meanings we give to the location. More specifically, these meanings are remembered and sustained in the narratives we create about these places.

Landscapes are more mental than physical. Western mentality thinks of landscape primarily in terms of who owns what. As a result, boundaries become one of the most significant aspects of landscapes – and the *significance* of boundaries is greater than their physical manifestations. Although not everything in a landscape is necessarily created by people, the idea – or, rather, ideas – of landscape are most certainly entirely invented by people. Clearly we construct landscapes by planting trees and hedges, clearing and managing woodland, digging ditches, ploughing and planting crops, erecting buildings, and – increasingly with the advent of mechanisation – we have transformed landscapes with canals, railways, roads, cities, suburbs, motorways, airports, industrial estates, derelict areas, and all the rest. But the way we *think about* landscapes is more important still. While we may only be constructing ideas and concepts, these are fundamental to our notions of 'reality'.

The sacred places explored in this book might be thought of as existing within both 'real' and 'perceived' landscapes. However, such a distinction is unreal, as the term 'landscape' essentially refers to the way we perceive and experience that landscape for ourselves, and our understanding of the 'reality' within that landscape. And to do that we need to walk through a landscape – a process which takes time – to explore it effectively.

Even if the entire world is seen as sacred, certain places may offer easier access to the deities or the Otherworld. In many societies mountains are seen not only as the cosmic axis, but also the places where Earth comes closest to the deities. Moses went to the summit of Mount Sinai to speak to Yahweh and receive the Ten Commandments. The Japanese national icon is the snow-capped peak of Mount Fuji (although many other mountains in Japan are also sacred). The Maoris regard the volcanoes at the heart of the Tongariro National Park as so sacred that no humans can venture there (a belief supported by UNESCO when, in 1993, Tongariro became the first property to be inscribed on the World Heritage List under the revised criteria describing cultural landscapes).

Natural sacred places 'evolve' into temples and tombs, and thence to churches and mosques. The columns of early temples mimic the trees of sacred groves and, many centuries later, are still a dominant architectural feature of the interiors of medieval cathedrals and mosques. The earliest Neolithic long barrows have cave-like chambers. The grandeur of large caves is matched only by the interiors of major churches. All churches are cave-like constructions (more so before Gothic architecture enabled large windows) and their spires point to God in a manner shared by sacred mountains the world over.

Just like churches enclosed within a well-defined churchyard, so pre-Christian sacred sites in Europe seem to have been defined areas, usually referred to in Latin as a *temenos*. The Old English word seems to have been *frithgaerd*, literally, 'peace enclosure', but with the sense of 'sanctuary'. Various types of *frithgeard*, '... about a stone, or a tree, or a well ...', were prohibited in England under the tenth-century laws of Edgar and the eleventh-century laws for Northumbrian priests.

Modern mentality can usually recognise that springs, ancient temples, certain caves, stone circles and the like may once have been regarded in a similar way to the way we now 'respect' churches, cemeteries, mosques and the like. But there is a considerable difference between putting up an interpretation board which includes the words 'ancient sacred site' and actually believing in and experiencing the sense of sacredness of such places. Most professional archaeologists and 'heritage managers' are quite happy to bandy about the term 'sacred site'. However, their notions of 'sacred sites' often have little in common with what the phrase denotes for, say, modern-day pagans. This is not to say that such pagans necessarily have a well-developed understanding of sacred sites or even always behave in ways that other pagans consider appropriate (see Trubshaw 2005: chapter 5), but suffice to say that the words 'sacred site' have a richness of meaning and experience for pagans that are difficult for others to grasp.

In essence, sacred places are significant less for their practical significance than for what they signify. Sacred places originally signified where deities and the Otherworld could be accessed. An ancient monument such as Stonehenge or the smaller Neolithic henges or the variety of sites described in this book can be readily regarded as 'sacred' because there is a perceived continuity with how we regard, say, cathedrals. In the same way a Neolithic chamber tomb (even though excavated and all human remains removed) is perceived with the sanctity we might now approach cemeteries or war memorials.

This preface is a revised version of Trubshaw 2005: chapter 1.

EDITOR'S NOTE

It is only by visiting the sites that one can start to understand why certain places were seen as sacred and why monuments, sculptured stones or churches were erected where they were. Visit and add your experience to the real and perceived notions of these sites. Experience and appreciate the landscapes iden- tified — academically, physically or emotionally — and thus maintain that sense of sacredness, whether it be real or perceived.

INTRODUCTION

LINDA SEVER

Grey recumbent tombs of the dead in desert places
Standing stones on the vacant wine-red moor,
Hills of sheep, and the homes of the silent vanished races
And winds, austere and pure ...

From *To SR Crockett* by Robert Louis Stevenson

At first glance, this book might seem to be just a collection of discrete essays about different places, sites or monuments in the area that is loosely defined as the county of Lancashire. A closer reading, however, should reveal common pathways that link all the different approaches to and understandings of what has been (and to some is still) considered as sacred within the landscape. Secondly, these essays and the research carried out by the authors reveal an enthusiasm for and commitment to the different ways and methodologies of studying the 'sacred' landscape. Books such as this are often limited to one discipline. This was not the intention here. In my own career I have researched many disciplines, both academic and non-academic, some of which specialist scholars would dismiss as irrelevant. However, this book is intended for the general reader as well as for those with specialist interests in the landscape and for this reason the following chapters include a variety of approaches, including archaeology, ecology, history, art history, place-name studies and folklore. The aim is not necessarily to construct a picture of the past in a particular area, nor to discuss what was considered as sacred by early peoples – here we can only speculate or attempt to interpret from the remains, artefacts and art that have been left behind. It is an attempt to show what and where was important in the Lancashire landscape for different groups of people who lived there, important enough for them to decide to site their stone circles and burial mounds, to give special names to places and areas, to erect and carve images and patterns in stone crosses, and to construct their early churches. Therefore, there is no apology for being so interdisciplinary in content.

Nevertheless, it should be noted that in introducing the chapters in this book, the terms 'sacred', 'sacred landscape' and 'sacred sites', in whichever context they are used here, are 'value laden and constructed' (Wallis 2003), and the idea of the sacred does needs 'further unpacking and theorising' (Wallis & Blain 2002). So it should be acknowledged that the phrase 'Sacred Landscape' is used loosely to bring together the contributions from academics from a wide variety of disciplines. Some give purely academic readings of a particular monument, site or group of sites; others include an experiential approach to the understanding of a part of the landscape. Therefore, this book is not only about the 'sacred' and the 'landscape'. To borrow the phraseology used by Blain, Ezzy and Harvey, it is also about 'academia and its disciplines, theoretical approaches, epistemologies, methodologies and methods' (Blain *et al*, 2004).

What gives a place identity and meaning? What makes it more than just an area or a region? The transition into a 'place' is summed up by Orton and Wood as follows:

> 'Place' is the area of one's being-in-the-world: of being-alongside-things; of being-with others and being-one's-self; of feeling and understanding one's relations with other things and other individuals. It's part of a region brought close to one's being-in-the-world. It's the general whereabouts of something. A human individual arrives in a region and gets to know the natural things or mere things there, the earth, rocks and soils, springs, rivers and lakes, plants, trees and animals that are present-to-hand there, and that individual opposes himself or herself to them … (it) becomes changed by them and changes them: he or she builds there and dwells there, cultivates crops and rears animals, puts up structures, comes to understand what is there and represent it in language and is engaged in it every day; he makes a 'place' there.

> Orton, Wood & Lees 2007:14

Vaughan-Thomas (1980:7) saw the landscape of the British Isles as a palimpsest – a manuscript written on, scraped off, then used again and again by the long procession of races that moved across these islands for thousands of years of our history. They have left traces of their presence, sometimes clearly superimposed, sometimes with the early remains almost obliterated by later occupation of the same site. This book will expose some of the layers of the palimpsest in Lancashire and in its journey will cover a period of a few thousand years, from the earliest detectable presence of people: those who built the round barrows, burial mounds and stone circles and farmed the land in the Neolithic, Bronze and Iron Ages, followed by the arrival in the landscape of the Celts, the Romans and Anglo-Saxons. It will journey through the fragmented period of history of the Dark Ages (where coherent theories can only be built up with much specu-lation) and on to the period when we get the first written records of the people who lived in the British landscape, ending in the early years of the tenth century when groups of Vikings arrived and settled in northwest England, as evidenced by place-names and stone sculpture. Many of these sites have not been widely documented in the past. However, it is important to remember that it is not always the well-documented sites that set the imagination racing; it is often at the smaller, more remote sites, where few visitors or tourists come, that the past seems to merge with the present and our ancestors seem very near.

The journey starts in the first chapter, where John Lamb, ecologist and con-servation officer with Lancashire Wildlife Trust, demonstrates the paucity of previous discussion of the prehistoric sites in Lancashire and seeks to redress the balance. The second part of John's contribution is the most comprehensive list-ing of sites to date, the state of the remains and their accessibility. In the second chapter, local historian, archaeologist and place-name expert Sara Vernon points to evidence where in some cases all that remains is the field or place-name. It is acknowledged by some academics in the discipline of archaeology and history that place-name study is not always one of the most reliable of sources for evi-dence, as one cannot always state definitively the origins of the name. But this form of research helps to illuminate further the importance given to particular areas of the landscape and reveals how a place or site considered sacred by an earlier group of people or culture was appropriated and used by a later group. In her article on the reuse of Bronze Age sites by the Anglo-Saxons, archaeologist Sarah Semple states that the 'archaeological investigation (as well as the study of historical, literary and linguistic sources) is revealing a consistent tradition of Anglo-Saxon secondary activity, occurring at Bronze Age burial mounds and Neolithic long barrows' (Semple 1998). Sara Vernon's research also contributes to this discourse of appropriation and reuse.

In Chapter 3, archaeologist and practitioner of Romano-British spirituality, Nick Ford, turns his attention to Ribchester, where he discusses the signifi-cance of the Roman presence in this small, but historically and archaeologically important town and, in particular, how their spiritual world view added an extra layer of understanding of the sacred within in the landscape. Nick does not just provide an academic overview of the Roman presence in Ribchester, but also an interesting personal and experiential account of what is understood (or felt) as sacred at a particular historic site today. Researcher and folklorist, Aidan Turner-Bishop, then takes the reader on a fascinating and comprehensive jour-ney around fairy and boggart sites in Lancashire, through folklore, legend and place-name research. Mythologies surrounding fairy and otherworldly beings have permeated many traditions and cultures in these Isles over the centuries, often the only remaining legacy being in the names given to springs, wells, valleys or hills. Lancashire can even boast the only park in the country named after one of these supernatural beings, Boggart Hole Clough, in Blackley, north of Manchester.

Chapter 5 gives an overview of scholarly and archaeological work that has been carried out in the discussion and examination of boundaries and early church sites. The second part of the paper takes Bolton as a case study to loosely examine whether anything can be detected of earlier Christian or pre-Christian boundaries from current and existing parish and territorial boundaries marked on OS and road maps. The aim is to attempt to show how early boundaries can be detected in the current landscape and how early church sites were sited within them. The paper also discusses the importance of stone sculpture in early Christian church sites and is followed by a listing of stone sculpture sites in the South East Lancashire area and across into Greater Manchester. This links into the two subsequent chapters, by Felicity H. Clark and Heather Rawlin-Cushing, who take two very different approaches to the study of Anglo-Saxon stone sculpture in the county.

Dr Clark's paper explores the interesting possibility that, as part of the named land grants read out by Bishop Wilfrid at the dedication of the newly-built stone church at Ripon in the 670s, the 'other places' referred to could be the Lune Valley in West Lancashire. As evidence of this Felicity points to a wide variety of archaeological, topographical and historical evidence, particularly based around a group of five sites which have produced pre-Viking stone sculpture, where there is strong corroborative evidence that these might have been the sites of monastic communities in the early medieval period. It also includes some other interesting discoveries uncovered by Felicity during the course of her research. Art historian Heather Rawlin-Cushing's chapter revisits the carved cross shaft at Urswick and attempts to provide a re-evaluation of its figurative imagery and overall function. The Urswick Cross bears a commemorative inscription following a formula that is particular to a small and scattered group of pre-Viking sculpture, but it also features an unusual and enigmatic image of two male secular figures conversing. Heather discusses this, alongside other motifs on the cross, to argue that both religious symbolism and secular concerns were equally important in terms of the dissemination of certain messages to the wider lay community.

In the final chapter, Derek Berryman takes a tour of carvings, hogback stones and stone crosses of mainly West Lancashire and across the border into Cumbria, focusing on the stories and mythology of Norse deities depicted on these monuments produced during the Anglo-Saxon and Viking period. Derek gives an overview of some of these well-known Norse myths, tales of cunning and deceit, tales of battles and of humour, and tales of the supernatural and human interaction with the gods, dwarves and dragons. The stories Derek retells, such as that of Sigurð and that of the god Thor's fishing expedition are as fresh and interesting today as they were when they were carved into the stone crosses over eleven centuries ago like comic strip stories – all the more interesting when juxtaposed with the Christian iconography also carved onto the stones.

I hope you enjoy reading these chapters as much as I have enjoyed compiling them. I hope it serves in some way as a memorial to those who, in the past, have seen or visualised some form of 'sacredness' within the Lancashire landscape. In the long-forgotten and long-abandoned moorlands and valleys of Lancashire our ancestors lived, worked, fought, worshipped and died. All that remains in some of the sites are a few tumbled stones (such as Pike Stones on Anglezarke moor) or a broken wall and a shattered cross (as in St Peter's Church, Bolton or Whalley churchyard). The people who passed their lives here may have left no recorded history, yet these monuments and ruins tell as much of a story as do the great cathedrals and deserve to be equally documented and remembered.

1

LANCASHIRE'S PREHISTORIC PAST

JOHN LAMB

INTRODUCTION

Lancashire isn't known for its prehistoric remains. Indeed *The Modern Antiquarian* by Julian Cope has no entries, Aubrey Burl's guide to stone circles includes just two sites and Cunliffe's 1991 map of Iron Age settlements draws a blank. However, there are over 100 sites on *The Modern Antiquarian* website and Lancashire's Sites and Monuments Record (SMR), and the Historic Environment Record (HER), administered by Lancashire County Council (2007), has over 730 prehistoric entries. The gazetteer of Lancashire's prehistoric sites (printed at the end of this chapter) lists 285 sites, of which fifty-one are Scheduled Ancient Monuments and ninety-four are on the National Monuments Record. This is only really scratching the surface of what is an important county for its prehistoric remains.

The SMR includes stone/hut circles, hillforts, burial sites, enclosures and settlements. The entries also include flint-chipping evidence and discovery of solitary implements, including arrow/spearheads, querns, adzes, jewellery, urns, knives/scrapers, swords, canoes etc., but details of chipping sites and solitary finds are not included here. Instead, some of the forty best sites are summarised.

Of these forty sites, twelve are on upland hill-slopes (2, 3, 6, 8, 29–36), eleven are on former wetland or river valley/floodplains (1, 4, 10, 11, 19, 20, 22/23, 25/26, 38), nine are on hill-summits (7, 16–18, 24, 27, 28, 39, 40), four are carved stones (12–15), two are caves (9, 37), one is a promontory non-hill summit (5) and one (Boar's Den) doesn't fit any of these categories. Hence the surviving prehistoric sites in Lancashire appear to be concentrated on hills and upland slopes and on the edges of rivers, former lakes and associated wetland habitats. But why were these sites sacred to our ancestors and why were particular locations picked to construct the stone circle, barrow or cairn? In the absence of written text or 'concrete' evidence we can only speculate. Possible reasons include alignment to points of the landscape visible or more prominent at certain times of the year, or its location relative to the cycle of the moon or position to the stars. Another reason is the view across the landscape, which would have been very different to the artificial agricultural/industrial/residential one we see today. The view(s) must have been especially important for sites used for trading and celebrating. The visibility of the site from where people lived may have been critical, as would the location if people lit fires or beacons on particular nights of the year. Other reasons could include the site being the favourite spot of the person buried, or the grieving family, the actual location where the person was injured or killed, the spot where a particular plant grew or animal was seen or found or because it was a dry spot surrounded by wetland.

Wetlands would have been important for fuel (timber and peat), thatch/roofing materials, willows for baskets, building timbers, hunting, fishing, herbs and medicinal plants, transportation, bathing/swimming, hiding/storage and aesthetics, etc. Trackways and possibly jetties were constructed and could have been used for ritual purposes as well as for crossing the wetland(s). It should be borne in mind that our ancestors would have depended upon the environment and nature for their food, water, shelter, medicines, clothing, etc. Today only fragments of the habitats that they knew survive in the artificial landscape that has been created and only a proportion of the sites that were sacred to them have not been destroyed.

Many of Lancashire's best sites can be visited, including Bleasdale circle – one of only 100 timber circles in Britain – hillforts at Castercliffe and Warton Crag, Summerhouse Hill Stone Circle, Boar's Den Barrow, Torrisholme Barrow and Pike Stones Chambered Long Cairn. In summary, this is a listing and a celebration of prehistoric sites including some of the best stone circles, burial, defensive and settlement sites that can be visited. The following timeline is used to introduce the types of site:

Late Upper Palaeolithic	40000 BC–10001 BC
Mesolithic	10000 BC –4001 BC
Neolithic	4000 BC–2201 BC
Bronze Age	2500 BC–701 BC
Iron Age	700 BC–AD 42

LATE UPPER PALAEOLITHIC

Before the last Ice Age, Lancashire was inhabited, but the development of thick ice sheets, deposition of glacial materials and subsequent erosion redefined the landscape that Palaeolithic people knew. The earliest evidence comes from the end of the Ice Age, during the Upper Palaeolithic. Evidence in northwest England is sparse and mainly confined to caves overlooking Morecambe Bay (Kirkhead) and in the Yorkshire Dales (Kinsey and Victoria). Early evidence of human activity in Lancashire comes from Poulton.

1. The Poulton Elk (Horace), Poulton-le-Fylde, Blackpool (SD331386): In July 1970 the remains of an elk was found with barbed points embedded in the skeleton and is dated to around 10250 BC. The skeleton had seventeen lesions and studies of these suggest that the animal was hunted, unsuccessfully, two or three weeks before its death. It is thought that flint-tipped projectiles, blunt implements and possibly something resembling an axe might have been used. The final hunt was unsuccessful, since the complete skeleton was found in a series of aquatic deposits, suggesting that the elk died in a pool inaccessible to its hunters. Horace is on display in the Harris Museum in Preston and a visit is highly recommended.

MESOLITHIC

Lancashire has a diverse range of habitats with large upland areas and the coastal plain in close proximity, which provides opportunities for a range of activity that isn't possible in many counties. Lancashire could be of national significance for understanding Mesolithic social and economic patterns (Cowell 1996). Mesolithic evidence comes from Anglezarke Moor, Burnley and Silverdale.

2. Rushy Brow Mesolithic Hunting Camp, Anglezarke Moor (SD633177): In 1985 excavations at Rushy Brow investigated the site of a small scatter of chert flakes found on an erosion patch in blanket peat. The clearance of 100 square metres of peat revealed a dense and well-defined scatter of lithic material dateable to the Early Mesolithic (8000 BC), clearly associated with a semi-circular stone setting – a possible shelter. Removal of the underlying soil revealed a second scatter of lithic material associated with an arc of five probable stakeholes, apparently enclosing a slightly raised area. It is suggested that such scatters and associated structures represent briefly-occupied hunting camps of small hunter-gatherer groups. The location of the site and the 'hunting type' composition of lithics, i.e. mostly waste from producing and maintaining tools, supports this interpretation.

3. Sheddon Clough Mesolithic Camp, Burnley (SD895295): At the Long Causeway end of Sheddon Clough fieldworkers in August 1984 revealed the remains of a small late Mesolithic campsite (4000 BC), which included the remains of a campfire associated with pieces of worked chert. Large stones still *in situ* may have been used as anvils.

4. Storrs Moss Mesolithic Settlement, Silverdale (SD484757): A possible Neolithic timber structure was discovered during excavations in 1965/67 by the University of Liverpool at Storrs Moss. Although the results were inconclusive, both archaeological and palaeoecological studies produced evidence for Neolithic settlement in the area, with the recovery of flint and chert artefacts associated with cut features and a layer of wood, some of which was worked. The wood was dated 3694–3384 BC, although disturbance by roots of reeds (*Phragmites*) made this a minimum and a true date on stratigraphic grounds was considered nearer 4300 BC. Subsequent work on the site revealed possible late Mesolithic occupation below the Neolithic strata.

Possible Mesolithic sites include hut circles at Cow Close Pasture, Littledale (SD544618) and excavations at Heysham Head (SD409616) in 1992 discovered approximately 1,180 flints, of which eighty-five per cent were waste, but some blades, microliths and blades were also found, which is indicative of a late Mesolithic settlement.

Other flint chipping sites have been found on Burnley's Moors (Deerplay, Extwistle, Great Hameldon, Heald Moor, Thieveley and Worsthorne), Bolton Moors (Turton), Chorley Moors (Great Hill, Grain Pole Hill, Rivington), in Pendle (Trawden, Boulsworth Hill, Pendle Hill, Claremount-Pendleton), on the Bowland Fells (Bowland Knotts, Grizedale Fell), in Rossendale (Scout Moor and the Haslingden Valley), in Lancaster District (Heysham Head, Hornby, Crook o' Lune, Lathom) near Lytham and at Blackmoor-Mawdesley in West Lancashire.

NEOLITHIC

This period covers the earliest farming communities, with their origins as the hunters and fishers of the late Mesolithic (*c.*4000 BC), to the developed and established farming systems of the Bronze Age from 2500–701 BC. The change from Mesolithic to Neolithic included the use of leaf-shaped arrowheads, introduction of polished axes, first use of pottery and formal burial structures in the form of long barrows and cairns. Neolithic pottery finds are poorly represented in Lancashire with the best finds from Portfield Camp near Whalley, where excavations found shards of plain bowl pottery.

5. Portfield Camp (SD745355): Portfield Hillfort or Planeswood Camp, near Whalley, is situated on a south-facing promontory on the eastern side of the valley of the River Calder and includes a flat enclosure, defended by banks and ditches on all sides except the west, where steep-slopes afford natural protection.

The enclosure measures 165m northwest–southeast by 110m northeast–south-west and appears to have been artificially levelled. The defences survive best at the northwest corner and consist of an inner bank or rampart to 1.5m high, outside which is a berm or levelled area 6m wide. Beyond this berm is a ditch up to 6m wide, then a second earthen bank 4m wide, then another ditch with a third earthen bank beyond. Limited excavation in 1957 found evidence for an earlier defensive rampart on the northern side and indicated that the hillfort was originally defended by a single rampart then extended and more complex defences added, i.e. the original univallate hillfort was modified into a small multivallate hillfort. A cobbled pavement comprised the entrance through the northern defences. In 1966 workmen discovered a hoard of Bronze Age artefacts including a gold bracelet, a gold 'tress or lock' ring, and a number of bronze objects including socketed axe heads. Excavation in the 1960s and 1970s found Roman and medieval pottery, flint and chert objects from the Bronze Age and Neolithic. Thus the site shows evidence of human activity/occupation from Neolithic times to the present.

Few burial structures have been found in comparison to Cumbria and Derbyshire, however, very little work has been carried out on Lancashire's uplands and most low-lying evidence will have been destroyed by drainage and cultivation. Only two long barrows are known from Lancashire and both are located on Anglezarke Moor, above Chorley. The best known is Pike Stones, which is the only claimed example of a Cotswold-Severn tomb north of the Cotswolds. The second tomb is on the same moor.

6. Pike Stones (SD627172): A chambered long cairn that has been robbed, with much of the stone having been removed, making it difficult to determine the exact perimeter. It is of the usual pear-shape, with the larger end to the north-northwest and is constructed out of gritstones and glacial erratics up to 0.4m high. It is aligned almost north–south and is up to 48m long by 19m wide at the northern end and 14m wide at the southern end, but widens at the centre due to disturbance and slippage to 29m. The two ends are best defined, the north end being very clear with the ground outside denuded of turf and almost bare of stones. The south end is demarcated by a distinct line of stone. The east and west perimeters can only be traced intermittently. There is no retaining kerb although some of the perimeter stones appear to be larger than the stones of the cairn. At the northern end, the cairn consists of a double wall, the outer being of slightly larger stones than the inner, that curves across and inwards to form an entrance or forecourt. This entrance leads into the cairn where there are remains of an inner burial chamber, which has five surviving gritstone slabs, 4.5m long by 1m wide, that would originally have been roofed with horizontal slabs and covered with

Pike Stones on Anglezarke Moor. Photograph by Phil Davies

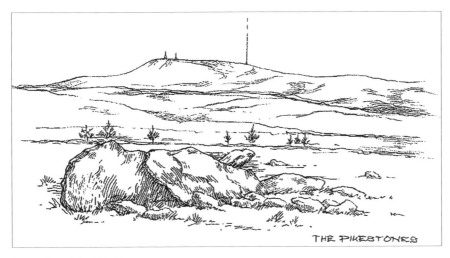

THE PIKESTONES

Illustration of the Pike Stones

rubble. Around the inner end of the chamber is a circular area of stones 25m in diameter, the stones larger than those in the cairn. This feature suggests the presence of a circular structure behind the chamber, or around part of it, similar to that found at chambered cairns in the Gloucestershire area.

Other Neolithic sites are found near Burnley and Warton.

7. Burwain's or Broad Bank Camp/Enclosure, Shuttleworth Pasture, Burnley (SD902352): A prehistoric defended early Neolithic to Iron Age settlement on a hilltop west of Broad Bank Hill, on the northern side of Thursden Valley. It includes a circular enclosure surrounded by an inner ditch and outer bank. The enclosure is approximately 45m in diameter, the ditch 0.3m wide by 0.25m deep, and the outer bank 2m wide and 0.3m high. There are opposed entrances through the bank and across the ditch on the west and east sides. Beneath the bank a small hearth was found together with a deposit of charcoal and burnt earth indicating earlier prehistoric activity.

8. Hazel Edge Cairn, Worsthorne, Burnley (SD905316): A cairn situated northeast of Cant Clough Reservoir on Worsthorne Moor. The cairn was excavated between 1935 and 1945, and a cremation and a number of flint implements of Mesolithic to Bronze Age date were found. The simple prehistoric burial consisted of a shallow hole 0.6m in diameter and 0.45m deep, containing a mixture of fine charcoal and fragments of calcined bones. Two concentric circles of stone were placed over the burial, which was then covered with a cairn of small boulders.

In 1912 a quern was found on the site of a Neolithic Barrow at Broadshaw Farm (SD870350). Stone lintels of possible Neolithic date were found at Gibson's Farm (SD471442) in 1982/3.

9. The Dog Holes Cave, Warton Crag (SD483730): This cave has evidence of use from the Upper Palaeolithic, Neolithic and Roman eras. The present entrance is a vertical shaft down from a ledge of limestone pavement. The mouth is roughly rectangular, 2.4m by 2.1m at the surface. Before excavation the shaft was 4m deep and consisted of a mass of debris sloping down on two sides into passages to the north and southwest. The debris on the southwest side sloped sharply for nearly 6m into a chamber called the Swirl Hole. From there a passage of three chambers ran in a southwesterly direction. These were named West Fissure, Bone Chamber and Upper Chamber, their length totalling about 21.3m. Bone Chamber was excavated between 1909 and 1912 and the bones of about 140 people from the Neolithic period, presumably buried in the cave

earth, were found. One small sherd of first-century Beaker pottery was found. Later occupation debris was found in the surface soil, especially at the foot of the entrance shaft, where a hearth was located and a large amount of animal bone was spread around the hearth. Other finds included antler, iron weaving combs, an iron sickle, iron knives, a bronze button and part of a bronze scabbard. Cave-earth deposits of the Pleistocene Age were found to contain the bones of extinct rodents and land molluscs.

Other types of Neolithic evidence include human remains and cup and ring-marked stones. Human heads have been found at Preston, Pilling and Poulton-le-Fylde.

10. Preston Docks Findspot (SD512296): In the considerable excavations for the construction of Preston Docks in the River Ribble from 1885–1889 various objects were discovered at depths of 3–6m below the surface, including a Bronze Age socketed spearhead, two dug-out canoes, wild ox bones and twenty human skulls and associated bones. The date range of skulls is at least early Neolithic to early medieval (4000 BC–AD 1065). The spearhead and skulls are on display in the Harris Museum, Preston.

11. Kentucky Farm Findspot, Pilling (SD442462): A bog burial was found on Pilling Moss in 1824 close to the Garstang Road. The head of a female was found 1.8m below ground wrapped in coarse yellow cloth, with strings of beads. She is described as having a great abundance of hair, of a most beautiful auburn, which was plaited and of great length; the braids had been cut by a heavy cutting instrument. The beads were in two links, one of jet, in cylinders about half an inch in length, and the thickness of a goose quill. The other link was also of jet, except for one large round amber bead, the beads in this link also cylindrical, but of irregular lengths, some being over 2cm but others less than 1cm.

Other skulls have been found in Red Moss and Chat Moss on the outskirts of Manchester. Most famous of all is Lindow Man, discovered during commercial peat harvesting from Lindow Moss in 1984. Unfortunately this destructive and unsustainable practice is still continuing in Cheshire, Lancashire and Greater Manchester and destroying not only an important ecological habitat and archaeological resource, but also releasing thousands of tonnes of carbon into the atmosphere year on year.

Unlike areas in West Yorkshire, e.g. Addingham Moors and Keighley, there are few examples of cup-and-ring-marked stones in Lancashire, but candidates have been found near Rivington, High Bentham, Burnley and Wycoller, with a possible example on the Bowland Fells.

12. Anderton Cup-and-Ring-marked Boulder, Rivington (SD627134): A boulder with several cup-marks and one, possibly two, cup-and-ring engravings was found along the eastern edge of the Lower Rivington Reservoir, about 10m below the high water mark, at a time of unusually low water level. The boulder is approximately 80cm long, 55cm wide and 50cm deep and the decoration is on one face only. In 1999 the boulder was moved to the Anderton Centre near Horwich. Bolton Archaeological Society investigated the site where the boulder was found, and natural boulder clay was dicovered beneath a surface scatter of stones.

13. Great Stone of Fourstones Cup-marked Stone, High Bentham (SD669662): A huge natural rock on the border between Lancashire and North Yorkshire, approximately 150m west of the Slaidburn Road and clearly visible to passing traffic (weather-depending). The stone is over 9m round and 3.6m high. A number of cup-markings are present on the top surface, but there are no discernible rings. Three other stones stood nearby but were broken up for sharpening scythes or building stone.

14. Hameldon Pasture Cup-marked Stone, Burnley (SD891326): The Calderdale historian J. A. Heginbottom described and made an illustration of a simple cup-marked rock approximately 90m northwest of the old circle on Wasnop Edge.

15. Wycoller Packhorse Bridge (SD932393): Four of the stones on the bridge have cup-markings. J. A. Heginbottom described them in his survey of the prehistoric rock-art of upper Calderdale.

A large boulder on Wolfhole Crag at SD632578 on Mallowdale Fell in Bowland has a pattern of grooves and cups. They are superficially similar to others on Ilkley Moor and Rombalds Moor, which are from 4000 BC to AD 42, but they may just be weathering patterns.

BRONZE AGE

From 3200 BC many changes started to happen, from farming communities becoming more stable and stratified, with evidence of social elitism, along with the development of a range of ceremonial monuments with henges and circles appearing for the first time and individual burials in mounds. Unfortunately all of Lancashire's stone circles have been damaged and some have been destroyed. Remnants are found on Turton Moor, Worsthorne Moor, Haslingden Moor and Silverdale.

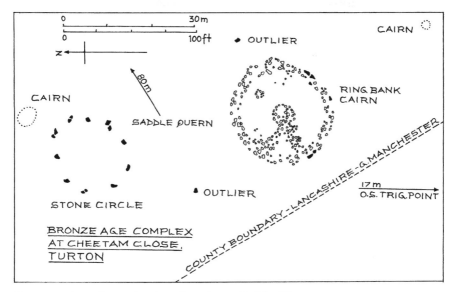

Illustration of complex at Cheetham Close, Turton. By John Dixon

16. Cheetham Close Stone Circle, Turton Moor (SD716158): Unfortunately none of the ten primary stones are *in situ* or completely intact, most of the stones having been buried, toppled or broken. However, there are three stones in the centre of the circle, which are no taller than 0.1m.

17. Delf Hill Stone Circle, Extwistle Moor, Burnley (SD900337): A small circle in enclosed moorland 80m east of Delf Hill. The circle of seven stones, some standing and some fallen, is 7m in diameter. The tallest stone stands 0.5m high. Within the circle is a partially mutilated cairn 2.4m in diameter and 0.2m high, surrounded by a central ditch. Limited excavation of the cairn in 1842 found three unglazed urns, human remains and flint arrowheads. It is one of the earliest excavations in Burnley.

18. Summerhouse Hill Stone Circle, Silverdale (SD500743): An impressive circle on the plateau summit of Summerhouse Hill, west of Yealand Conyers. The circle encloses an area of 2.3 hectares. Four stones and thirteen slight depressions, which mark the socket holes of stones that have been removed, are on a circle 140m in diameter. The stones are of local limestone ranging from 2.1–3.3m long by 0.9–1.8m wide and 1.3–1.6m high. Some of the socket holes lie on the circumference, some are slightly inside and others slightly outside. On the northwest side of the circle there are traces of a ditch 3m wide and 0.4m

deep which originally flanked the stone circle on all sides except the east. Two outlying stones are present 30m west and 48m east–southeast.

The Bleasdale circle near Chipping has at least three elements: a large outer palisaded timber enclosure, a circular ring of timber posts and an inner barrow. The post circle and barrow have been dated to 2200 BC.

Summerhouse Hill stone circle. Photograph by John Lamb

Bleasdale timber circle. Photograph by John Lamb

19. Bleasdale Timber Circle (SD 577459): The circle is situated in the centre of a former peat moss known as Edmarsh at the foot of Fairsnape Fell. It was discovered in 1898 by J. Kelsall and S. Jackson, and partly excavated by them in 1898–1900. In 1933–5 re-excavation of the whole site was carried out under the direction of W. S. Varley. The circle comprises an inner structure within an outer palisade. The inner structure has a central grave, which marks the only burial. The grave goods (discovered in 1899) consisted of two inverted linear urns, 21.5cm and 20cm high, with overhanging rims, dating to the middle Bronze Age. Inverted in the mouth of the larger urn was an incense or pygmy cup and all were filled with charcoal and small particles of calcined human bones. The central grave was surrounded by eleven oak posts forming a ring 11m in diameter. The ring is surrounded by a straight-sided and flat-bottomed ditch lined with birch poles laid in the bottom. The rounded ends of the ditch are flanked by a row of three posts to each end, the space between them forming a causeway into the burial site. The outer palisade is roughly circular, having a diameter of 45.7m with a break in the southwest marked by especially large posts; it nearly touches the inner circle opposite the causeway. The palisade is made up of 'minor posts' set contiguously within a straight-sided, flat-bottomed trench separated by larger 'principal posts', which probably stood much higher than the 'minors'. Following excavation the timbers started to decay and they were replaced with concrete marker posts that are still there today. Also in the Harris Museum are fragments of cloth, shown by the British Museum Research Laboratory to be linen.

From 2200 BC metalwork became increasingly popular and was concentrated in the lowlands, with seventy-five per cent of finds in Lancashire found in wetlands, mainly rivers and mossland. The earliest metalwork finds in Lancashire are flat axes, such as that from Manor Farm, Borwick (destroyed site), dated to 1,740–1640 BC. Axe marks on timbers found in Kate's Pad trackway suggest that metal axes may have been in use by 2345 BC.

20. Kate's Pad, or Dane's Pad (SD409446): A wooden trackway, found under 3.7m of peat, was traced by Revd Banister (1850) and Revd Thornber (1850–2) crossing the mosses of Rawcliffe, Stalmine and Pilling. Both describe it as being formed of split oaks, hollowed by use, lying on cross-sleepers and pegged together. Banister claimed it ran four miles (6.5km); Thornber claimed it could be traced for 1.5 miles. In 1950 the Pilling Historical Society traced about 64m of trackway, which consisted of split oak trees over 5m long and 2.4–4.6m wide, but with no evidence of cross sleepers as previously described. Sobee (1953) claimed that Thornber's sketch plan is pure imagination, and questioned how the track could be traced 1.5 miles under deep peat. Mr Sobee discovered split oak trunks 5m long with a hole roughly cut through, near to one end. He said the causeway was found at about 1.5m below ground and suggested that the peat had shrunk down from 3.7m due to drainage and drying out over the 100-year period. What was probably the last surviving fragment of Kate's Pad was examined on Moss Cottage, or Iron House Farm, between 1949 and 1967. Samples were taken for pollen analysis, specimens of timber preserved and radiocarbon dated to 2760 BC +/- 120.

Examples of barrows are found at Dangerous Corner, Gisburn Forest, Morecambe and near Hurst Green.

21. Boar's Den Bowl Barrow, Dangerous Corner (SD517111): A bowl barrow located on gently undulating ground 150m south of Boar's Den Farm. It includes a slightly oval mound of earth and stones 1.8m–2.5m high, with maximum dimensions of 66.5m east–west by 62m north–south.

22 & 23. Brown Hills Beck Bowl Barrows, Gisburn Forest (SD756602 and 756603): Two round barrows immediately west of Brown Hills Beck. They are well preserved and conical in shape with no trace of ditch and no stone visible through the vegetation cover. The northern barrow is more regular than the southern and comprises an oval earthen mound 25m by 15m and 8m high. The southern barrow is an oval earthen mound 40m by 30m and 10m high.

24. Torrisholme Bowl Barrow, Morecambe (SD459642): Located on the summit of a small hill east of Torrisholme village. It includes a flat-topped circular mound

Boar's Den. Photograph by John Lamb

Torrisholme. Photograph by John Lamb

of earth and stones measuring 32m diameter and 2.3m high on the steeply sloping east side, where it incorporates the remains of an old field boundary, and 1.4m
high on the north side. An Ordnance Survey triangulation station is located on
the summit.

25 & 26. Winckley Lowes, near Hurst Green (SD706374 and 708372): Two Bronze
Age barrows lying within a bend on the flood plain of the River Ribble, between
the confluences of the Rivers Calder and Hodder. The meeting of three rivers
probably held special significance to the people at that time. The western bowl
barrow includes an irregularly shaped mound of earth and stones 60m southwest–northeast by 35m southeast–northwest and 2.5m high. Limited investigation
in 1894 by members of Stonyhurst College found several inurned cremations. The
primary burial consisted of a cairn of large stones beneath which a partly cremated
human burial without pottery was found at ground level, lying on a thin layer of
charcoal. Three secondary inhumations were also found at various levels in the
barrow, one of which was accompanied by a small flint knife or scraper and several
pieces of pottery, one with thumbnail decoration. The eastern barrow, called Loe
Hill, is an oval earthen mound 44m north-northwest–south-southeast by 35m
south-southwest–north-northeast and 6m high. Limited excavation on its summit
in 1894 did not find any archaeological deposits and the results indicate that the
mound may be of glacial origin. However, its location adjacent to the proven
Bronze Age barrow would make this conclusion doubtful, and further investigation, including detailed examination of the excavation records, is required.

Relatively simple earthen barrows have also been found, including Astley Hall,
Chorley (SD574184) and Weeton Lane Heads (SD392345), both destroyed sites,
in which an earth mound surrounded by a ditch covered a central burial and
possibly satellite burials. The huge Round Loaf on Anglezarke Moor (SD673182)
and Carve Hill Tumulus (SD754158) may also fall into this category, though there
are doubts as to whether or not these are natural. A similar sized and unexca-
vated cairn can be found at Thieveley Pike (SD872270).

Examples of cairns are found on Bleara Moor, Leck Fell and Longridge Fell.

27 & 28. Bleara Lowe and Tumulus, Bleara Moor (SD926453 and 924453): Bleara
Lowe is a round cairn on the summit of the Moor. It includes a slightly oval
mound of peat and heather-covered stones 21m east–west by 19m north–south
and 1.4m high. The Tumulus, 230m west of the Lowe, is a round cairn 23m
north-northeast–south-southwest by 21m west-northwest–east-southeast and
1.2m high. It has a bank around the edge with traces of an inner ditch 0.4m
deep and 18.5m in diameter.

Round Loaf. Photograph by Phil Davies

29–33. Eller Beck Cairns, Leck Fell (SD6477–6478): A run of four late Neolithic–early Bronze Age burial cairns along the Eller/Leck watershed from 173–159m AOD and situated amidst the High Park Romano-British settlement. Another (fifth) cairn at SD646783 doesn't form part of the central cairn line, but nevertheless still occupies a prominent position on top of a small knoll above the steep-sided valley, and is a late Neolithic–early Bronze Age burial mound. This cairn is much smaller, at 12m in diameter and 0.6m high, but it has been robbed and its centre removed to ground level.

34. Longridge Fell Cairn (SD645404): A round cairn 36m in diameter and 0.5m high on Thornley Hall Fell. The northern part has been disturbed and a small pile of loose stones has been dumped on its summit. Despite thick heather cover the perimeter can be traced for most of its length, but is clearest to the south. Fires have revealed that the cairn has a well-defined, consolidated base. There is no trace of a ditch or kerb.

35. Winter Hill Kerbed Round Cairn (SD655149): A round cairn of earth and stone 19.2m in diameter and 0.3m high, approximately 400m west-northwest of the summit. Chorley Archaeological Society carried out preliminary investigations in 1957. The tumulus appears to have been robbed at an early date. Excavations located a central stone cairn 2.5m in diameter and 1.5m high surrounded by a continuous low outer wall/kerb, approximately 18m in diameter and 0.4m high. Construction details and pollen analyses suggest a date of 1600–1400 BC. The mound has been badly mutilated on the south and east faces, but a retaining circle of stone boulders is visible. Approximately 12m of the outer wall/kerb is visible in the southeast perimeter, but the rest of the cairn is covered by peat, vegetation and rubble.

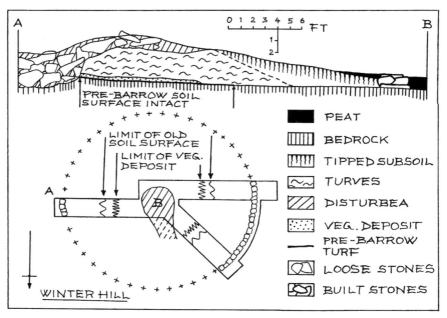

Diagram of Winter Hill. By John Dixon

36. Noon Hill Round Cairn, Rivington Moor (SD646149): A round cairn with cremations and grave goods on the northern edge of the summit of Noon Hill. Limited excavation in 1958 and 1963–4 located the primary burial at the centre, which comprised three cremations interpreted as an adult male, adult female and a child, located beneath a collapsed enlarged food vessel and inserted into a central stone cist. Three or four secondary cremations and a number of flint tools including barbed and tanged arrowheads, scrapers and a knife were also found. The cairn is a slightly oval mound of earth, with stones 21m north–south by 19m east–west and 1.3m high. Three exposed boulders in the south-south-east are the remains of a kerb.

Smaller cairns on Anglezarke, Chorley, and the Worsthorne Moors in Burnley have been excavated and contained inurned burial cremation burials. Caves continued to be used, with evidence found at Whitewell.

37. Fairy Holes Cave at Whitewell (SD655467): The cave is located near the top of a steep wooded bluff formed in a limestone cliff some 10m high overlooking the River Hodder towards Longridge Fell. The cave entrance can be seen from the road on the opposite side of the river. It was excavated in 1946 and produced evidence of occupation as a dwelling in the Middle Bronze Age.

The cave passes straight into the rock for nearly 20m, is about 1.8m wide and 3m high at the mouth, then becomes narrower before terminating in a round chamber 2.4m in diameter and 3.7m high. A platform in front of the cave drops away almost vertically for 6m and then curves away to the river. The platform, excavated down to the bedrock through 60–90cm of earth and fallen rock, yielded all the pottery. About 3.4m in from the entrance, a stone wall was found, approximately 45cm high and 60cm thick, built of large pieces of rough limestone. Over 1m further in is a second wall capped by flat stone slabs, 7.5cm thick and 45cm wide. Charcoal was found in all areas from the platform to the low passage, but by far the greatest amount being over 7m in from the entrance where a possible hearth was found, with several half-charred branches.

Activity falls off sharply after about 1400 BC and there is little Bronze Age metalwork present after about 950 BC.

38. Briarfield Nursery Findspot, Poulton-le-Fylde (SD337389): In 1998 a human skull was found in the section of a newly cut drain at Briarfield Nursery. The skull had been located in a layer of silty wood peat *c.* 1m deep, containing hazelnuts, wood fragments and some charcoal. During excavation through brushwood, worked wood fragments were found, some of which indicated animal (beaver) activity. The skull belonged to a male twenty-five–thirty-five years old. Radio-carbon dating of the skull established it was late Bronze Age, as were the hazelnuts and worked wood, whereas the beaver-gnawed timber was dated to early Iron Age. The lower

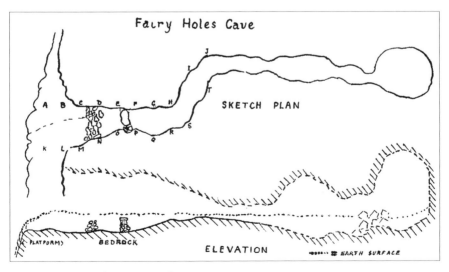

Diagram of Fairy Holes Cave. By John Dixon

horizons of the peat deposits contained intact root systems of dense hazel, indicating that the organic peat material resulted from the rapid flooding of a relatively dry landscape. The exact cause of this inundation remains uncertain, although the effect of beaver damming is a strong possibility.

IRON AGE

The Iron Age was characterized by the climate becoming colder and wetter – not so good for people, but great for peat bog development. Less land was suitable for farming and living on, hence competition for land increased. Tribes began to protect their territories and sites were fortified against neighbours or intruders. There are more than 3,000 hillforts in Britain dating from around 400 BC, and they were used as settlements, for storage, and for trading.

Knowledge of the Iron Age in Lancashire is poorer than almost any other part of England. The National Monuments Record lists only four sites excavated before 1980 in Lancashire that have Iron Age features, easily the lowest total for any English county. Lancashire can only claim to have two excavations out of 200 in Northern England carbon dated 900 BC–AD 70, and both of these, from Castercliffe Hillfort, are more akin to the late Bronze Age than the Iron Age (Haselgrove 1996).

39. Castercliffe, Nelson (SD884383): A small oval Iron Age multivallate 'Vitrified' hillfort enclosing c. 2 acres. It is located on a mound overlooking the valley of the River Calder and includes an oval-shaped internal plateau measuring approximately 115m by 76m, which is enclosed on all sides except the north by three rubble ramparts, each up to 1.5m high and situated on the slope of the hill, with an external ditch up to 1.5m deep in front of each. The maximum width of the whole rampart and ditch system is 46m. On the north side the defences are incomplete and mainly consist of a single rampart and ditch. However, some short lengths of triple rampart and ditch separated by areas of undisturbed ground are also visible here. Limited excavation of the defences indicated that the inner rampart was revetted with stone and also timber-laced. It has been suggested that the hillfort was built in two stages, the second of which was not completed. Very faint traces of two circular or sub-circular platforms are visible on aerial photographs.

Other hillforts are present at Portfield (site 5) and near Carnforth.

40. Warton Crag Hillfort, Carnforth (SD491728): Warton Crag is a prominent limestone hill, naturally defended on three sides by rock terraces, overlooking Morecambe Bay. The summit has an Iron Age small multivallate hillfort including

a sub-rectangular enclosure of roughly 3.2 hectares, and is defended by a combination of rock scarps and steep slopes to the south and west, and three stone ramparts curving to the north and east. The ramparts measure 3–7m wide and up to 1.3m high, and are set roughly parallel to each other approximately 50–60m apart. Within the enclosure are boulder foundations of three sub-rectangular huts constructed against a long, low rock escarpment. Immediately outside the inner rampart are a further two hut foundations located against the same escarpment. To the south, below the summit of the crag, faint traces of a bank and ditch have recently been observed along the edge of a limestone shelf. To the north of the outer rampart antiquarian sources noted the existence of numerous oval tumuli. The walls were constructed of unhewn stone with a rubble core. There are a number of entrances. The inner wall appears to contain a 1.5m-diameter chamber. Three possible hut sites are evident, and the former existence of 'innumerable small oblong barrows of earth and many sepulchral cairns, two with stone cists, cremated remains and pottery' is recorded. John Hodgson has painted an impression of how the hillfort may have looked. Today the northern hill-slope is densely wooded and the ramparts heavily overgrown so that individual features or construction details are no longer obvious.

Other possible hillfort sites may exist at Boilton Wood, Fishwick, Guyfield Bank, Hawksclough, Hindley House, Mete House, Red Scar, Selbourne Street and Six Acres. There are a number of other defended settlements at Burnley, Caton, Leck, Whittington and Worsthorne. Other possible Iron Age enclosures/settlements are found at Askew Heights (SD527623), Fair Oak (SD647458), High Park (several sites in SD64–78) and Sellet Bank (SD605773).

END OF THE IRON AGE AND ROMAN INVASION

When Claudius invaded England in AD 43, the population of Lancashire was presumed to have formed part of the wider group of people known as the Brigantes, as described by the Roman geographer Ptolemy. The Brigantian kingdom collapsed in AD 69 and there followed a swift Roman expansion, as shown by evidence from Ribchester and Carlisle, and by the early AD 70s, the whole of the area to the west of the Pennines had passed into Roman control.

Romano-British sites include Beadle Hill, Bomber Camp, Claughton Enclosure, Eller Beck, Twist Castle and Ringstones Camp. Possible Romano-British settlements are found in Burnley (New Barn, Ringstones, Twist Castle), Lancaster (Cantsfield, Claughton, Collingholme, Kellet Lane, Lancaster University, Longfield Barn, Low Barn, Scotforth and Queens Square), South Ribble (Potter Lane) and Wyre (Burn Hill).

A GAZETTEER OF LANCASHIRE'S PREHISTORIC PAST

Lancashire's Sites and Monuments Record (SMR), or Historic Environment Record (HER), administered by Lancashire County Council, has 731 prehistoric entries, which include the various stone and hut circles, hillforts, burial barrows and cairns, bog bodies and the remains of trackways, enclosures, settlements and field systems. The entries also include flint-chipping evidence and the discovery of solitary implements such as axeheads, spearheads, arrowheads, hammerheads, maceheads, querns, adzes, jewellery, pins, urns, scrapers, mallets, knives, swords, daggers, canoes and harpoons.

This gazetteer attempts to catalogue the above sites, excluding the flint-chipping sites and solitary finds. It also includes some, but not all, of the additional sites on *The Modern Antiquarian* website, which are not included in the SMR/HER.

The place-name 'Lowe' suggests the possibility of a Bronze Age ritual or burial site in the vicinity and the SMR/HER includes Hog Lowe, Pike Lowe and Three Lowes as possible prehistoric sites. The author trawled through the Ordnance Survey Landranger 1:50,000 and Explorer 1:25,000 scale maps that cover the post-1974 County of Lancashire and noted any additional 'Lowe' place-names. An extra thirteen 'sites' were found and are included here as possible prehistoric sites.

Note that in some cases Lowe has been changed or corrupted to Low or Law, as in, for example, Knave Low Barrow, Low Barn Enclosure/Settlement, Low Hill House (Ashleigh Barrow), High Law and Law House Cairns. Any additional Low and Law place-names on the Ordnance Survey maps are not included here since, in many cases, they may refer to low (as in opposite of high) and law (as in the legal system), and the number of such sites would run into the hundreds.

Instead this gazetteer includes 285 sites, broken down into four categories as below, of which fifty-one are Scheduled Ancient Monuments (SAM), ninety-four are on the National Monuments Record (NMR) and 159 are entries in the HER/SMR.

Surviving sites	104
Other sites (findspots)	8
Destroyed sites	23
Possible sites	150

Surviving sites in alphabetical order

Site name and type	Grid ref (SD)	Time-scale(s)	Location	District	SAM ref.	NMR ref.	HER/SMR ref.	Access
Anderton Cup- and Ring-marked Boulder	627134	4000–2201 BC	Adlington	Chorley	–	–	PRN4279	Private but visible by arrangement
Askew Heights Enclosure	527623	1000 BC–AD 42	Caton	Lancaster	SM23760	SD56SW17	PRN2755	Private
Badger Wells Cairn	783396	–	Pendle Hill	Ribble Valley	–	–	–	Open Access – Crow Act
Beadle Hill Bowl Barrow A	891340	2500–701 BC	Worsthorne	Burnley	SM23726	SD83SE3	PRN241	Private; nearest footpath 100m
Beadle Hill Bowl Barrow B	891341	2500–701 BC	Worsthorne	Burnley	SM23725	SD83SE3	PRN240	Private; nearest footpath 100m
Beadle Hill Romano-British Farmstead	889341	701 BC–AD 409	Worsthorne	Burnley	SM23738	SD83SE3	PRN252	Private; nearest footpath 100m
Bleara Lowe	926453	2500–701 BC	Earby	Pendle	SM23717	SD94NW5	PRN337	Open Access – Crow Act
Bleara Moor Tumulus	924453	2500–701 BC	Earby	Pendle	SM23718	SD94NW5	PRN336	Open Access – Crow Act
Bleasdale Timber Circle	577459	4000–701 BC	Chipping	Wyre	SM23749	SD54NE1	PRN115	Concessionary Footpath
Boar's Den Bowl Barrow	517111	2500–701 BC	Dangerous Corner	West Lancashire	SM23706	SD51SW17	PRN279	Private but with permitted access
Bomber Camp	842476	701 BC–AD 409	–	Pendle	SM27680	–	PRN317	Private

Site name and type	Grid ref (SD)	Time-scale(s)	Location	District	SAM ref.	NMR ref.	HER/SMR ref.	Access
Bonds Farm Occupation Site	419468	2500–701 BC	Scronkey, Pilling	Wyre	–	–	PRN1565	Private; nearest footpath 200m
Borwick Round Cairn	523728	2500–701 BC	Carnforth	Lancaster	SM23716	–	PRN2696	Private; Borwick Lane 100m
Bottoms Lane Round Cairn	469756	2500–701 BC	Silverdale	Lancaster	–	–	PRN12106	Private; nearest footpath 100m
Bradshaw Lane Farm Stone/Hut Circle	415462	4000 BC–AD 42, 2500–701 BC	Pilling	Wyre	–	SD44NW7	PRN367	Private; nearest footpath 100m
Bride's Chair Cave	482732	500,000 BC–AD 42, 1000–701 BC	Warton Crag	Lancaster	–	–	PRN1215, PRN3613	?
Brink Ends Cairn	942379	2500–701 BC	Wycoller	Pendle	–	–	PRN18878	On edge of Open Access land
Broadshaw Farm Barrow	870350	4000–2201 BC, 2500–701 BC	Worsthorne Moor	Burnley	–	SD83NE27	PRN696	Private but path around field edge
Brown Hills Beck Bowl Barrow East	756602	2500–701 BC	Gisburn Forest	Ribble Valley	SM23714	–	PRN9537	Access land in woodland area – Crow Act
Brown Hills Beck Bowl Barrow West	756603	2500–701 BC	Gisburn Forest	Ribble Valley	SM23713	–	PRN3690	Access land in woodland area – Crow Act
Burns Wood Bronze Age Settlement	519479	2500–701 BC	Barnacre with Bonds	Wyre	–	–	PRN26371	Private
Burwain's or Broad Bank Camp	902352	4000–2,201 BC, 2500–701 BC, 800 BC–AD 42	Colne	Pendle	SM27677	SD93NW8	PRN265	Private; Halifax Road 25m

Site name and type	Grid ref (SD)	Time-scale(s)	Location	District	SAM ref.	NMR ref.	HER/SMR ref.	Access
Cant Clough Round Barrow	896311	500,000 BC–AD 42, 2500–701 BC	Hurstwood	Burnley	–	–	PRN2320	Open Access – Crow Act
Carriers Croft Bronze Age cremation	755395	2500–701 BC	Pendleton	Ribble Valley	–	SD73NE4	PRN2087	Private
Carve Hill Tumulus	754158	2500–701 BC	Hawkshaw	Blackburn with Darwen	–	SD71NE8	PRN175	Private; nearest footpath 50m
Castercliffe Hillfort	884383	800 BC–AD 42	Nelson	Pendle	SM22507	SD83NE7	PRN224	Crossed by public footpaths
Castle Hill Enclosure/Settlement	650779	800 BC–AD 42	Leck	Lancaster	SM23769	SD67NE1	PRN672	Private; nearest footpath 50m
Cheetham Close Stone Circle and Cairns	716158	2500–701 BC	Turton	Blackburn with Darwen	SM23732	SD71nw2, SD71nw14	PRN169–170, PRN20124–20127, PRN20146–20149	Open Access – Crow Act
Claughton Enclosure	572663	800 BC–AD 409	Carnforth	Lancaster	SM23761	SD56NE30	PRN1197	Private; nearest footpath 100m
Collingholme Enclosed Hut Circle Settlement	638748	701 BC–AD 409	Leck	Lancaster	SM23763	SD67sw18	PRN3332	Private
Cow Close Pasture Mesolithic Hut Circles	544618	10,000–4,001 BC	Littledale	Lancaster	–	–	PRN25207	Private; Littledale Rd 50m, footpath 100m
Delf Hill Stone Circle and Cairn	900337	2500–701 BC	Worsthorne	Burnley	SM23719	SD93SW1	PRN267	Open Access – Crow Act

Site name and type	Grid ref (SD)	Time-scale(s)	Location	District	SAM ref.	NMR ref.	HER/SMR ref.	Access
Devil's Apronful Ring Bank Cairn	778394	500,000 BC–AD 42	Pendle Hill	Ribble Valley	–	–	PRN1838	Open Access – Crow Act
Dog Holes Cave	483730	500,000 BC–AD 42, 40,000–10,001 BC, 4000–2201 BC	Warton Crag	Lancaster	Lancs 84	SD47SE2	PRN511	?
Dutton's Farm Late Prehistoric/Romano-British Settlement	464104	800 BC–AD 42	Lathom	West Lancashire	–	–	PRN444	Private but close to A5209
Ell Clough Ring Cairn	901341	500,000 BC–AD 42, 2500–701 BC	Extwistle Moor	Burnley	SM23728	SD93SW2	PRN269	Private but adjacent to a public footpath
Ell Clough Saucer Barrow	901341	2500–701 BC	Extwistle Moor	Burnley	SM23727	SD93SW2	PRN270	Private but adjacent to a public footpath
Eller Beck Bell Cairn	645786	2500–701 BC	Leck	Lancaster	SM32848	SD67NW23	PRN2513	Private
Eller Beck Oval Cairn	641778	2500–701 BC	Leck	Lancaster	SM32848	SD67NW7	PRN2512	Private
Eller Beck Platform Cairn	644784	2500–701 BC	Leck	Lancaster	SM32848	SD67NW24	PRN2515	Private
Eller Beck Round Cairn 1	643781	2500–701 BC	Leck	Lancaster	SM32848	SD67NW26	PRN2514	Private
Eller Beck Round Cairn 2	646783	2500–701 BC	Leck	Lancaster	SM32848	SD67NW24	PRN2516	Private
Fairy Holes Cave	655467	1600–1001 BC	Whitewell	Ribble Valley	–	SD64NE1	PRN162	Private; nearest footpath 150m

Site name and type	Grid ref (SD)	Time-scale(s)	Location	District	SAM ref.	NMR ref.	HER/SMR ref.	Access
Great Stone of Fourstones Cup-marked Stone	669662	–	High Bentham	Lancaster	–	–	–	Open Access – Crow Act
Hameldon Pasture Cup-marked Stone	891326	–	Wasnop Edge	Burnley	–	–	–	Private; nearest footpath 100m
Hazel Edge Burial Cairn	905316	500,000 BC–AD 42, 4000–2201 BC, 2500–701 BC	Worsthorne	Burnley	–	SD93SW15	PRN275	Open Access – Crow Act
High Law Cairn/Round Hill Barrow	876308	2500–701 BC	Mereclough	Burnley	–	SD83SE17	PRN247	Private; nearest footpath less than 50m
High Park House Platforms	645785	2500–701 BC, 800 BC–AD 42	Leck	Lancaster	–	–	PRN25041	Private
High Park Iron Age Earthwork/Field System	643782	100 BC–AD 42	Leck	Lancaster	–	–	PRN25061	Private
High Park Platforms	640779	800 BC–AD 42	Leck	Lancaster	–	–	PRN25054	Private
High Park Prehistoric Field System	643782	500,000 BC–AD 42, 1000–701 BC	Leck	Lancaster	–	–	PRN25060	Private
High Park Settlement North	640781	800 BC–AD 42	Leck	Lancaster	–	–	PRN25036	Private
High Park Settlement West	637780	800 BC–AD 42	Leck	Lancaster	–	–	PRN25039	Private
High Park Settlement East	642779	100 BC–AD 42	Leck	Lancaster	–	–	PRN25053	Private

Site name and type	Grid ref (SD)	Time-scale(s)	Location	District	SAM ref.	NMR ref.	HER/SMR ref.	Access
High Park Settlement South	640778	800 BC–AD 42	Leck	Lancaster	–	–	PRN25059	Private
High Park Unenclosed Settlement	640782	800 BC–AD 42	Leck	Lancaster	–	–	PRN25034	Private
Hurst Hill Cairn	623173	500,000 BC–AD 42	Anglezarke	Chorley	–	–	PRN4029	Open Access – Crow Act
Jeppe Knave Grave	759378	2500–701 BC	Wiswell	Ribble Valley	–	SD73NE3	PRN187	Open Access – Crow Act
Kate's Pad Wooden Trackway	409446	2500–701 BC, 800 BC–AD 42	Out Rawcliffe	Wyre	–	SD44SW5	PRN84	Private
Lancaster University Romano-British farmstead	483565	100 BC–AD 409	South West Campus	Lancaster	–	–	PRN30347	Private; nearest footpath 100m
Law House Cairns	872302	2500–701 BC	Mereclough	Burnley	–	–	PRN2321	Private but Red Lees Road passes through the site
Leighton Park Cairn	488740	2500–701 BC	Yealand Conyers	Lancaster	–	–	PRN3520	Private but with public footpath very close by
Little Hameldon Long Barrow	794293	4000–2201 BC	Hapton	Burnley	–	–	PRN16262	Open Access – Crow Act
Little Painley Bowl Barrow	828501	2500–701 BC	Gisburn	Ribble Valley	SM23746	SD85SW5	PRN330	Private; the A682 & Ribble Way are 250m away
Longridge Fell Cairn Circle	645404	2500–701 BC	Longridge Fell	Ribble Valley	SM32845	SD64SW21	PRN165	Open Access – Crow Act

Site name and type	Grid ref (SD)	Time-scale(s)	Location	District	SAM ref.	NMR ref.	HER/SMR ref.	Access
Noon Hill Kerbed Round Cairn	646149	2500–701 BC	Belmont	Chorley	SM23708	SD61SW32	PRN134	Open Access – Crow Act
Parlick Pike Round Cairn	595450	2500–701 BC	Chipping	Ribble Valley & Wyre	SM23751	–	PRN8100	Open Access – Crow Act
Parsonage House Bronze Age Burial Site	648351	2500–701 BC	Ribchester	Ribble Valley	–	–	PRN4219	Private but adjacent to a Bridleway
Pike Lowe Bowl Barrow and Tumulus	894342	2500–701 BC	Worsthorne	Burnley	SM23720	SD83SE4	PRN242	Private; nearest footpath 100m
Pike Stones Chambered Long Cairn	627172	3500–2701 BC	Anglezarke Moor	Chorley	SM23731	SD61NW6	PRN278	Open Access – Crow Act
Pinder Hill Barrow	727435	2500–701 BC	Waddington	Ribble Valley	–	SD74SW17	PRN305	Private; clearly visible from the nearest footpath 50m
Pleasington Cemetery Inurned Cremation Site	649269	2500–701 BC	Pleasington	Blackburn with Darwen	–	–	PRN7118, PRN7862	Within the Cemetery
Portfield Hillfort	745355	4000–2201 BC, 2500 BC–AD 42, 800 BC–AD 42	Whalley	Ribble Valley	SM27676	SD73NW22	PRN181 PRN1176	Private; adjacent to Portfield Lane
Revidge Tumulus	673294	2500–701 BC	Blackburn	Blackburn with Darwen	–	SD62NE1	PRN141	Private
Ringstones Camp	886330	700 BC–AD 409	Worsthorne	Burnley	SM23739	SD83SE11	PRN254	Private with a public footpath along the edge

Site name and type	Grid ref (SD)	Time-scale(s)	Location	District	SAM ref.	NMR ref.	HER/SMR ref.	Access
Ringstones Mound/Stone Circle	885329 885330	2500–701 BC	Worsthorne	Burnley	–	SD83SE13	PRN259	Private with a public footpath alongside
Round Loaf Round Barrow	637182	2500–701 BC	Anglezarke Moor	Chorley	SM23707	SD61NW2	PRN127	Open Access – Crow Act
Rushy Brow Mesolithic Hunting Camp	633177	500,000 BC–AD 42, 10,000–4001 BC	Anglezarke Moor	Chorley	–	–	PRN4875	Open Access – Crow Act
Sandhole Wood Barrow	512424	2500–701 BC	Claughton	Wyre	SM27843 Claughton hlaew	–	PRN119	Private but adjacent to Lodge Road
Sellet Bank Enclosure	695773	2500 BC–AD 42	Whittington	Lancaster	SM 23762	SD67NW33	PRN2682	Private; nearest footpath 200m
Sheddon Clough Mesolithic Camp	895295	10,000–4001 BC	Worstorne Moor	Burnley	–	–	PRN11179	Open Access – Crow Act
Slipper Hill Stone Circle	884327	2500–701 BC	Worsthorne	Burnley	SM23723	SD83SE14	PRN244	Private; nearest footpath 100m
Standing Stones Hill Stone Circle	646173	500,000 BC–AD 42, 2500–701 BC	Belmont	Chorley	–	SD61NW17	PRN128	Open Access – Crow Act
Storrs Moss Mesolithic Settlement and Causeway	484757	500,000 BC–AD 42, 10,000–4001 BC, 4,000–2,201 BC	Yealand Redmayne	Lancaster	–	SD47NE11	PRN508	Private but adjacent to Storrs Lane
Summerhouse Hill Kerbed Round Cairn	501742	2500–701 BC	Yealand Conyers	Lancaster	SM23730	SD57SW1	PRN603	Private; nearest footpath 100m, 50m from Peter Lane

Site name and type	Grid ref (SD)	Time-scale(s)	Location	District	SAM ref.	NMR ref.	HER/SMR ref.	Access
Summerhouse Hill Stone Circle & Cairn	500743	3000–1001 BC	Yealand Conyers	Lancaster	SM23729	SD57SW2	PRN604	Private but a public footpath passes through
Sweet Well House Barrow	893340	4000 BC–AD 42	Worsthorne	Burnley	–	–	PRN4667	Private but close to the Burnley Way
Tatham Park Enclosed Settlement	610684	2500 BC–AD 42	Wray	Lancaster	SM23764	SD66NW11	PRN2678	Private
The Clough Long Mound	690323	500,000 BC–AD 42	Wilpshire	Ribble Valley	–	–	PRN15016	Private nearest footpath is less than 100m
Thieveley Pike Beacon	872270	2500–701 BC	Deerplay Moor	Burnley	–	SD82NE8	PRN209	Open Access – Crow Act
Thirteen Stone Hill Stone Circle	766242	2500–701 BC	Haslingden	Rossendale	–	–	PRN1096	Open Access – Crow Act
Torrisholme Bowl Barrow	459642	2500–701 BC	Morecambe	Lancaster	SM23715	SD46SE2	PRN429	Concessionary
Twist Castle Barrow	890337	2500–701 BC	Worsthorne	Burnley	–	SD83SE27	PRN249	Private; nearest footpath is 200m
Twist Hill Bowl Barrow	889337	2500–701 BC	Worsthorne	Burnley	SM23724	SD33SE2	PRN239	Private; nearest footpath is 100m
Twist Castle Romano-British Farmstead	888337	–	Worsthorne	Burnley	SM23750	SD83SE6	PRN253	Private; nearest footpath is 75m
Warton Crag Hillfort	491728	500,000 BC–AD 42, AD 42, 800 BC–AD 42	Warton	Lancaster	SM23643	SD47SE4	PRN513	Concessionary part of Warton Crag Nature Reserve

Site name and type	Grid ref (SD)	Time-scale(s)	Location	District	SAM ref.	NMR ref.	HER/SMR ref.	Access
Wasnop Edge Bowl Barrow	891326	2500–701 BC	Worsthorne	Burnley	SM23721	SD83SE16	PRN246	Private; nearest footpath is 100m
Wasnop Edge Round Cairn Southwest	891325	2500–701 BC	Worsthorne	Burnley	SM23722	SD83SE15	PRN245	Private; nearest footpath is 50m
Whitelow Hillock Cairn	805162	2500–701 BC	Shuttleworth	Bury	–	–	PRN1939	Private; nearest footpath is 50m
Winckley Lowe Barrow West	706374	500,000 BC–AD 42, 2500–701 BC	Brockhall Village	Ribble Valley	SM23711	SD73NW3	PRN180	Private but visible from the Ribble Way 200m
Winckley Lowe Barrow East (Loe Hill)	708372	2500–701 BC	Brockhall Village	Ribble Valley	SM23712	SD73NW2	PRN179	Private but visible from the Ribble Way 150m
Winter Hill Kerbed Round Cairn	655149	2500–701 BC	Rivington Moor	Chorley	SM23709	SD61SE18	PRN139	Open Access – Crow Act
Worsaw Hill Barrow and Cave	779432	2500–701 BC	Downham	Ribble Valley	–	SD74SE7	PRN194	Private; nearest footpath is 150m
Worsthorne Moor Burial Cairn	910300	500,000 BC–AD 42, 2500–701 BC	Worsthorne	Burnley	–	SD93SW25	PRN272	Open Access – Crow Act
Worsthorne Moor Cairn	90–30–	2500–701 BC	Worsthorne	Burnley	–	–	PRN2343	Open Access – Crow Act
Wycoller Packhorse Bridge Cup-marked Stones	932393	–	Wycoller	Pendle	–	–	–	In Wycoller Country Park

Other sites/findspots in alphabetical order

Site name and type	Grid ref.(SD)	Time-scale(s)	Location	District	SAM ref.	NMR ref.	SMR ref.	Access
Backridge Findspot	719427	500,000 BC–AD 42	Bashall/ Waddington	Ribble Valley	–	SD74SW13	PRN304	Private
Briarfield Nursery Findspot	337389	500,000 BC–AD 42	Poulton-le-Fylde	Wyre	–	–	PRN15564	Private
Fowler's Farm Findspot	453453	500,000–4001 BC	Nateby	Wyre	–	–	PRN26106	Private
Jollies i'th Dean Farm Findspot	524063	500,000 BC–AD 42	Upholland	West Lancashire	–	–	PRN15047	Private
Kentucky Farm Findspot	442462	500,000 BC–AD 42	Garstang/Pilling	Wyre	–	–	PRN1876	Private
Poulton Elk Findspot	331386	40,000–10,001 BC	Poulton-le-Fylde	Wyre	–	–	PRN2663	Private
Preston Docks Findspot	512296	4000 BC–AD 409, 2500–701 BC	River Ribble	Preston	–	SD52NW2	PRN6	No Access – underwater!
Skippool Marsh Findspot	357409	500,000 BC–AD 42	River Wyre	Fylde	–	SD52NW	PRN51	Private (Saltmarsh) but close to Wyre Way

Destroyed sites in alphabetical order

Site name and type	Grid ref. (SD)	Time-scale(s)	Location	District	NMR ref.	SMR ref.
Ashleigh or Low Hill House Round Barrow	696208	1600–1001 BC	Darwen	Blackburn with Darwen	SD62SE22	PRN144
Astley Farm Burial Site	574184	4000 BC–AD 42, 2500–701 BC	Chorley	Chorley	–	PRN2569
Bank Lane Cairn	805172	2500–701 BC	Shuttleworth	Rossendale	–	PRN1940
Bone Hill Hut Circle	43–46–	2500–701 BC	Pilling	Wyre	SD44NW1	PRN358
Broadshaw Farm Barrow	870350	4000–2201 BC, 2500–701 BC	Haggate	Burnley	SD83NE27	PRN696
Brockhall Wood Tumulus	699375	2500–701 BC	Brockall Village	Ribble Valley	SD63NE27	PRN149
Catlow Quarry Cremation Urns	885368	2500–701 BC	Nelson	Pendle	SD83NW25	PRN222
Cliviger Laithe Urns	867311	2500–701 BC	Southeast of Burnley	Burnley	–	PRN1993
Derby & Whitprick Hills Barrow	397339	2500–701 BC	Weeton Lane,	Fylde	SD33SE2	PRN37
Ell Clough Ring Cairn	902341	2500–701 BC	Extwistle Moor	Burnley	–	PRN268
Extwistle Moor Burial Mound	900330	500,000 BC–AD 42	Extwistle Moor	Burnley	SD93SW26	PRN1160

Site name and type	Grid ref. (SD)	Time-scale(s)	Location	District	NMR ref.	SMR ref.
Hapton Earth Circle	80–30–	500,000 BC–AD 42 2500–701 BC	Hapton	Burnley	SD83SW15	PRN232
Lancaster Barracks	487608	2500–701 BC	St Martin's College	Lancaster	SD46SE16	PRN441
Lancaster Moor Urnfield	488613	2500–701 BC	Williamson Park	Lancaster	SD46SE15	PRN440
Manor Farm Cairn	522725	2500–1501 BC	Borwick	Lancaster	–	PRN2691
Moseley Height Stone Circle	879300	2500–701 BC	Mereclough	Burnley	SD83SE34	PRN250
Penny Street Bridge Cinerary Urn	477612	2500–701 BC	Lancaster	Lancaster	–	PRN1999
Penny Street Urnfield	477613	2500–701 BC	Lancaster	Lancaster	–	PRN2000
Queen's Square Cremation Urn	476614	2500 BC–AD 200	Lancaster	Lancaster	SD46SE51	PRN473
Ring Stones Hill Stone Circle	892366	2500–701 BC	Nelson	Pendle	SD83NE24	PRN1937
Stonyhill Lodge Round Cairn(s) and Wells	311321	2500–701 BC	Blackpool	Blackpool	SD33SW3	PRN36
Warton Crag Cairns	490730	2500–701 BC	Warton	Lancaster	SD47SE15	PRN522
Weeton Lane Heads Round Cairns	392345	2500–701 BC	Weeton Lane	Fylde	SD33SE7, SD33SE8, SD33SE9, SD33SE10	PRN38, PRN39, PRN40, PRN41

Possible sites in alphabetical order

Site name and possible site type	Grid ref. (SD)	Time-scale(s)	Location	District	NMR ref.	HER/SMR ref.	Access
Bad Grove Burial Mound	711520	–	Slaidburn	Ribble Valley	–	–	Private; between public and concessionary paths
Boilton Wood Promontory Fort/Enclosure	584314	4000 BC–AD 42	Preston	Preston	–	PRN15241	In a Local Nature Reserve with footpath adjacent
Brown Hill End Circle	716491	–	Easington Fell	Ribble Valley	–	–	Open Access – Crow Act
Brown Lowe place-name (Barrow/Tumulus)	68-19-	–	Darwen Moor	Blackburn with Darwen	–	–	Open Access – Crow Act
Bull Bank Farm Settlement	622718	500,000 BC–AD 409	Wennington	Lancaster	–	PRN2667	Private
Bull Hill Barrow or Flint Manufacturing Site	767187	500,000 BC–AD 42, 4000–2201 BC	Ramsbottom	Rossendale	SD71NE3	PRN1074	Access Land but within a firing and test range. Observe warning notices
Burn Hill Enclosed Settlement	332443	4000 BC–AD 42, 2500 BC–AD 409	Thornton	Wyre	–	PRN26074	Private; close to Fleetwood Road (B5268)
Burwain's Farm Stone Circle, Camp or Cairn	888358	–	Colne	Pendle	–	–	Private; footpath nearby
Byroe Hill Barrow	441607	4000 BC–AD 42	Heaton	Lancaster	–	PRN30032	Private
Cantsfield Prehistoric or Romano-British Enclosure/Settlement	624722	3000 BC–AD 409	Cantsfield	Lancaster	–	PRN2654	Private
Carterplace Hill Barrow	786245	500,000 BC–AD 42	Hud Hey	Rossendale	–	PRN30270	Private

Site name and possible site type	Grid ref. (SD)	Time-scale(s)	Location	District	NMR ref.	HER/ SMR ref.	Access
Cartridge Pasture Bronze Age Cairn	890278	2500–701 BC	Cliviger	Burnley	–	PRN20150	ON edge of Access Land with Bridleway adjacent
Cat Knot Barrow	721598	2500–701 BC	Hasgill Fell	Ribble Valley	–	PRN13167	Open Access – Crow Act
Charters Moss Settlement	695165	–	Darwen	Blackburn with Darwen	–	–	Open Access – Crow Act – close to a plantation
Claughton Manor Enclosure	574661	500,000 BC–AD 42	Lune Valley	Lancaster	–	PRN9007	Private; nearest footpath 50m
Clow Hill Cairn, Nutshaw Hill	817287	2500–701 BC	Dunnockshaw	Burnley	–	PRN15336	Open Access – Crow Act
Commissary's Farm Henge	538178	4000–2201 BC	Euxton and Eccleston	West Lancashire	–	PRN3025	Private; nearest footpath 100m
Coverdale Enclosures/ Settlement	849468	500,000 BC–AD 42	Barnoldswick	Pendle	–	PRN1918	Private; nearest footpath 50m
Cowpe Lowe place-name (Barrow/ Tumulus)	82–20–	–	Waterfoot	Rossendale	–	–	Private
Crag Hole Settlement	484534	4000 BC–AD 42	Ellel	Lancaster	–	PRN11260	Private; but close to the Lancaster Canal
Cuckoo Wood Bee-hived Pits	452426	800 BC–AD 42	Rawcliffe Moss	Wyre	–	PRN30273	Private; nearest footpath 250m
Deeply Vale Cairn	824149	4000 BC–AD 42	Bury-Rochdale	Rossendale	–	PRN30126	?
Deeply Hill Cairns	824148	4000 BC–AD 42	Bury-Rochdale	Rossendale	–	PRN30127 PRN30128	?
Dock Acres Quarry Enclosure	511726	2500–701 BC	Warton	Lancaster	–	PRN2556	Private between A6 and railway line

Site name and possible site type	Grid ref. (SD)	Time-scale(s)	Location	District	NMR ref.	HER/ SMR ref.	Access
Dovecote Farm Settlement	571234	4000 BC–AD 42	Clayton-le-Woods	Chorley	–	PRN19290	Private
Dry Hill Barrow	747241	2500–701 BC	Oswaldtwistle Moor	Hyndburn	–	PRN20309	Open Access – Crow Act
Eagland Hill Stone Circle, Birks Farm	425449	500,000 BC–AD 42	Southeast of Pilling	Wyre	SD44SWM	PRN1639	Private with a public footpath close by
Fair Oak Settlement	647458	800 BC–AD 42	Bowland with Leagram	Ribble Valley	–	PRN3089	Private with minor road to south
Fishwick Allotments Promontory Fort	559294	500,000 BC–AD 42	Preston	Preston	–	PRN12914	Private; nearest footpath 150m
Fulwood Hall Lane Barrow or Motte	549321	4000 BC–AD 42	Fulwood	Preston	–	PRN15265	Private but adjacent to a minor road
Gibson's Farm Findspot	471442	4000–2501 BC	Nateby	Wyre	–	PRN26087	Private nearest footpath 50m
Grain Pole Hill Round Cairns,	625180	Undated	Anglezarke Moor	Chorley	–	PRN4065 PRN4066 PRN4067 PRN4068	Open Access – Crow Act
Grain Pole Hill Round Cairn	626180	Undated	Anglezarke Moor	Chorley	–	PRN4069	Open Access – Crow Act
Grain Pole Hill Round Cairn (North)	625182	Undated	Anglezarke Moor	Chorley	–	PRN4070	Open Access – Crow Act
Grain Pole Hill Round Cairn (North)	626181	Undated	Anglezarke Moor	Chorley	–	PRN 4071	Open Access – Crow Act
Grain Pole Hill (West) Round Cairn and Mounds	622181	Undated	Anglezarke Moor	Chorley	–	PRN4077	Open Access – Crow Act

Site name and possible site type	Grid ref. (SD)	Time-scale(s)	Location	District	NMR ref.	HER/ SMR ref.	Access
Green Lowe place-name (Barrow/Tumulus)	68-18-	–	Turton Moor	Blackburn with Darwen	–	–	Open Access – Crow Act
Guyfield Bank Promontory Fort	575306	500,000 BC–AD 42	Brockholes Wood	Preston	–	PRN15240	Local Authority Woodland Nature Reserve
Hameldon Pasture Trackway	886330	4000 BC–AD 42	Worsthorne	Burnley	SD83SE12	PRN255	Private but adjacent to a footpath
Hawksclough Hillfort	574240	4000 BC–AD 42	Clayton Brook	Chorley	–	PRN19289	Private; in Country Park adjacent to concessionary footpath
Hellbank/Hallbank Long Barrow	499706	4000–2,201 BC	Carnforth	Lancaster	–	PRN3382	Private; in an urban fringe setting
Heysham Barrow North	414605	4000 BC–AD 42	Middleton Road, Heysham	Lancaster	SD46SW4	PRN2548	Private; in an urban fringe setting
Heysham Barrow South	414603	4000 BC–AD 42	Trummacarr Primary School, Heysham	Lancaster	–	PRN2549	In school grounds
Heysham Head Late Mesolithic Settlement	409616	10,000–4,001 BC	Heysham	Lancaster	–	PRN26083	Open Access – Crow Act
High Park Platforms	638781	1000–701 BC	Leck	Lancaster	–	PRN25040	Private
High Park Burial Cairn	646784	4000–2201 BC, 2500–1501 BC	Leck	Lancaster	–	PRN25042	Private
High Park Short Long Cairn	646784	4000–2201 BC	Leck	Lancaster	–	PRN25043	Private
High Park Round or Burial Cairns	647785	500,000 BC– AD 42, 1000–701 BC	Leck	Lancaster	–	PRN25044	Private

Site name and possible site type	Grid ref. (SD)	Time-scale(s)	Location	District	NMR ref.	HER/ SMR ref.	Access
High Park Huts or Pens	643781	100 BC–AD 42	Leck	Lancaster	–	PRN25050	Private
Higher Broad Clough British Camp	863243	4000 BC–AD 42	Higher Broad Clough	Rossendale	–	PRN30286	Private; nearest footpath 100m
Higher Height Ring Cairn	668143	500,000 BC–AD 42	Belmont	Blackburn with Darwen	–	PRN25076	Open Access – Crow Act
Higher Swineherd Lowe Farm place-name (Barrow/Tumulus)	77–23–	–	Thirteen Stone Hill	Rossendale	–	–	Private farm but with footpaths through
Hindley House Promontory Fort,	552231	4000 BC–AD 42	Kitchen Green, Fulwood	Preston	–	PRN15263	Private; in an urban setting
Hoarstones Stone Circle	824375	4000 BC–AD 42	Fence/Nelson	Pendle	–	PRN1903	Private
Hodder Bank Fell Enclosures	673491	500,000 BC–AD 42 4000 BC–AD 42	Hodder Bank Fell	Ribble Valley	–	PRN15391	Open Access – Crow Act
Hog Lowe Pike place-name (Barrow/ Tumulus)	747214	500,000 BC–AD 42, 10,000–4001 BC	Haslingden Grane,	Blackburn with Darwen, Rossendale	–	PRN12557	On boundary of Open Access – Crow Act
Horse Hey Farm Bronze Age Settlement site	693426	500,000 BC–AD 42, 2500–701 BC	Bashall Eaves	Ribble Valley	–	PRN1875, PRN2303	Private; nearest footpath 200m
Hurst Hill Long & Round Barrows (Southwest)	623174	Undated	Anglezarke Moor	Chorley	–	PRN4022–4026	Open Access – Crow Act
Hurst Hill Round Cairn (Northeast)	630180	Undated	Anglezarke Moor	Chorley	–	PRN4030	Open Access – Crow Act
Hurst Hill Long Cairn	624176	Undated	Anglezarke Moor	Chorley	–	PRN4054	Open Access – Crow Act

Site name and possible site type	Grid ref. (SD)	Time-scale(s)	Location	District	NMR ref.	HER/ SMR ref.	Access
Hurst Hill Round Cairn	624177	Undated	Anglezarke Moor	Chorley	–	PRN4055	Open Access – Crow Act
Hurst Hill Ring Cairn	625174	Undated	Anglezarke Moor	Chorley	–	PRN4059	Open Access – Crow Act
Hurst Hill Round Cairn (West)	624177	Undated	Anglezarke Moor	Chorley	–	PRN4072	Open Access – Crow Act
Hurst Hill Round Cairn	624176	Undated	Anglezarke Moor	Chorley	–	PRN4074	Open Access – Crow Act
Hurst Hill (East) Platform	631179	Undated	Anglezarke Moor	Chorley	–	PRN4079	Open Access – Crow Act
Hurst Hill Round Cairn	631178	Undated	Anglezarke Moor	Chorley	–	PRN4080	Open Access – Crow Act
Hurst Hill Round Cairn	629178	Undated	Anglezarke Moor	Chorley	–	PRN4082	Open Access – Crow Act
Hurst Hill Round Cairn	628178	Undated	Anglezarke Moor	Chorley	–	PRN4085	Open Access – Crow Act
Hurst Hill Long Cairns	631179 & 631180	Undated	Anglezarke Moor	Chorley	–	PRN4088, PRN4089, PRN4080	Open Access – Crow Act
Hurst Hill Round Cairns	631180 & 631181	Undated	Anglezarke Moor	Chorley	–	PRN4091, PRN4092	Open Access – Crow Act
Hurstwood Brook Valley Cairn	897323	2500–701 BC	Wasnop Edge, Worsthorne	Burnley	–	PRN15294	Open Access – Crow Act
Ireby Fell Settlement	672771	500,000 BC–AD 42	Ireby	Lancaster	–	PRN11327	Open Access – Crow Act
Jepson's Gate/Hurst Hill Long & Round Cairns	624173	Undated	Anglezarke Moor	Chorley	–	PRN4031, PRN4036	Open Access – Crow Act

Site name and possible site type	Grid ref. (SD)	Time-scale(s)	Location	District	NMR ref.	HER/ SMR ref.	Access
Jepson's Gate/Hurst Hill Long Cairns	625173	Undated	Anglezarke Moor	Chorley	–	PRN4046, PRN4047, PRN4048	Open Access – Crow Act
Kellet Lane Romano-British Settlement	483644	2500 BC–AD 409	Halton	Lancaster	SD46SE88	PRN2677	Private; nearest footpath 100m
Knave Hill Mound	895371	500,000 BC–AD 42	Nelson	Pendle	–	PRN15378	Private; nearest footpath less than 100m
Knave Low Barrow	727245	2500–701 BC	Belthorn	Hyndburn	–	PRN20308	Open Access – Crow Act
Know Hill Barrow	460744	2500–701 BC	Silverdale	Lancaster	–	PRN2935	Private land
Lad Lowe Hill place-name (Barrow/ Tumulus)	87-44-	–	White Moor, Salterforth	Pendle	–	–	Open Access – Crow Act
Langden Head Barrow	581507	4000 BC–AD 42	Forest of Bowland	Wyre	–	PRN2625	Open Access – Crow Act
Leck Hall Enclosure/ Settlement	649767	500,000 BC–AD 42	Leck	Lancaster	–	PRN2584	Private; nearest footpath 200m
Longfield Barn Settlement	590779	100 BC–AD 409	Whittington	Lancaster	–	PRN4334	Private land
Longridge Fell Round Cairn/Field System/ Settlment	637396	2500–701 BC	Northeast of Longridge	Ribble Valley	–	PRN12817	Open Access – Crow Act
Low Barn Enclosure/ Settlement	647756	500,000 BC–AD 409	Wire Gill, Leck	Lancaster	–	PRN10217	Private; nearest footpath 100m
Lowe Hill place-name (Barrow/Tumulus)	70-18-		Cadshaw	Blackburn with Darwen	–	–	Private but crossed by a footpath
Lower Apronful Hill of Stones Cairn	777390	–	Apronful Hill, Pendle Hill	Ribble Valley	–	–	Open Access – Crow Act

Site name and possible site type	Grid ref. (SD)	Time-scale(s)	Location	District	NMR ref.	HER/ SMR ref.	Access
Many Pits Wood Bowl Barrow	478329	500,000 BC–AD 42	Newton with Clifton	Fylde	–	PRN12875	Private land
Midgery Lane Ring Ditch Earthwork	547334	500,000 BC–AD 42	Fulwood	Preston	–	PRN15214	Private; in an industrial estate
Mellor Brow Mound	651310	2500–701 BC	Mellor	Ribble Valley	–	PRN20296	Private; in an urban fringe setting
Mete House Wood Promontory Fort/ Enclosure	564294	500,000 BC–AD 42	Fishwick	Preston	–	PRN15239	Private
Much Hoole Charcoal Pit	460227	4000 BC–AD 42	Much Hoole	South Ribble	–	PRN30498	Private; nearest footpath 50m
Nateby Lodge Findspot	462443	2500–701 BC	Nateby	Wyre	–	PRN26095	Private but close to footpath
New Barn Farm Settlement	808300	500,000 BC–AD 409	Hapton	Burnley	–	PRN3498	Private
Old Laund Booth Stone Circle	824375	4000 BC–AD 42	Fence	Pendle	–	PRN1903	Private; in an urban fringe setting
Old Park Wood Earthwork	471565	4000 BC–AD 42	Thurnham	Lancaster	–	PRN26485	Private
Over Kellet Iron Age or Romano–British Settlements (Northeast)	522712	800 BC–AD 42	Over Kellet	Lancaster	–	PRN4721	Private
Over Kellet Iron Age or Romano–British Settlements (Southwest)	520711	800 BC–AD 42	Over Kellet	Lancaster	–	PRN4721	Private
Pike Lowe place-name (Barrow/Tumulus)	734229	2500–701 BC	Haslingden	Rossendale	–	PRN12535	Open Access – Crow Act

Site name and possible site type	Grid ref. (SD)	Time-scale(s)	Location	District	NMR ref.	HER/SMR ref.	Access
Pike Lowe place-name (Barrow/Tumulus)	62-22-	–	Brinscall	Chorley	–	–	Private but surrounded by footpaths
Potter Lane Iron Age or Romano-British Round Houses	582286	800 BC–AD 409	Cuerdale	South Ribble	–	PRN30131	Private but close to footpath
Red Scar Wood Promontory Fort/Enclosure	581319	4000 BC–AD 42	East Preston	Preston	–	PRN15242	Adjacent to footpath (Ribble Way)
Roscoe Lowe place-name (Barrow/Tumulus)	61-13-	–	Adlington	Chorley	–	–	Private but adjacent to New Road/Roscoe Lowe Brow
Rushy Brow Round Cairn	633175	Undated	Anglezarke Moor	Chorley	–	PRN4094	Open Access – Crow Act
Rushy Brow Stone Cist/Structure	634174	Undated	Anglezarke Moor	Chorley	–	PRN4093	Open Access – Crow Act
Saddle Fell Circular Bank/Hut Circle	610462	4000 BC–AD 42	Chipping	Ribble Valley	–	PRN12352	Open Access – Crow Act
Saddle Fell Reveted Bank	611464	4000 BC–AD 42	Chipping	Ribble Valley	–	PRN12348	Open Access – Crow Act
Salwick Barrows	462314	2500–701 BC	Newton with Clifton	Fylde	SD43SE19	PRN68	Private; north of Church Lane
Scotforth Enclosure Iron Age or Romano-British Farmstead	479588	500,000 BC–AD 42	Scotforth	Lancaster	–	PRN243	Private; in urban fringe setting close to A6
Scotforth Barrow	475582	2500–701 BC	Scotforth	Lancaster	–	PRN30003	Private but adjacent to footpath
Scout Moor Boundary Marker	824187	4000 BC–AD 42	Scout Moor	Rossendale	–	PRN26141	Open Access – Crow Act

Site name and possible site type	Grid ref. (SD)	Time-scale(s)	Location	District	NMR ref.	HER/SMR ref.	Access
Selbourne Street Promontory Fort	543286	500,000 BC–AD 42	Frenchwood	Preston	–	PRN12913	In Frenchwood Gardens public park
Six Acres Promontory Fort	543324	4000 BC–AD 42	Preston Golf Course, Fulwood	Preston	–	PRN15249	Private; in golf course with footpath within 50m
Skelshaw Earthwork	719504	–	Rye Clough, Slainburn	Ribble Valley	–	–	Private; nearest footpath 50m
Slipper Lowe place-name (Barrow/Tumulus)	661202	–	Tockholes Plantation	Blackburn with Darwen	–	–	Private; nearest footpath 150m
Stump Cross Standing Stone	877301	–	Mereclough	Burnley	–	–	On roadside verge
The Flatt Stone Circle	628173	Undated	Rushy Brow, Anglezarke Moor	Chorley	–	PRN4078	Open Access – Crow Act
The Lowe place-name (Barrow/Tumulus)	61-19-	–	White Coppice	Chorley	–	–	Private but surrounded by footpaths
The Lowe place-name (Barrow/Tumulus)	88-27-	–	Cliviger	Burnley	–	–	Open Access – Crow Act
The Sandpit Neolithic Settlement	478148	4000–2501 BC	Blackmoor, Mawdesley,	Chorley	–	PRN2778	Private but close to Black Moor Road
The Sluice Findspot, Fiddler's Ferry, Hundred End	380206	500,000 BC–AD 42	North Meols	West Lancashire	SD32SE1	PRN1281	Private
Three Lowes place-name (Barrows/Tumuli)	718167	4000 BC–AD 42	Turton	Blackburn with Darwen	–	PRN1865	Private but crossed by footpath

Site name and possible site type	Grid ref. (SD)	Time-scale(s)	Location	District	NMR ref.	HER/ SMR ref.	Access
Trough Plantation Neolithic Settlement	482759	4000–2501 BC	Silverdale	Lancaster	–	PRN2769	Private
Turn Lowe place-name (Barrow/Tumulus)	67–19–	–	Darwen Moor	Blackburn with Darwen	–	–	Open Access – Crow Act
Turton Moor Findspot	680180	500,000 BC–AD 42	Belmont/ Darwen	Blackburn with Darwen	SD61NE	PRN1857	Open Access – Crow Act
Uglow Farm Prehistoric Site	748210	4000 BC–AD 42	Turton North	Blackburn with Darwen	–	PRN11979	Private; nearest footpath 50m
Wasnop Edge Cairn	893326	2500–701 BC	Ben Edge, Worsthorne	Burnley	–	PRN15277	Open Access – Crow Act
Wasnop Edge Round and Linear Cairns	893327	2500–701 BC	Worsthorne	Burnley	–	PRN15296	Open Access – Crow Act
White Coppice Cairnfield SMR No.	625189	Undated	North of Dean Black Brook	Chorley	–	PRN1835	Open Access – Crow Act
White Ledge Hill Long Cairn	636173	Undated	Anglezarke Moor	Chorley	–	PRN4095	Open Access – Crow Act
Winter Hill Round Cairn	656143	Undated	Rivington	Chorley	–	PRN3037	Open Access – Crow Act
Winter Hill Oval Mound, Rivington	656143	Undated	Rivington	Chorley	–	PRN3038	Open Access – Crow Act
Wolfhole Crag Cup-marked Stone	632578	4000 BC– AD 42	Mallowdale, Fell	Ribble Valley	–	PRN26030	Open Access – Crow Act
Worsthorne Moor Cairn	900306	2500–701 BC	Worsthorne Moor	Burnley	–	PRN15285	Open Access – Crow Act
Worsthorne Moor Cairns	904306	2500–701 BC	Worsthorne Moor	Burnley	–	PRN15286, PRN15287	Open Access – Crow Act

2

PLACE-NAMES AND THE SACRED IN THE LANCASHIRE LANDSCAPE

SARA VERNON

The research for this paper initially came out of talk I gave on place-names that have a pre-Christian element. These consisted of over 100 place-names that denote some pre-Christian etymology. Places denoting strange past activities such as ridges haunted by goblins, hills protected by demons, valleys belonging to witches, sacred groves belonging to heathen gods; cliffs, banks, hills and mounds possessed by evil spirits; hills where elves and fairies danced, sacred trees with a personal attachment to a saint, crosses depicting safe passage routes, blessed boundary stones, hills with crosses, holy wells and springs, hills blessed by saints, pre-Conquest churches miraculously placed nearby Roman roads and major water ways. With this in mind, I decided to rewrite my former paper and systematically go through Cameron's,[1] Ekwall's,[2] Gelling's,[3] A.D. Mills'[4] and David Mills'[5] written works, thus creating a new comprehensive catalogue specific to pre-Christian and pre-Conquest sacred sites in Lancashire.

Past cultures can be embraced, explored and debated in many ways, such as is found in romantic, historical literature and archaeological, demographical, environmental and palaeoethnobotany studies, but the main understanding must come from the study of place-names and their placing upon the landscape. Buy any Ordnance Survey map and the first notable features you see are the many field and place-names, their etymology often distorted over the years.

Before starting to unravel the studied place-name it is essential that all earlier spellings of the place must be obtained from historical sources such as the Domesday Book, *The Anglo-Saxon Chronicles*, Subsidy Rolls, Pipe Rolls, Bede, Beowulf, Chaucer, Chartulary Records, and other early Monastic, Ecclesiastical Records.

Identifying early Christian sites within a modern landscape is not a task for the faint-hearted. Early church sites follow a topographical pattern, and they are often sited by riverbanks or a watercourse, which may point to the continuation of a tradition from pre-Christian times. If no river is nearby, the church is often sited near to a well. Early churches are located on the edges of settlements, with the churchyard giving its own clues to an earlier origin, many appearing to have originated as sacred enclosures. These are easily picked out with their circular boundaries, with the centre of the churchyard being used as a fixed central point and the church becoming the new central point. A sign of this is to look out for the 'drop off' where the old graves meet the new; this is an indication that the graveyard has been extended. Walking around the edge of the old graves one may become aware of going round in a circle. This is likely to be the church's medieval boundary before Georgian, Victorian and Edwardian extensions occurred. Another feature of an early church can be found just outside the church gates, where you can discover a widening of the road. This would have been where the town's medieval market once operated after Sunday worship. Often walking around inside and outside the church can throw more light upon a church's early origins, as one can observe medieval wall paintings, stone crosses, carved crossbone and skull sculptures and stone coffins.

Over forty years ago, Professor Margaret Gelling undertook a survey of West Midland place-names ending in 'low'. Her studies showed that place-names with an Old English personal name attached to the suffix 'low' will indicate an early burial site. For example, in Shropshire, Gelling unearthed seven 'low' suffixes indicating early burial sites. A quick look at the relevant Ordnance Survey map will reveal the distribution pattern of the noted place-names and their geographical placing upon the Shropshire landscape – it quickly becomes apparent that all the mentioned tumuli are located on high ground and often form boundaries between the old administrative hundreds. Gelling also notes that some Old English personal words that are attached to the suffixes of 'hlāw' and 'hlæw', both meaning hill, could indicate an ancient site. Place-names with the first element of 'burh' and the dative of 'byrig', both meaning 'bury', and with no immediate Anglo-Saxon settlement nearby, could denote a prehistoric fort. With prehistoric forts can come detached prehistoric burial sites.

Place-names with suffixes 'hām' and 'tūn' are often confused, with the former denoting a homestead and the latter being representative of a farmstead or later hamlet, village and manor. 'Hām' suffixes are often coined earlier than 'tūn' names. Tūn-named sites with a Celtic prefix often denote a hamlet or a village, whereas tūn-named places with a pre-Conquest personal or surname, or a compound suggestive of royalty, may indicate a manor.[6] Kenneth Cameron notes that English place-names with the suffix 'hām' and an Old English folk-name as the prefix often denote an early Anglo-Saxon settlement, and that most compound names are of a genitive nature mirroring a person or tribal group that settled there.[7]

Cameron's studies have shown that there is a dividing pattern, with early pre-Conquest names being more widespread in the east and uncommon in the west due to late settlements.[8] Denise Kenyon also notes that most hām place-names are often found near the vicinity of a Romano-British settlement, with the Anglo-Saxons preferring to settle near pre-existing settlements.[9] This study is based on her findings in the southern and midland counties of England.[10] Her Lancashire studies showed a topographical pattern with the twelve studied hām sites being located near or by coastal river inlets where crossings could take place, but more importantly where water could be taken, fish could be caught and fertile agricultural land existed thus creating good trading routes.[11] Along these trade routes came early Christian sites – Kenyon claims that fifty per cent of hām-named settlements lying to the south of the sands became, by the end of thirteenth century, important ecclesiastical centres, this being compared to places with the suffix 'tūn' returning sixteen per cent.[12] Dr Mary C. Higham carried out similar fieldwork studies that confirmed Kenyon's research by revealing that eleven out of fourteen hām-named sites were pre-Conquest in date, with the remaining three being coined between AD 1100–1300.[13] Out of the pre-Conquest hām-named sites, only eight are listed as parishes, with four not listed as parishes and two being listed as anomalous. Higham's fieldwork surveys produced a similar topographical pattern to that of Kenyon's, with the studied names being located along coastal routes, above rivers, along old lake beds and on cliffs overlooking water routes. Seven pre-Conquest hām-named sites revealed curvilinear graveyards, with one being unchecked due to not being a parish centre, and the remaining three of the eleven hām sites needing further investigations; none of the three post-Conquest sites were checked due to not being a parish centre. Higham's field studies also revealed that out of the eleven pre-Conquest hām-named sites, only half have Roman roads located nearby with four having pre-Conquest sculptures. None of the fourteen studied hām-named sites were listed as nucleated villages.

Ekwall cites 1,764 Lancashire place-names, of which only 181 are pre-Conquest in date; out of these only twenty-nine are with personal prefixes, suggesting early settlements.[14] Of these 181 pre-Conquest named sites, only eleven have religious simplex compounds. These are Bispham (Amounderness), Great and Little Crosby, Kirkby, Kirkdale, Kirkham, Lancaster Priory, Great and Little Eccleston, Preston and St. Michael's on Wyre. One may note that two have the common Celtic prefix of 'eglēs', modern-day 'eccles', referring to Romano-British Christian churches, and Preston has the Old English prefix of 'prēost', modern-day 'priest'. One site also has the Old English prefix of 'biscop', today's word for 'bishop'; one has a saint-dedicated name; one denotes a priory; two are named after the Old Norse 'kirkja', modern-day 'church'; and a further two reflect the Old English word 'cros', modern-day 'cross'.

'SACRED' PLACE-NAMES

Bispham (*Biscopham* – the bishop's estate) was coined in 1086. Bispham lies near Blackpool overlooking the Irish Sea.

Crosby, Great and Little (farmstead, village or settlement with crosses),[15] was coined in 1086. Simply, Great and Little Crosby refers to a place where crosses stood. Little Crosby houses no less than six stone crosses.

Kirkby (*Cherchebi* – village with a church) was coined in 1086.[16] Kirkby is located near Liverpool, by the Irish Sea. The present church is dedicated to St Chad, the seventh-century Anglo-Saxon saint Ceadda, and the Old Norse 'by' form may replace an earlier Old English name. Before 1766, when the modern-day church was built, Kirkby was a chapelry, but places with a chapel of ease were not usually called Kirkby and the name probably suggests a church independent of the Liverpool parish at Walton.

Kirkdale (*Chirchedele* – the valley with a church) was coined in 1086. Kirkdale lies along the Mersey.[17]

Kirkham (*Chicheham* – homestead or village with a church) was coined in 1086.[18]

Lancaster Priory (*Landc* – the city on the Lune) was coined by 1035, and by 1086 Lancaster was being written down as *Loncastre, Chercaloncastre*. Later etymology translates to Kirk Lancaster. Lancaster Priory stands almost side-by-side with the Roman fort. Lancaster Priory houses no fewer than fifteen stone cross fragments, one with ninth-century interlace design having the description in Latin now housed at the British Museum – a replica has been placed by Lancaster's city museum in the market square.

Little Eccleston (*Eglestun* – church town). This pre-Conquest hamlet lies south of the Ribble adjacent to Great Eccleston, both of which are placed within the larger parish of St Michael's on Wyre. Remarkably the Domesday Book does not cite Great Eccleston (*Eglestun Parva*) having a pre-Conquest church, yet the name suggests an early Christian site being located near the Kirkham to Ribchester Roman road overlooking the Wyre River.

Preston (*Prestune* – farmstead of the priests). An old rectory manor lying north on the bank of the Ribble; nearby is the Kirkham to Ribchester Roman Road. Priest Hutton (*Hotune* – priest was added later to distinguished it from Hutton Roof) lies in the ancient parish of Warton, being situated on a spur of land in a sheltered position from the elements (Irish Sea), in close proximity to Warton Crag with its ancient beacon hill and earth-works and with the River Lune lying to the south.

The Domesday parish of St Michael's (*Michelescherche* – church dedicated to St Michael) overlooks the River Wyre and has a circular graveyard.

Other pre-Conquest sites with pre-Conquest sculpture but without religious prefixes or suffixes are Aighton, Aughton, Bolton-le-Sands, Caton, Gressingham, Halton, Heysham, Hornby, Melling, Overton, Pennington, Ribchester, Stydd and Whalley.

Aighton (*Actun* – oak tree tūn) has an undecorated stone cross.[19]

Aughton (*Acheton* – farmstead where oak trees grew). A Norman doorway can be seen at Aughton church.

Bolton-le-Sands (*Bodeltone* – village by the sands). The village overlooks Morecambe Bay. The church itself houses a Viking hogback tomb with carvings depicting a serpent and figure seen as a representation of the story of Eve being tempted in the Garden of Eden.

Caton (*Catun* – farmstead or village of a man called Káta). The church at Caton houses one of Lancashire's finest Norman arches; nearby is the Roman town of Lancaster.

Gressingham (*Ghersinctune* – homestead or enclosure with grazing or pasture). Like Aughton, Caton and Overton this church at Gressingham houses a Norman doorway.

Halton (*Haltune* – tūn in the bend of a river). The village stands on the River Lune and the name of Halton refers to a sharp bend in the river about one and a quarter miles to the east. The village churchyard houses one of Lancashire's finest pre-Conquest stone crosses, one side of the shaft depicts a flock of sheep while the other side tells of the saga between Sigurd, the fearless son of Odin, the great Viking god, and Regin, the youngest son of the dwarf King Hreidman, where Sigurd is apparently victorious.

Heysham (*Hessam* – homestead or village among the brushwood).[20] Heysham is the home of two pre-Conquest churches, namely St Patrick's and St Peter's. According to folklore, St Patrick himself was once shipwrecked there and the chapel was built to overlook the place where the saint came ashore. Whether this legend is founded on fact or not, this promontory at Heysham has been seen as a sacred ground for well over 1000 years. This Saxon-styled chapel is unique to England (except in Cornwall) as a single-celled chapel, being similar both in style and position to many of the tiny Irish churches. Interesting, too, is the row of graves hewn out of solid rock, each with its socket for the cross that marked the position of the grave. Evidence of the reverence paid to this holy ground is strengthened by the close proximity of another Saxon-styled church, namely St Peter. Near to the entrance of St Peter's graveyard is a curiously carved Saxon stone which serves as a further reminder of the antiquity of this early church. One side of this stone, once part of a much taller cross, has a representation of Christ in Majesty; on the other a shrouded figure stands in the doorway of a house complete with windows and a chimney. This possibly depicts the biblical story of the raising of Lazarus. Heysham is also famous for its Viking antiquities.[21]

Overton (*Ouretun* – higher farmstead). Like Caton, Overton church houses a Norman doorway. Overton overlooks the River Lune with Heysham nearby.

Whalley (*Hwælleage*). In the churchyard is another pre-Conquest stone cross depicting combinations of Christian and pagan loyalties. Depicted is the Dog of Berser, the Norse symbol of eternity sharing a sculptured stone with the Ascending Christ, with another two stone crosses carved with a scroll and Anglo-Saxon documents noting the burial of a Bishop at Wagele in AD 664. Whalley lies east of Ribchester and south of Clitheroe with the River Ribble flowing nearby. The name Whalley being coined by 789, by 1086 it was being written down as *Wallei*. Whalley Abbey dates to 1296.

Post-Conquest coined places with pre-Conquest sculpture are Anderton, Bispham (West Derby), Bailey, Blackrod, Bolton (formerly Bolton-le-Moors), Burnley, Chaigley, Cliviger, Colne, Halliwell, Foulridge, Ormskirk, Urswick and Walton on the Hill.

Anderton (*Eanred's tun*) was coined in 1212. John Rawlinson gives a vivid account of the Anderton Stone, stating: 'the stone is more than a yard high and half a yard wide with a curved front'.[22] The carving is in two halves, one above the other. The top half portrays God the Father clad in an embroidered cloak, holding a sphere surmounted by a cross in his right hand and a manuscript in his left hand; an excellent illustration for the text from St Matthew, XXVIII: 19. Near his right foot the lion and the lamb lie down side-by-side, and near to his left foot is an acrostic SATOR, AREPO, TENET, OPERA, ROTAS. Rawlinson gives a simple explanation that this is an old benediction, as the same acrostic is inscribed on the wall of an old church in Gloucestershire and was also found cut on a wall of one of the catacombs in Rome.[23] The lower half rather crudely portrays the Crucifixio. Over the head of the crucified Christ is the inscription *INRI* meaning *Jesus of Nazareth, King of the Jews*, and near his right hand is carved the name Jesus. Underneath this name are two groups, evidently coats of arms, the top group depicting weavers' combs and the bottom group illustrating trees resembling yews or firs. On the other side of the design are two groups of shack-bolts, illustrating the two arms of Anderton Hall of Anderton Ford. This small hamlet also houses some unique Roman carvings.

Rawlinson states that by the lych gate of the parish church lies carved stones; on the left-hand side of the footpath the first one appears to be part of a doorway or porch. The bottom face is cut concave and sloping inwards with a cross cut in the concave face. Perhaps it was the top of a small niche or alcove like that over a built-in holy stoup or the niche for a small statue. There is a figure of the Lion of Judah and a bunch of grapes on the front face and on the sloping side what looks like an illustration of the Good Samaritan. The second stone is in two sections, the bottom one containing three illustrations of special interest. First from the left is a wheel with a background of letters, the most prominent of which are P and R. On the rim of the wheel are several small symbols and the Roman numerals DCLXVIII, evidently a date; the centre of the wheel contains seven spokes and a round boss also in seven parts. The second illustration is of a baptism; the sculptor evidently took the baptising of Jesus by John the Baptist in the River Jordan as his inspiration. The third illustration carved in stone depicts three legs joined to a common centre, like to the arms of the Isle of Man. Rawlinson's translation of these designs are first that the wheel is reflecting eternity, the Roman numerals denoting the date 668 when an important event in the history of Rivington took place. The letters of P and R are the initial letters of Pilkington and Rivington, and the initials of Richard Pilkington who had the church rebuilt in 1540. The second design tells us that the event that took place in 668 was an important baptism, and the third design, the legs of a man, were used by the House of Stanley from 1405–1736, when they were Kings of Man.

Another stone bears the likeness of a bishop's head, complete with mitre, as well as the heads of an ox and an ass. One of the other stones resembles a large lintel 5ft 6in long, 1ft 2½in deep and 9in thick, on which has been carved an indecipherable design or inscription of letters, crosses, two heads of monkish type and various other symbols, and cut over a part of the original design is the date 1666. Archaeologists, to whom Rawlinson submitted a drawing of this stone, described it as a 'farrago of nonsense'.[24]

The village of Anderton lies between the villages of Adlington and Rivington, where another stone carving once stood,[25] namely the Headless Cross. Dr Ben J.N. Edwards gives a long written account detailing the carvings.[26] He states the lowest part of the shaft of a cross was surmounted by a flat quadric-lateral stone, which served at the time as the base for a sundial used as a direction post. It is said to have been erected by the first Lord Leverhulme, who had at his Rivington bungalow a collection of carved stones. Edwards note that the Headless Cross is recorded in the eighteenth century. He carries on by describing the fragment bearing a moulding near its base like that in Bolton Parish Church, the difference being that above the moulding is the lower half of a human figure. Two aspects only of this figure are clear: it wears a skirt-like garment finishing above the knees and it wears strikingly depicted footwear. This seems to link to a carved stone unearthed in a garden of a house called Hollowforth (north of Preston), forming the upper part of the shaft of which the Headless Cross from Anderton was the lower portion.[27]

Bailey (*Baillee* – lēah where berries grow) was coined in 1204. Bailey houses an undecorated stone circle.[28]

Bolton (*Boelton* – settlement with a special building) was coined in 1185. The church dedicated to St Peter stands overlooking the winding River Croal with a circular boundary.[29] Inside the church there is a complete stone coffin and stone cross fragments supposedly depicting Adam and Eve. The Roman road (Watling Street) lies to the east.

Burnley (*Brunlaia* – probably woodland clearing by the River Brun) was coined in 1124. Brun simply refers to the colour brown.[30] Burnley houses a plain stone cross, located on Godley Lane.[31]

Chaigley (*Chadelegh* – the clearing of the broom, gorse brushwood) was coined in 1336. A plain stone cross is housed within Chaigley's church.[32]

Above left: Stone carving of Roman Wheel in Rivington Parish church

Above centre: Signpost for Rivington

Above right: Topography of Rivington

Circular boundary round
Bolton Parish Church

Cliviger (*Cliveracher* – cultivated land by a slope) was coined in 1196. Cliviger houses an undecorated stone cross.[33]

Colne (*Calna* – place by the River Calne) was coined in 1124. Mills is uncertain about the meaning of this river.[34] Housed inside the parish church there is a pre-Conquest stone cross.

Halliwell (*Haliwalle* – the holy well) was coined in 1200. Sadly Halliwell's holy well is underneath a car park. Nearby in St Peter's Church, a solitary stone cross stands, and flowing nearby are the Rivers Croal and Tonge.

Foulridge (*Folric* – ridge where foals graze) was coined in 1219. Like Bailey, Foulridge has an undecorated stone cross.[35]

Ormskirk (*Ormeschirche* – Orm's church) was coined in 1190. In the churchyard stands a stone preaching cross symbolising where Christian open-air meetings took place. Ormskirk lies approximately 10 miles inland from Formby, with Kirkby and Crosby situated nearby. Ormskirk overlooks the Irish Sea.

Urswick (*Ursewica* – the village by the bison lake) was coined in 1150. Urswick houses at least two tenth-century stone crosses, both of which are preserved in the church.

Other post-Conquest-coined names reflecting religious sites without known pre-Conquest sculptures are Abbey Village, Abbeystead, Abbot Reading, Bispham, Church, Church Coniston, Churchtown in Kirkland, Churchtown in Southport, Chapel Island, Cockersand Abbey, Conishead Priory, Crossens, Croston, Eccles, Eccleshill, Eccleston near Chorley, Eccleston near Prescot, Furness

Abbey, Hunts Cross, Kirkby Ireleth, Kirkland, Kirkthwaite, Lytham St Annes, Monk Coniston, Prescot, Prestolee, Priest Hutton, Priestwath, Prestwich, St Annes on Sea, St Helens and Simms Cross.

Abbey Village takes it name from the 1840 cotton mill, namely Abbey Mill. The first word refers to Stanlow Abbey, later transferred to Whalley-held land in the township of Withnell, within which the village is located.[36]

Abbeystead (*Abbey* – the site of the abbey). Named after the house of Cistercian monks in Wyresdale, which was founded by monks from Furness Abbey during Henry II's reign. The place-name was coined in 1323; this date also corresponds to the recorded vaccary. Abbeystead overlooks the Wyre River.

Abbot Reading (*Abbot Ridding* – abbot's clearing) was coined in 1661.

Bispham (*Biscopham* – the bishop's hām) was coined in 1219. Bispham is located near to Rufford. Back in the early thirteen century, Bispham did not have village status and was probably a small hamlet containing a few homesteads, of which one belonged to the Bishop.

Church (*Chirche* – place at the church) was coined in 1202.

Church Coniston (*Chirche Coningeston* – the king's tūn with a church); unknown date of coinage.

Churchtown in Kirkland was coined in 1786 and Churchtown in Southport in 1725. The actual site of earlier churches, as inferred in their names, are not documented, but existing churches in both places stand on earlier foundations, giving evidence of an earlier church site pre-dating the cited dates.

Chapel Island (date of coinage unknown). This island stands mid-channel of the Leven estuary, taking its name from a chapel used by monks and medieval travellers crossing the Leven Sands to Conishead or Cartmel.

Cockersand Abbey (*Cocresha* – the abbey on sandy land by the River Cocker). This early thirteen-century abbey was built on a previous religious site, namely Askell(es) Cross, 'Askell' being an Old Norse personal name. The name 'Cockersand Abbey' was coined by 1207.

Conishead Priory (*Cuningesheued* – King Hill). Conishead Priory overlooks Morecambe Bay.

Eccles (*Ecclesia, eglēs* – church) was coined *c.* 1200.

Eccleshill (*Eccleshull* – church hill) was coined in 1246.

Eccleston near Chorley (*Aycleton* – the church tūn) was coined in 1094 and had become Eccleston by 1180.[37]

Eccleston near Prescot (*Ecclistona* – the church tūn) was coined in 1190.

Furness Abbey (*Fuththernessa* – headland by the rump-shaped island) was coined by 1150.

Kirkby Ireleth (*Kirkebi* – church village) was coined by 1175. Ireleth was added by 1180 to distinguish it from Kirkby in Lonsdale and other Kirkbys.

Kirkthwaite (*Kyrkwythe* – church clearing, meadow or paddock) was coined by 1535. Kirkthwaite stands a distance away from Colton Church. Thwaite simply refers to the Old Scandinavian word meaning clearing, meadow or paddock (Mills 2003). Could Kirkthwaite be an old church site that belonged to an abbey or a priory?

Prescot (*Prestecota* – the priest's cottage) was coined in 1178.

Prestolee (*Prestawe* – the lēah belonging to Prestall) was coined in 1618. There is a Prestall near Farnworth. Simply, Prestall translates to 'the hall belonging to the priest'.[38]

Priest Hutton (*Presthotone* – village that belonged to a priest by a spur of land) was coined in 1307. Priest Hutton is unusual due to the second element being coined pre-Conquest, with 'Priest' later added to distinguish it from nearby Hutton Roof.[39]

Priestwath (*Presreguet* – priests ford) was coined by 1094. Priestwath is now known as Scale Ford (a place where fish could be caught).

Prestwich (*Prestwich* – the priest's wīc) was coined in 1194. *Wīc* is the Old English word that translates to an early Romano-British settlement with a special building or industry.[40]

St Annes on Sea (*Kilgrimol* – Kelgrim's hollow) was coined in 1190. The modern name takes its name from the church, built in the 1870s dedicated to St Anne.

The church was the first building to be constructed in a new planned town. St Annes on Sea was formerly christened Kilgrimol; during the fourteenth century Kilgrimol's churchyard succumbed to the Irish Sea.[41]

St Helens (chapel dedicated to the Saint) was coined in 1552.

Simms Cross (Simm being a nickname for Sigemund, today's Simon) – coinage date unknown. Simply, Simms Cross relates to the cross belonging to Simon. A cross once stood on the crossroads.[42]

The Anglo-Saxon, and later Viking, invaders were heathens, worshipping gods such as Frig, Thor, Tiw and Woden, whose memory is perpetuated in the days of the week. There have been suggestions that animal-named places could reflect animal sacrifice to these heathen gods. Animal-named sites make up seven per cent of the total Lancashire place-names listed by Ekwall. Ekwall (1922) cites 108, with a further seven being pre-Conquest in date. Out of these pre-Conquest names, only Hart Carrs – '*Hert*' being translated to 'the hart of a dog' – could refer to animal offerings.[43] Of the post-Conquest-named places, none refer specifically to animal offerings; the majority of animal-named places refer to hills resembling horses, cat's tails or hills where pigs and oxen were kept, or where wolves, deer, foxes, hares and rabbits roamed, and hawks flew. A quick calculation of the animal-named sites revealed places denoting pigs, deer and wolves being common. Further topographical and etymological research at field-name level is needed to pinpoint fields where possible animal sacrifice took place.

There are certain places that denote more mystical phenomena. These are Armetridding, Deadwin Clough, Dragley Beck, Harhum, Harrock Hall, Graveoak, Grimshaw, Laffog, Spellow, Tarbock, Thrushgill, Thursden, Thursland and Wiswell. Armetridding (*de Armetheriding*) was coined in 1246. Simply, Armetridding is referring to 'the hermit's clearing'.[44]

Deadwin Clough (*Dedequenclogh*) was coined in 1324. This morbidly named place depicts 'a clough of the dead women'.[45]

Dragley Beck (*Dracklebecke*) was coined in 1596. In earlier documents Dragley appears as *Drakelow, c.*1270. The hamlet stands on Levy Beck. Ekwall suggests that Dragley Beck could be referring to 'a hill or mound of the dragon'.[46]

Harhum (*Harumcar*) was coined in 1298. This place is now lost, but may refer to a heathen temple. The first element being *hearg*, the Old Norse word for heathen, Ekwall acknowledges the first element could also refer to *horgr*, Old Norse for a heap of stones.[47]

Harrock Hall (*Harakiskar*) was coined *c.* 1260. The first element is referring to the Old English word *hār* meaning hoary, with the second denoting the Old English word *āc* meaning Oak; Harrock simply means the 'hoar oak'.[48]

Graveoak (*Gravoke Manor*) was coined in 1563. Simply Graveoak refers to a grave by the oak tree.[49]

Grimshaw (*de Grineshare*) was coined in 1265. The first element has three possibilities; first reflecting one of the names given to the heathen god, Odin/Woden, secondly, the Old Norse personal name of Grímr and thirdly referring to the Old English word of *Grīma* meaning spectre. If we take the latter etymology Grimshaw simply means 'the haunted grove'.[50] There is also a Grimshaw in Cliviger.

Laffog (*Lachok*) was coined in 1246. Ekwall treads carefully when explaining Laffog's etymology. He states Laffog could refer to the 'law oak', i.e. that this oak could have been a holy oak.[51]

Spellow (*de Spellowe*) was coined in 1306. The first element relates to 'speech', the second denotes a hill. Thus Spellow is simply referring to 'a hill where announcements were made or on which moots were held'.[52]

Tarbock (*Torboc*) was coined in 1086. There are two suggestions for Tarbock, which are 'the brook belonging to Thor' or the 'brook by the thorn'.[53] Thor was the pagan god who gave his name to Thursday. Ekwall prefers the latter etymology.

Thrushgill (*Thursgill*) was coined in 1631. The first element denotes the Old Norse word *Þurs* meaning 'giant', with the second element referring to the Old Norse word *gil* meaning ravine.[54] Could Thrushgill simply reflect a large ravine or does it have a more supernatural meaning?

Thursden (*Thirsedeneheved*) was coined in 1324. Thursden lies on the banks of Thursden Brook and refers to 'the giant's valley'.[55]

Thursland (*Thurselande*) was coined in 1320. Simply, Thursland means the 'land belonging to Thor'.[56]

Wiswell (*Wisewell*) was coined in 1207. Ekwall notes that there are several wells in the area, one denoting 'Old Molly's Well'. He states that the first element may be the Old English word *wise* referring to 'the wise one' or 'the wise women'. Ekwall does not ignore the possibility that 'wise' could reflect the Old English personal name *Wīsa*.[57]

Anglezarke signpost

Lancashire is awash with standing stones, cairns, barrows, tumulus and long chambered tombs at Anglezarke, Birkrigg Common, Blackrod, Bleasdale, Bowland with Leagram, Burwains, Coppull, Kenyon, Kirkby Ireleth, Makerfield, Mossborough, Nelson, Raisthwaite, Ringstonhalgh, Roseacre, Toppin Rays, Turton, Urswick, Warton, Wharles and Whalley.

Anglezarke (*Andelevesarewe* – Anlaf's shieling, hill pasture belonging to Anlaf, Anlaf being an Old Norse personal name) was coined in 1202.[58] High upon Anglezarke Moor are situated two ancient burial sites, namely Pike Stones Long Chambered Burial Tomb and Round Loaf Burial Mound.

Birkrigg Common (*Byrkeryg* – birch tree ridge) was coined in 1282.[59] On Birkrigg Common there are five barrows, mostly on the northeast side of the common. Excavations in 1911 and 1921 unearthed burnt patches where bodies may have been cremated, as well as a cobbled pavement immediately outside the inner circle, suggesting they may have been used for processions or dances.[60]

Blackrod (*Blakerode* – black clearing) was coined in 1201. This village stands south of Rivington, west of Bolton and the River Douglas flows nearby. Blackrod village stands on a hill of over 500ft; Blackrod church was originally a chapel or a chantry, hence Chauntry Brow. According to folklore, Blackrod was the site of a former battleground where King Arthur fought. A cairn was excavated on the alleged site of the battle, producing iron deposits (possible military weapons) and possible (human) cremation remains.[61] The cairn was visible in 1770, but through constant ploughing it has long since disappeared.

Bleasdale (*Blesedale* – bright valley) was coined in 1228. Situated amidst a plantation, this prehistoric site consists of a turf burrow measuring 11m in diameter and 1m in height, surrounded by a ditch lined with birch poles. Sticking out of the burrow mound was a ring of eleven oak posts (now marked by concrete pillars). At the centre was a grave measuring just over 1m in length and 0.5m deep. The circle measured a staggering 45m in diameter and was made up of a continuous circle of closely spaced posts with larger ones about every 4.5m. Radiocarbon dating for one of the oak posts gives us a suggestive date of between 1900–1720 BC.[62]

Bowland with Leagram (*Boelanda* – land in a bow; *Lathegrim* – mark indicating a road) – the two elements were coined in 1102 and 1282 respectively.[63] Fairy Holes stands on the southern slope of New Laund Hill; this small cave measuring 3m high, nearly 2m wide and 20m long was an important shelter for the Bronze Age inhabitants. Pottery, including a collared urn, was unearthed at the flat platform in front of the cave mouth.[64]

Burwains (*Burwens*) was coined far later in 1541. The place-name denotes a prehistoric burial or cairn.[65]

Coppull (*Cophill*) was coined in 1218. The first element of 'cop' refers to 'top', in this case a hill, heap, mound or tumulus. Coppull simply means 'peak hill'.

Kirkby Ireleth. On Kirkby Moor lies a bank of earth and stones measuring between 2–3m wide and 0.5m high, delimiting a circle measuring 22m in diameter. This is a ring cairn, partly retained on the inner eastern side by a kerb of stones. There is no obvious entrance, but 30m to the northeast lie three pairs of smaller stones forming the beginning of an avenue. About 300m north-east is a rough stone cairn measuring 24m in diameter and 1m high. It has a burial cist on its southwest side in which a cremation was found.[66]

Kenyon (*Kenien*) was coined in 1212. Ekwall is unclear about the etymology, noting the possibility that the name contains the common Welsh personal name *Einion*, earlier *Eniōn*. Ekwall gives the uncertain etymology of 'Einion's Mound'.[67]

Makerfield (*Macrefeld*) was coined in 1121. Within the bounds of Makerfield there are two named fields, namely 'the two Makerfields'. Both reflect two ancient burrows. Ekwall notes that the first element refers to a British word meaning wall or ruin.[68]

Mossborough (*Mossebarrowe*) was coined in 1516. The place-name Mossborough could refer to a prehistoric barrow, covered with moss.[69]

Raisthwaite (*Reisthuathec*) was coined in 1319. Ekwall refers to the first element being *hreysi*, the Old Norse word for cairn.[70]

Ringstonhalgh (*de Ryngestoneshalgh*) was coined in 1352. As the place-name suggests, Ringstonhalgh is simply referring to a stone circle.[71]

Roseacre (*Rascak, Raysak*) was coined in 1249. Roseacre is simply referring to 'an acre with a cairn', *hreysi* denoting the Old Norse word for cairn and *aker* being Old Norse for acre.[72]

Toppin Rays (*Toppinraise*) was coined in 1590. Simply, Topping Rays refers to 'a cairn on a hill', with the second element being the Old Norse word *hreysi*, meaning cairn.[73]

Turton (*Turton* – Thor's *tūn*) was coined in 1212. Within an area called Cheetham Close (named after the Cheetham Family) are two prehistoric stone circles lying at a height of 320m above sea level. The northern circle contains seven stones, all measuring less than 1m in height with a diameter of 15m. Approximately 12m to the southwest lies an outlying stone. The second circle lies 20m southwest and is smaller in size, being constructed of two concentric rings of stones, the outer being 11m in diameter and the inner measuring 10m across. Between them is a packing of rubble, suggesting this latter stone circle to be characteristic of a ring cairn concealing an earlier burial[74] (as discussed in Chapter 1).

Urswick is incredibly rich in its prehistoric sites. Situated in Little Urswick, all that remains of this important site are two large boulders that support a capstone. Additional strength is given by the use of packing stones. More stones are scattered nearby and probably formed another burial chamber.[75] Nearby lies Skelmore Heads, a grass-covered mound measuring 18.5m in diameter. Two large stones protrude from the eastern end and two others were found in alignment towards the west. In 1957 the mound was excavated, revealing that the site had been robbed of all artefacts. If there had been a burial, it must have been between the eastern stone, but no burial evidence remains. There were no signs of a kerb to the barrow, and there was no evidence of its original shape. The Tosthills burial chamber marked on the Ordnance Survey map is a natural rock outcrop.[76]

Wharles (*Quatlous*) was coined in 1249. Ekwall gives a long suggestive etymology for Wharles. He starts by suggesting that the second element was Old English *hlāw*, meaning 'hill', or if the first element ended in 'l', Old Norse for *haugr*. The first element being doubtful, it seems most probable that it began with '*hw*'. Possible sources are Old English *hwer*, Old Norse *hverr* (meaning 'kettle, basin'), Old English *hwearf*, Old Norse *hvarf* (simply meaning 'turning'), or Old English *hwerfel* (meaning 'circle'). Ekwall refers to Wharles as 'a hill with mounds forming a circle.'[77]

3

RIBCHESTER (*BREMETENACUM VETERANORUM*):
PLACE OF THE ROARING WATER

NICK FORD

ORDNANCE SURVEY GRID REFERENCE: SD649351; OS MAP: LR102/103

In Roman religion, there is no land that is not in some way sacred. By tradition, the Earth herself is believed to be a divinity (*Tellus Mater*). What sets some places apart from others is that they are deemed sacred in different ways, consecrated to different purposes. It would still be fair to say that some places are more sacred than others, but to a pre-Christian Roman, there is no hard-and-fast difference between parts of life – or land – that are 'spiritual' and parts that are not. There is an understanding that every place belongs, in some sense, to some entity or other, whether visible, or invisible: some are human, some are not; some are in spirit form, some are not. Sacred behaviour is simply a matter of approaching a certain place, whose purpose or whose ownership is known, respectfully and in an appropriate manner.

And for us, what makes a certain place a 'sacred site'? What we see, and what we feel at a place, informs the value we put on it. Seeing, and feeling, are believing, but it is also true that what we believe influences the way we think and feel, and our belief can also transform what we are actually looking at. Our belief may even make a thing visible or invisible.

Roman remains in Britain are even more challenging in this way than megaliths and barrows, or the well-preserved ruins of Pompeii; usually there is little or no lore attached to our Roman sites and mostly all you have to look at are the footings of a few walls, column bases and bits of pavement – a spring if you're lucky – but as with the ancient monuments of prehistory, to appreciate them fully you have to look at them in their proper context, their part in the history of the place, their importance in the landscape. The knowledge, or belief, of what happened there is a big part of that important sense of sacredness that can be unlocked from them, if one has the keys.

River Ribble, river of
the Goddess Belisama.
Photograph by Karen
Lawrinson

RIBCHESTER: THE PLACE, ITS NATURE, ITS HISTORY

The present-day little town of Ribchester lies about halfway between Preston
and Clitheroe, in the valley of the River Ribble, from which it derives its
modern name. It is recorded in the Domesday Book as Ribelcastre, which
translates simply as 'The Roman Fort (Anglo-Saxon *Ceastre*, from the Latin
Castrum,) on the [River] Ribble'.

To get an understanding of place, names are important, so it is worth men-
tioning here that the name for the Ribble itself seems to derive from the
Gallo-Brythonic (indigenous Celtic) *Rigabelisama* (*Riga-*, a queen, and *Belisama*,
a goddess-name widely used in Gaul, and often in connection with Minerva:
it is thought to mean 'Most Shining One'. See Rivet & Smith 1981).[1] Thus
the Ribble is 'Most Shining Queen', or possibly, 'Most Mighty Queen'. Most,
if not all, the names of Celtic divinities seem to be descriptive epithets rather
than 'real' names, and it would be a mistake to assume that because there are a
number of Belisamas in western Europe, there was therefore one goddess called
Belisama, who was worshipped widely across the Celtic world (although certainly to me, the river has very much her own divine presence).

Ribchester grew up as a river-crossing, which may well have been where the
bridge now stands, probably from the Bronze Age, since cremation urns from
that period have been found to the north of the village. By the first century CE,
it will have been connected by road to Lancaster, Manchester, Chester and York.
The Romans knew it as *Bremetenacum*, from the native *Bremetonacon*, 'place by
the roaring river',[2] and later as *Bremetenacum Veteranorum*, 'Bremetenacum of
the Veterans', probably because it became a place where many soldiers settled
on discharge from the army, presumably on lands granted them as part of their
severance pay.

At the time of the beginning of the Romanisation of northern Britain in the mid first century CE, the lands around the Ribble valley formed part of the territory occupied by the tribe (or possibly a confederation of tribes) known as the Brigantes, whose ruling queen Cartimandua was an ally of Rome. It may have become Imperial property during the reign of Antoninus Pius (c.CE 154–5), as the contemporary historian Pausanias states: 'Antoninus … took much of the territory of the Brigantes in Britain because they … had entered on a war of aggression by invading the Genounian part, (which was inhabited by people) subject to the Romans' (Pausanias, *Description of Greece*, VIII.43 3–4). It is uncertain, however, where 'Genounia' was, as the name occurs nowhere else in surviving writings or inscriptions. It seems likely that before this the military presence was light and the Brigantes were under civilian government. Then, the security threat posed by this Brigantian rebellion seems to have prompted the imposition of military rule and the expansion of Bremetenacum accordingly.[3]

Whether acting as a force of military occupation, or as allies of a native client ruler, it was general practice for the Romans in Britain to station small units of cavalry in forts, usually overlooking river-crossings, to police sections of the road network, and certainly a fort had been built for this purpose by the time of the Flavian emperors in the later first century, probably for a detachment of auxiliary cavalry from Asturia in what is now northwestern Spain.

There may of course already have been a native British town or village in existence before the arrival of a Roman military presence (and the name seems to suggest this, as do a number of coin finds pre-dating the military occupation by over a century), but even if this was not the case, the presence of soldiers who, during long, quiet periods of duty, had few ways of spending their pay, would quickly have attracted the kind of enterprising people who in all times and places have always seemed to be on hand to provide rest and recreational facilities for bored young men in military establishments. Such unofficial suburb-shanties immediately outside the forts, or *vici* as they were known, often developed into sophisticated townships with a large and varied population engaging in all kinds of economic activity. The first grants of land to veteran soldiers at Bremetenacum were made about the end of the second century CE, but the official status of Bremetenacum is not known; it certainly was not a *colonia*, a Roman city, usually founded by time-served Roman soldiers, whose citizens had full Roman legal rights, though it may have been a local administrative centre.

The mid second century, which saw the expansion of the Roman fort at Bremetenacum into a major cavalry base, also saw the arrival of an *ala* (cavalry division, literally 'wing') of Sarmatians, whom the Romans had recently encountered in a series of wars with the Dacians (a Celtic people living north of the Danube in what is present-day Romania and Hungary), as allies of the Dacians. They were accomplished heavy cavalrymen from the Hungarian steppe, horse and rider covered from head to foot in scale mail armour, and armed with lances and bows – heavy cavalry being a tactical advantage the Romans did not have at the time. Later, after the Dacian Wars, when Dacia had become a Roman province and the emperor Marcus Aurelius made a campaign into Sarmatia itself, after a truce with the Sarmati the Roman army lost no time in recruiting no fewer than 5,500 Sarmatian cavalrymen – these became the Roman *Cataphractes*, the prototype of the medieval armoured knight.[4] A Roman cavalry *ala* normally numbered 500 and there is no direct evidence of Sarmatian units being posted anywhere else, though some may have been deployed on the German frontier and others on the borders of the Empire with Mesopotamia; it is hard to imagine all 5,500 being posted to Britain, though not impossible.

On arrival in Lancashire, here this Hungarian-raised armoured division remained for at least the next 300 years. The *Notitia Dignitatum*, a list of military positions in the Roman Empire and datable to about CE 420, the end of Roman military presence in Britain, gives as one of the units *per lineam Valli* ('along the frontier of the Wall'), *Cuneus Sarmatarum, Bremetenraco* ('the formation of Sarmatians at Bremetenacum'). As the original enlisted men retired, they were given land grants in the area, becoming the veterans of Bremetenacum, and replacements would have been recruited more locally. Even so, throughout history, military units are notorious for keeping up their traditions, especially when these are useful, and so the equipment and training would have remained more or less the same, their exotic appearance no doubt adding to the unit's prestige. (For a parallel in more recent times, one has only to look at hussars in the armies of eighteenth- and nineteenth-century Europe, originally recruited from Hungary, who preserved their characteristic dress and hairstyle even when those regiments were nationals of, say, the French or British armies).

One interesting peculiarity of Sarmatian cavalry was their use of a dragon standard, with a metal head on a pole, its body made of cloth and shaped like a windsock. Its original purpose may have been to show the mounted archers the speed and direction of the wind, but one can imagine that it looked fearsome in its own right – especially if, as some have speculated, its teeth and/or tongue were designed to funnel the wind and make it roar or howl, like a *carnyx*, the Celtic war-trumpet.[5] One of these dragon heads has been found at Niederbieber, in west Germany. It is made of bronze, overlaid in silver and gold, and has been dated to the early third century and has a convex rim at its 'neck' which has holes for attaching cloth or leather; its underside is fitted for carrying on the end of a pole. Complete examples are shown on Trajan's Column in Rome, commemorating his wars against the Dacians in the early second century.

A similar gold dragon standard head was found in the Sargetia valley, Transylvania (part of modern Rumania), and is thought to have been part of the royal treasures of the Dacian king Decebalus, hidden in the early autumn of 106, at the end of the emperor Trajan's Second Dacian War.[6] None have yet been discovered at Ribchester, although a dragon-standard of similar design can be seen on a Sarmatian tombstone now in the Grosvenor Museum in Chester. It is tempting to speculate that here we might have the historical origin of Arthur Pendragon and his knights of myth and legend, although no other evidence, historical or literary, points to this.

The story that in the early fifth century the Romans left Britain is a myth. Historians have assumed that at least the actual legions of the Roman army were ordered out to defend Rome from the advancing Goths (or to support Constantine III in his claim for the Imperial throne), though the logistical effort of transporting upwards of 20,000 men, stores and equipment, uprooted from their homes and families, where they had been for over 300 years, across the English Channel and the North Sea, then supposed to have been swarming with barbarian pirates, is a challenging thing to try and imagine. It seems to me far more likely that denuded, skeleton legions remained at their stations, and that many, if not most, of the auxiliary troops also stayed behind; auxiliaries were, by this time, locally recruited, mostly cavalry and light infantry. By this time they were mostly garrison troops, living with their families in and around the forts and their surrounding towns, and in many cases will have been there for generations. Later, as the Imperial monetary system collapsed, they were paid not in cash, but in kind – chiefly in land – and here you can see the beginning of the feudal system of the Middle Ages. Even so, these people regarded themselves as being as Roman as anybody else – albeit they were British Romans.

In 410, Britain's actual rulers refused to acknowledge the Roman Emperor Constantine III, and appointed their own. For the next century or so, while a system of government resembling the old Roman administration still survived, Rome (making a virtue of necessity) actually recognised Britain's self-appointed rulers and it is possible that, like the offices of command in the army, these posts became hereditary – certainly military command was traditional in aristocratic Roman families. Under Rome, Northern Britain had always been run primarily by the military, and from the fifth to the seventh century, this might well have been the basis of rulership of the British kingdoms of the north that formed the main resistance to barbarian invasion.[7]

THE GODS OF BREMETENACUM

When looking at prehistoric sites, from which there is no contemporary written evidence, one can only make an educated guess as to what the site meant to the people who designed and used it, working from clues like its location, orientation and the discovery of artefacts, floral and faunal remains; and we can know even less of their religious beliefs. While we are more fortunate with Roman Britain in terms of inscriptions and other written evidence for the gods to which places of worship were dedicated, there is a danger in assuming that, because a god or goddess is named, that we can have much certainty about the way people interacted with those gods, or how they considered their nature; and, of course, we cannot assume that, because no inscription or image has been found of a god or goddess, that a particular divinity was not worshipped there.

The same holds true for other gods and goddesses one might expect to find evidence of – Epona, for example, has no known historical associations at Ribchester, yet she has many altar-dedications in many places throughout the Empire – east as well as west – where Celtic units serving as Roman cavalry were stationed. Wherever horses were kept, it is not unlikely that she, as a patron of horses, would have been honoured by a small wooden or clay image on a little shelf (see, for example, the second-century Roman writer Lucius Apuleius, *The Golden Ass*, 3.27).[8]

So popular was she, and so much Rome owed to the prowess of her Celtic horsemen, that she is the only deity of the Celts known to have been accorded her own festival date in the official Roman religious calendar. Of course, the Sarmatians may well not have been a Celtic people, but after the first recruits of the *Ala Sarmatorum*, the Sarmatian Division, came replacements who by majority certainly would have been. However, a small wooden image is unlikely to survive or, if it does come to light in an excavation, it may be misinterpreted. Perhaps, in time, an altar-stone inscribed to Epona will be discovered reused as part of a wall, or be ploughed up on nearby farmland.

THE DEAE MATRONES (THE MOTHER GODDESSES)

Dedications to the Mother Goddesses are common in the Western Empire, especially in areas of military occupation where Celtic troops were stationed, such as Hadrian's Wall and the frontier forts and towns of the German provinces. They are generally shown in threes, ladies of high status with elaborate hairstyles, seated, with baskets of food on their laps, though sometimes one holds a scroll or a baby. Their connection with fertility is obvious, though their role as a triad may extend into the three worlds, or past, present and future, or of the three passages of birth, marriage and death. This is from a second-century altar stone in Ribchester Museum:

> To all the Mother Goddesses, Marcus Ingenuius Asiaticus, *decurion* [troop commander] of the Second *Ala* [Wing] of Astures, willingly and deservedly fulfilled his vow.

> RIB 586

The badly worn inscription on this altar, now barely legible, represents the only written evidence of the presence of Asturian cavalry in Ribchester. The altar was first recorded by William Camden in 1580. The brass plaque records Camden's reading of the lettering.

Translation:
To the Mother Goddesses, Marcus Ingenuius Asiaticus, decurion of the Second Asturian Cavalry Regiment, willingly and deservedly fulfilled his vow.

Above left: Altar stone, dedicated to the Mother Goddesses, Ribchester Museum. Photograph by Karen Lawrinson

Above right: Inscription on altar stone. Photograph by Karen Lawrinson

APOLLO AND MAPONUS

Known from inscriptions elsewhere in northern Britain and in Gaul, the god Maponos is portrayed as a youthful figure with a harp or a lyre. As such he has been equated (as in the altar inscription below) with Apollo, whose music also brings sickness as well as healing, nightmares as well as dreams, madness as well as clarity. His name is Gallo–Brythonic, which simply means 'The Son'. He is assumed to be identical with the mythical figure Mabon Modron (Old Welsh meaning 'Mother's Son') in the Mabinogion legend of *Culhwch ac Olwen*, where he is rescued from imprisonment by Arthur and his companions. Maponus and Apollo have also been equated with the Irish god Angus Og ('Young Angus'), who has similar attributes. A further connection with the eloquent Gaulish god Ogmios and the Irish Oghma, is possible.

This octagonal altar stone, or possibly part of a plinth for a larger altar, is dateable to CE 241:

> To the holy god Apollo Maponus, and for the health of our Lord [i.e. the Emperor] and the unit of the Gordian Sarmatian Horse at Bremetenacum, Aelius Antoninus, centurion of the Sixth Legion, the *Victrix*, ['Victress'] from Melitanis [?] *praepositus* [provost] of the unit and of the region, willingly and deservedly fulfilled his vow. Dedicated on the first day of September when our Lord Imperator Gordianus Augustus – for the second time – and Pompeianus were consuls.

RIB 583

Above left: Carved stone head, Ribchester Museum. Photograph by Karen Lawrinson

Above right: Stone head, Ribchester Museum. Photograph by Karen Lawrinson

The shaft of a rectangular pedestal was found in Ribchester in 1578, then taken to Samlesbury Hall nearby, where it was incorporated into the fabric of the building. It was rediscovered in 1814 and acquired by St John's College, Cambridge, where it still resides. It is part of a larger structure, possibly an altar. The left side has lost its surface. On the right side is a relief of Apollo, nude except for a cloak draped from his shoulders and a headdress, which seems to be a Phrygian cap. He has a quiver on his back, but there is now no trace of his bow, which may have stood at his left. He rests on his lyre, at his right side. Perhaps it was Apollo's bow that endeared him particularly to the Sarmatian horsemen.

On the other side are two carved niches each containing a female figure, one facing the other. The one on the left is young, has flowing locks, and wears what may be a turreted crown. Her back and shoulders are draped; at the front she is nude from the thighs upwards. The right-hand figure wears a similar headdress, but is veiled and fully draped. She appears to be handing a box-like object to her younger companion. It has been speculated that they are personifications of the *Regio Bremetenacensis* (the area under military rule from Bremetenacum) and the province of Britannia Inferior, respectively. In my opinion, an entity shown wearing a mural crown is more likely to be the tutelary *genius* of a town or city; if this is the case, the younger would represent Bremetenacum, the other perhaps Belisama, the River Ribble. *Genii loci* are often shown at an altar, usually holding a *patera*, or plate for offerings. The box in this instance may be an incense-box, incense usually being burned on the altar accompanying prayer as a prelude to sacrifices, sometimes as a sacrifice in itself.

MARS

Mars is not merely a god of war, like the Greek Ares with whom he is con-fused: to the Romans, he is traditionally as much a god of agriculture, his role common to both functions being that of the protection of land, people, and crops – and in Roman Britain there is no other god so frequently equated with native Celtic (usually local) divinities.

This is an inscription from an altar stone, found in Ribchester, but now unfortunately lost:

> To Mars the Peacemaker, Elega … urba …[1] placed this on account of a vow.

> RIB 584

It has been suggested that 'Elegaurba' is the name of a Sarmatian, because it is not a Roman name. The surviving seventeenth-century transcription appears all on one line without any spacing, but this is not unusual for lower-status inscriptions, and neither is a high degree of unorthodox abbreviation. It may stand for Elegabalus Urbanus – or even Elegantia Urbana.

MINERVA

A small bronze bust of Minerva was found in the same hoard as the Ribchester Helmet, mentioned above. Usually armed, armoured but wearing a dress, Minerva was a favourite with all classes of the Roman armed forces as she is a patron not only of warfare, but also of shipbuilding, crafts, and generally of inventiveness. In her aspect of *Minerva medica*, she is also a goddess of healing.

Although in local guidebooks and on the internet you will find many references to a temple of Minerva at Ribchester (especially in connection with the reused pillars in the church and at The White Bull), the best evidence for this is a nineteenth-century mistranslation of an inscription reading 'PRAEP N ET REG' as *praepotenti numini et reginae* ('to the very mighty numen and queen'). It is probably the same inscription as RIB 587, and should be read as *praepositus numeris et regionis* (commander of the unit and the region). The pillars at The White Bull were also found in the river nearby, so a connection was made.[9]

VICTORY

Victoria is a goddess personifying victory in battle, equated with the Greek Nike. She is often shown winged, and holding out a crown of bay leaves, traditionally awarded to commanders of victorious armies. Nike is sometimes represented as perched on the hand of Athena, and Victoria can be associated similarly with Minerva in her martial aspect. This altar stone, now lost, was found as building material in Salesbury, a mile and a half from Ribchester:

> To the gods Mars and Victoria, for [?] ... our [?] [unit?] ... [?] ... the strongholds in [their?] care ...

RIB 585

AN UNKNOWN GOD

The inscription below is part of a slab, probably a dedicatory plaque, celebrating the restoration of a temple at Ribchester. It was found in the early nineteenth century, embedded in the northern bank of the Ribble, which in altering its course over the last 1,500 years has unfortunately destroyed much of Roman Ribchester – including, probably, the temple itself:

> [...] for the health of the Emperor Caesar Alexander, our Augustus, and for Julia Mamaea, the mother of our Lord and of the Strongholds, under the direction of Valerius Crescens Fulvianus, his pro-praetorian legate, Titus Florid(us) Natalis, legionary centurion in charge of the unit and the region, restored this temple from the ground upward in answer to the god, and dedicated it on their behalf.

RIB 587 (CE 225–35)

Frustratingly, Floridus does not mention which god – but then, at the time, everyone would have known. It is a pity we do not. There is a hint that it may be Jupiter Dolichenus, which, given the Syrian origins of the then ruling Severan dynasty, seems plausible.[10]

Jupiter Dolichenus is a conflation of the Roman Jupiter Optimus Maximus ('the Greatest and Best'), with Dolichenus, who is thought to be of Hittite origin, and in Roman times was widely worshipped in Syria, where he seems to have been conflated with Baal. He is portrayed wielding a double-headed axe, sometimes also with thunderbolts, and often standing on the back of a bull. He became popular elsewhere in the Roman Empire during the reign of Septimius Severus (CE 193–211), especially among soldiers from the provinces around the Danube (this may account for his popularity with the Sarmatians at Ribchester).[11] In Britain, his worship is mainly attested by military dedications in the north (effectively, for much of the time a military zone), and it has been speculated that these dedications to him indicate places of iron production.[12]

Several other altar dedications have been found where the names of the god or gods are missing. Elsewhere in the North, notably in the forts along Hadrian's Wall, many altar inscriptions on behalf of units brought from overseas – Celtic, Germanic, African – exist to their gods whose names are otherwise unknown, and it is disappointing that there is no evidence of the Sarmatians naming the gods of their own land and people in this way. Either they have not survived, or are yet to be discovered, or possibly these steppe nomads came with no tradition of making stone altars or even of fixed places of worship, but it seems likely that, after a period of inclusion in the Roman army, common Roman religious practices would have been adopted – especially after a generation or two in Britain, when the troopers of the Sarmatian Division were no longer native-born Sarmatians. The following is a tombstone, so it is unlikely that in its original form it would have included any dedication to gods other than the *Di Manes* (the deified spirits of the dead):

> To the spirits of the departed (and) [...] decurion of the Sarmatian Wing.
>
> RIB 595

Here is another, probably from the third century:

> This earth seals up Aelia Matrona, who lived for twenty-eight years two months and eight days, and Marcus Julius, son of Maximus, fifty years old. Julius Maximus, *singularius consularis* of the Sarmatian *Ala* (literally, a wing, or division), husband of an incomparable wife, and son of a most devoted father, placed this in memory of the most steadfast of companions.
>
> RIB 594

A *singularius consularis* was a high-ranking officer nominally appointed to the staff of the consular governor (who at that time had control of the military forges in the province), for special duties. Normally a cavalry unit would have been commanded by a *praefectus*, and it is possible that the Sarmatians at this time were commanded by this very senior officer Julius Maximus because of the recent armed rebellion of the Brigantes, and/or the importance of what was then a very new fighting unit at the cutting edge of military practice – like the first tank regiment. There may also have been a special programme for the breeding of heavy horses. It may also have had something to do with the repu- tation the Sarmatians had at the time for being a wild lot, even for barbarians.

WHAT IS THERE NOW?

In addition to the slow obliteration of the fort of Roman Ribchester by the river, the present-day village covers most of what was once the adjoining civil- ian town, or *vicus*, and in consequence there is not a lot left to see on the ground, apart from the excellent museum close to the church (which also covers a large portion of the fort). The museum houses many interesting finds, including a replica of the famous bronze full face cavalry parade helmet, the original of which is now in the British Museum. The Ribchester Helmet is one of the finest Roman cavalry artefacts found in Britain to date.

Near the museum you can see the footings of the military granaries, and if you follow the path by the river across from Church Street, there is a complex of Roman baths, built outside the fort but probably by the military for the use of the local population as well. A section of the northwest rampart and defensive ditch can also be seen along the footpath leading to the public car park, but most of the fort itself now lies beneath the museum, the church, the graveyard and the vicarage. Reused Roman building materials can be found all over Ribchester. There are column bases and capitals outside the museum, the remains of a Roman well not far away (unfortunately now in a private garden), and there are columns around the portico of the White Bull Inn in Church Street, going towards the village centre. The parish church is also partly constructed of Roman masonry, including the pillars supporting the gallery at the back of the church. Other Roman pillars can be seen in the Shireburn Almshouses in the hamlet of Stydd, at the northeast end of the village.

Ribchester is a quiet place nowadays, and hard to imagine as a cavalry base for at least 500 horsemen and their mounts, with training-rings and assault course for horse and rider, stables, granaries, armourers, smiths, leather workers and saddlers, a large parade ground where the regiment sacrificed to Rome's official gods – possibly a distribution centre for all the heavy cavalry horses

Remains of Roman Bath House. Photograph by Karen Lawrinson

used by the Roman military in Britain, and perhaps beyond – kitchens, head-quarters buildings with the treasury and the shrine of the standards where the spirit of the regiment lives, and beyond its lime-washed, battlemented walls and moat, the town with its couple of thousand civilian inhabitants, its temples, its shrines, and festivals. Voices calling in Latin, Brythonic, Sarmatian; full dress parades for visiting dignitaries, gilded and polished bronze scale armour brilliant in the sunshine, red dragon-standards writhing like flames in the breeze... But you can stand by the river and look at the fields and woods beyond, listen to the birdsong and the sounds of water rushing over rock, feel the Roman stone pavement beneath your feet, the sun, wind or rain on your face – and, with your eyes closed, 2,000 years have passed away like a breath.

Some things are unchanging: the three worlds, of earth, sky and water. No less changing is our need to connect with the sources of being, the roots of our past. And Riga-Belisama is still there, as she was before the Bronze Age folk chose this place to bury the urns of their dead. To me, it is a sacred place, above all because it is the cradle of Arthurian legend, and a place where humans, not so very different from you or me in their concerns and values, have prayed to their gods for millennia.

4

FAIRY AND BOGGART SITES IN LANCASHIRE

AIDAN TURNER-BISHOP

Lancashire has a rich tradition of fairy and boggart tales, many of which are linked to specific sites. Of all the English counties indexed in Westwood and Simpson's *The Lore of the land* (2005), only Northumberland and Derbyshire 'score' as highly as Lancashire for tales of fairies and sprites, and there are many tales not recorded in their guide.

Before we consider why Lancashire's fairy lore is so extensive, and before we look at some of the tales, it is useful to define the county and to be clear about different types of fairies, boggarts and other spirits. By Lancashire we mean the traditional County Palatine, which stretches from the Furness district to the banks of the Mersey. Local government reform in 1974 added parts of the Craven district of Yorkshire, including Bashall Eaves, to the reduced county. At the same time, parts of Saddleworth in Yorkshire, including the Greenfield Fairy Holes, were joined to Greater Manchester. Parts of Lancashire, such as Winwick, were added to a reduced Cheshire. Remember that Lancashire's Victorian folk-lorists always had in mind the County Palatine.

Andrew Lang (1911), the editor of the series of coloured fairytale books (Blue, Yellow, Olive, etc), defined fairies as 'a supposed race of supernatural beings who magically intermeddle in human affairs'. *Chambers Dictionary* (1993) refines this by 'generally of diminutive and graceful human form'. The word fairy derives from the French *fée* or *faerie*, from Medieval Latin *fatare*, to enchant, and originally from the Latin *fatum*, fate or destiny. The modern image of a fairy – as a delicate, often winged, creature – largely derives, via Disney Studios, from J.M. Barrie's *Peter Pan* (1904), Richard Dadd's fairy paintings, Doyle's *In Fairyland* (1870), illustrations by Arthur Rackham, Cicely Mary Barker, Edmund Dulac and many others. Shakespeare's *A Midsummer Night's Dream* and *The Tempest*, Shelley's *Queen Mab* and many literary works create a fey, even whimsical, image. This is reinforced by modern marketing of 'faerie' products.

Yet there could be a darker side. Crosby (2000), following Hardwick (1872), defines Lancashire *feeorins* as 'frightening or fearful things; ghost or boggarts, evil spirits or fairies'. However, *feeorin* could just be a dialect plural of fairy with an -en ending, like oxen or children. In Edwin Waugh's dialect ballad 'What ails thee, my son Robin?' (1865), Robin denies that his love-lorn melancholy is 'fairy stricken':

'Tisn't lung o'th feeorin'
That han to do wi th' dule.

One of the most common types of *feeorin* is the boggart, an often mischievous, even malevolent, house brownie. Crosby (2000) notes that, 'Until recently, boggarts were common in the folklore of many parts of the county, and there was scarcely an old house or a lonely valley which did not have its terrifying tales of creatures which roamed, shrieked and caused havoc'. A terrifying spirit, related to boggarts, was the barguist, which often manifested as a large creature, especially a black dog, such as the Bezza Shriker, of Bezza in Samlesbury; 'Owd Scrat' in Brindle; or the Radcliffe Shag. Elves, dwarves and goblins also occur widely; often they live underground. Harland and Wilkinson (1867) record a dwarf sighting on top of Mellor Moor: 'a dwarf-like man, attired in full hunting costume, with top-boots and spurs, a green jacket, red hairy cap, and a thick hunting whip in his hand'.

Water sprite tales include Jenny (or Jinny) Greenteeth, a spirit with long, green weed-like hair, that lives in ponds and deep water and entraps unfortunate children. Arkholme, by the River Lune [589718], is a Jenny Greenteeth site (Carr 1977). Dobbies, as readers of J.K. Rowling's Harry Potter books know, are usually helpful house elves or goblins. However, the White Dobbie of Bardsea, recorded by Bowker (1883), was more sinister. It looked like a gaunt, unhappy pilgrim and it frequented the coastal road from Bardsea to Rampside. It had feverish eyes and it would hurry along the road without speaking. A 'ghastly-looking scraggy white hare with bloodshot eyes' ran before it. The White Dobbie appeared, in the belfry of Bardsea church [302745], before a funeral with its hare as the passing bell was rung. Locally the White Dobbie was said to be the ghost of a murderer. Katherine Briggs (1976) distinguished between dobbies – hobgoblins, like brownies – and dobies (with one 'b') who were less intelligent than brownies.

Why has Lancashire such a rich boggart and fairy tradition? Some folklorists suggest that fairies may be of Celtic origin, reflections of pagan Celtic spirits. Silver (1999: 34) notes that 'Irish interest in what was perceived as a national and ethnic inheritance – one the English could not expropriate – is not surprising'. For those involved in the Celtic Revival – W.B. Yeats, Lady Wilde,

Lady Gregory, George Russell, for example – 'belief in fairies was almost a political and cultural necessity'. Lancashire's Celtic heritage may today be over-looked, but Crosby (1998) notes that 'post-Roman Lancashire, like pre-Roman Lancashire, was a Celtic land whose inhabitants, the Cumbri (their name survives in 'Cumberland' and 'Cumbria') spoke Cymric, a British tongue closely related to Old Welsh'. Parts of Lancashire – perhaps as far as the Ribble – were in the kingdom of Rheged until the Anglo-Saxon conquests in the seventh century. Kenyon (1991) describes Lancashire as 'the last of the English counties to emerge'. The County Palatine was not established until 6 March 1351.

For centuries Lancashire was a poor, remote area. Remoteness, coupled with spiritual conservatism, may have helped the survival of so many boggart tales. This may also be reflected in a firm local belief in witchcraft, shown in the Pendle and Samlesbury witches trails of 1612 and 1633 and, perhaps, in the stubborn survival of pre-Reformation Catholicism in the county. A belief in boggarts and fairies was not incompatible with Christianity. Catholic priests, as in the Towneley Hall case, were sometimes called to 'lay' boggarts. 'Laying' a boggart stilled its mischief. The Hothersall Hall [632347] boggart is laid under a laurel tree and it was fed milk to assuage it and to preserve the power of the spell (Harland & Wilkinson 1867). The church tower of St Mary's, Newchurch-in-Pendle [824394], built in 1544, has an 'Eye of God' set in it as protection against evil spirits.

The Industrial Revolution profoundly affected Lancashire. Not only did manufacturing industries and mining penetrate remote country districts, but also many people migrated from rural areas into the rapidly growing towns. The late eighteenth and early nineteenth centuries would have seen many former country folk, with their beliefs in boggarts and fairies, working in the industrial towns. At the same time, a generation of folklore scholars – perhaps influenced by Romantic ideas of the authenticity of folk tales and legends – were collecting, recording and exchanging fairy and boggart tales. Silver suggests that 'nostalgia for a fading British past' motivated the recording of local traditions: 'The nation was growing too industrial and technological, too urban and material for their health and welfare. It was important to locate the elfin peoples and to record their acts before they departed forever' (1999: 34). It may be no accident that the lifespans of Lancashire's most important folklore authors coincided with the most rapidly changing period of the county's industrialisation. John Roby (1793–1850), Thomas Turner Wilkinson of Burnley (1815–1875), Charles Hardwick (1817–89) and John Harland (1806–68) were active in this period, followed by James Bowker's publication, in 1883, of his *Goblin tales of Lancashire*. The nineteenth-century revival of interest in folklore was not confined to Lancashire; it was Europe-wide. The Grimms, for example, first published their *Kinder und Hausmärchen* fairy tales in 1812, many of which were collected from farmers and peasants, including the 'Fairytale-Wife' Dorothea Viehmann, the source of many famous fairy tales. The rapid changes in Lancashire, the world's first industrial society, may have contributed to its rich, collected folklore.

Folklorists often classify tales by common themes or motifs.[1] One typical motif is that of the fairy funeral, of which Lancashire can record two sites. Fairy funerals may have an unhappy outcome if humans disrupt the funeral. The poet William Blake was said to have witnessed a fairy funeral when he lived at Felpham, in Sussex, from 1800 to 1802: 'I saw a procession of creatures, of the size and colour of green and grey grasshoppers, bearing a body laid out on a rose leaf, which they buried with songs and then disappeared'.[2] Lancashire fairy funerals were more tragic. Bowker's (1883) account of a funeral in Penwortham records that two men were walking home, very late on a moonlit night, along a lane by Penwortham Woods [525291]. They heard the bell of St Mary's tolling for a funeral. It rang twenty-six times, the same age as Robin, one of the pair. They saw a group of small figures, dressed in black, but wearing redcaps, carrying a little coffin. It contained a dead fairy, which looked just like Robin. He cried out in alarm but the procession vanished. Robin became depressed and a month later he fell off a haystack and died. The Extwistle Hall [876338] fairy funeral (Williamson 1957) is specific to a date and a historic person. In 1715 Captain Robert Parker, a former High Sheriff of Lancashire, was reputed to have seen a goblin funeral procession bearing a coffin with his name. In March 1717 he was drying gunpowder in the hall when there was a severe explosion from which he died. He was 'much damnified by gunpowder, and two rooms much damaged', according to an original account.

The Fairy Lane in Penwortham where the fairy funeral was seen. Photograph by Karen Lawrinson

The Fairy Funeral

Fairylore is often linked to caves and the underground. There was a wide-spread belief, in Victorian times and the early twentieth century, that fairies and dwarves were originally an early race of 'little people' displaced by more recent humans; a folk memory of prehistoric races of small people. This theory was popularised by David MacRitchie's *The testimony of tradition* (1890). MacRitchie's euhemeristic theories used archaeological exploration as evidence of the existence of prehistoric 'little people'.[3] In Ireland, for example, Elizabeth Andrews (1913) argued that dwarves built the souterrains (caves roofed with large slabs of stone) which are found in Ulster and elsewhere in Ireland. The little people, or *sidhe*, were memories of a 'Turanian' race that once occupied the island. Silver (1999) notes that the 'pygmy theory' of fairy origin was reinforced by dis-coveries — for Europeans at least — of Aka Pygmies in Africa. Accounts in Henry Morgan Stanley's *In Darkest Africa* (1890) fed the public imagination. Fantasies — often overtly racial and quasi-Darwinian — about races of dwarves occur in many nineteenth-century accounts. The oddity and alleged sub-humanity (after Darwin, science was searching for a missing link between humans and apes) of dwarves was pandered to by exhibitions of dwarves in fairs and sideshows.[4] In the early 1800s — admittedly before Darwin — 'Lady Morgan, the celebrated Winsdor fairy', was exhibited in Blackburn (Hind 1911). Images of 'savage' dwarves, ugly dark-skinned, malevolent goblins,[5] racial prejudice, post-Darwinian beliefs and anxieties, and selective archaeology swirl around the entrances to 'fairy caves'.

Lancashire's best-recorded caves are the Little Bolland Fairy Holes, above the River Hodder, overlooking Whitewell [656467]. The cave is in a small limestone knoll at New Laund Farm. It has a nearly straight passage into the rock about 65ft (19m) deep. Reginald Musson led an archaeological excavation of the site in 1946. Remains of animals, but not of humans, were found together with fragments of pottery: parts of a rim of a collared urn. There was a possible hearth about 16ft (5m) inside the cave. Two interior wall remains were uncovered. The archaeologists concluded that the cave was occupied in the Middle Bronze Age. Gilks (1985) calculated that the urn might have dated from 1700–1300 BC.

Lofthouse (1948) records local fairy sightings, retold by Mr Weld, a local landowner, from a farmer called Leeman who lived at Saddle End, in the eighteenth century. Fairies were seen dancing and washing in a stream at Buck Banks (Self Weeks, 1920). A fairy husband, according to Leeman, travelled from Dinkling Green to Clitheroe to find a midwife for his fairy wife. She was blindfolded and taken to the wife, whom she assisted with the birth. As her reward she was given a bag of fairy gold. Fairy midwife tales are reported elsewhere (Aarne-Thompson motif, ML 5070) and nearby Fair Oak Farm [648461] is said, by Lofthouse and Self Weeks, to be the site of a fairy oak.

Greenfield Fairy Holes, in Saddleworth, are on Alderman's Hill [SE014045]. They were explored in 1871 by Mr Robinson who found a network of caves and passages but with no evidence of human or animal occupation.[6] An account in *Notes and queries* (5 February 1870) records that 'Raura Peena', the last 'fairee' in the parish of Saddleworth, was said to live there by a local man who died in the mid-nineteenth century.

Boggart and fairy holes occur elsewhere, often in tantalising passing references. The 1960s 'Geographia' street plan of Bolton, for example, records a 'Boggart Hole' near Eagley Brook, opposite Waters Meeting Bleach Works [723111].

Fairies and boggarts also lived by streams, bridges, wells and in wooded valleys and cloughs. Perhaps there is a hint of Celtic water spirits about these stories? The Fairy Bridge at Bashall Eaves [703435] is supposed to have been built in a night to help an old woodcutter being pursued by witches (Self Weeks 1920). The Towneley Hall Bridge [852308] boggart was said to be the soul of Sir John Towneley who, in the sixteenth century, enclosed common land into his park, to the distress of local people. Nadin (1991) records that, to appease the boggart, a pact was made that he could seize the soul of the first creature to cross the bridge on New Year's Day. It was planned to send a chicken over but, as the clock struck twelve, an unsuspecting pedlar crossed the bridge and he disappeared, leaving only a strong smell of brimstone.

Fairy Bridge,
Bashall Eaves.
Photograph by
Karen Lawrinson

The Boggart
Bridge near
Towneley
Hall, Burnley.
Photograph by
Karen Lawrinson

The Fairy Glen, at Appley Bridge [515108], is a pleasant wooded nature reserve, with a waterfall, now managed by West Lancashire District Council. No legends have yet been recorded for the site. Perhaps the word 'Glen' – normally a Celtic word – suggests a Victorian origin of the name, inspired by holidays in North Wales (there is a Fairy Glen near Betws-y-Coed) and on the Isle of Man.

A significant water spirit legend is that of 'Peg [or Peggy] o' th' Well' at Waddow Hall, on the banks of the Ribble, near Clitheroe [735426]. Harland and Wilkinson (1867) tell of an evil spirit at the well that was said to inhabit a stone figure. Misfortunes were blamed on Peggy. One day, Mrs Starkie – the lady of the Hall – angered by the near-drowning of a visiting preacher, hurried to the malevolent statue and severed its head from the body. Henderson (1866) was told that Peg was the ghost of a servant girl at the Hall who, cursed by her mistress, slipped and broke her neck or drowned on the stepping stones. Fairies favoured waterfalls too. Dixon (2004) records that fairies inhabit the wooded ravines at Whitehalgh and, 'on a cool summer's evening, their singing, carried on the balmy air, can be heard as they feast and make merry by the waterfall in Sheep Bridge Brook'.

Calf Hey Well, near Cockden, close to the Roggerham Gate Inn [875348], is a fairy site, as is Jam Hole Well [876324] at Worsthorne (Nadin 1991). When, in 1819, a company was formed to build a reservoir near Heasandford, the Calf Hey Well fairies vanished. Bennett (1947), in the official history of Burnley, records that the fairies of Jam Hole Well used little milk cans and made tiny pats of butter. The latest recorded appearance of fairies, he noted matter-of-factly, was in 1829 when a woman from Bottin [870331] saw fairies playing at Brown Side. Another Fairy Well was at Craggs Farm, Sabden (Self Weeks 1920).

Bowker (1883) tells a tale of a Preston woman who travelled to the Fairies' Well near Blackpool, to draw water from the well because of the water's healing powers. Her daughter was going blind. As she was filling her bottle a little man, dressed in green, gave her a box of ointment which, he said, would cure her child. He then disappeared. Because the woman was unsure about the ointment's powers, she tested it on her own eye first. It seemed harmless so she used it on her child who soon recovered her sight. Some years later she saw the same little man in Preston market, apparently stealing corn from a sack. She went to thank him for the ointment, but he angrily asked her in which eye she could see him. She told him which was her good eye and he struck the eye, blinding her. After that, her daughter, who had used the ointment on both her eyes, was always wary of letting any fairies she saw know that they were being watched.

Vales, ravines and cloughs were often boggart and fairy sites. Probably the most famous one is Boggart Hole Clough, Blackley, in Manchester, which is now a City Council-run park [867025]. Originally a farmhouse stood on the site. It was the home of a troublesome boggart according to Roby (1829). Westwood and Simpson (2005) suggest that the tale may have been supplied to Roby by the Irish folklorist Thomas Crofton Croker (1798–1854), who recorded many Irish *sidhe* and leprechaun tales. The story is that a boggart pestered the farmer, George Cheetham, so much that he decided to move house. The boggart frightened children, indulged in practical jokes – sometimes quite malicious ones – like a poltergeist, and had a 'small and shrill' voice that could be 'heard above the rest, like a baby's penny trumpet'. As the farmer, on his laden cart, left the farm with his family, a neighbour called out, 'Well, Georgy, and soa you're leaving th' owd house at last'. As he was replying, a shrill voice called out, from a churn on the cart, 'Ay, ay, neighbour, we're flitting, you see'. The farmer turned to his wife and said, 'We may as weel turn back again to th' owd house, as be tormented in another not so convenient' (Hardwick 1872).

Above left: Boggart Hole Clough in Blackley, North Manchester. Photograph by Karen Lawrinson

Above right: Healey Dell, Rochdale. Photograph by Karen Lawrinson

An important fairy site, located in a wooded valley by a stream, is the Fairies' Chapel at Healey Dell [882168]. Roby's account (1829) is elaborate and probably largely invented, based on the history of the Chadwick family. The River Spodden flows through the narrow, deep 'Thrutch', or channel, in Healey Dell. It powered a corn mill that was once inactive during a deep frost. Roby says this was in Edward IV's time (1461–83). The unoccupied miller, Ralph, decided to catch a hare, but his intentions were overheard by the fairies. When he thought he had caught the hare it turned into 'something black and "uncanny", with glaring eyes'; he had been lured into the Fairies' Chapel. He was told that he would lose his soul if he failed to return to the Dell with Eleanor Byron for the 'Elfin King'. He obeyed and managed to bring Eleanor to the Dell, but she resisted signing away her soul in her blood. She screamed and was rescued by her fiancé, Oliver Chadwick, whom she later married. Alas, on the wedding day, Oliver was killed in a battle with the Trafford family. The fairies had wreaked their terrible revenge. Another version (Marshall 1976, based on Dr Oakley's account) is that, one night in 1180, a witch summoned Robert of Huntingdon. She told him where he could find a ring that would confirm his rights to be the heir to his late uncle, the Earl. He refused her offer but he did look into the holy well of St Chad to see his future. He saw an image of himself as the outlaw Robin Hood. He tried to kill the witch but she flew away. The Fairy King, however, helped Robin by giving him his uncle's ring which he was told to throw into the witches' cauldron in the Thrutch. He did so and the cauldron shattered and fell into the river. The Fairy King shrivelled the witches into hideous elves who disappeared into a crack in the rock. The Fairies'

Chapel was hidden behind a ledge of rocks until a flood in 1839. This exposed a 'pulpit', 'reading desk' and 'seats'. On a visit in 2007, the author noticed posies of flowers laid in the Chapel which may suggest a modern, active fairy cult at the site. Healey Dell is now a nature reserve managed by Rochdale Council. The modern boundary between Lancashire and Greater Manchester bisects the Dell; Fairies' Chapel is on the Lancashire side.

Other fairy and boggart sites in dells and cloughs include those at Hollin Hey Clough, Briercliffe (Eyre 1974) – perhaps a conflation of the Towneley Hall boggart tale; Kitchen Clough, Platting (Roeder 1907); and Clough Head Wood at Grindleton [754450] (Self Weeks 1920). The last may also be a 'fairy steps' site. According to the Vicar of Grindleton, the Revd F.G. Ackerley, the two boys, Tom S. and Richard B., who heard the fairies 'singing beautifully', said that the little men wore 'green coats and red caps running up to a peak'. Other steps are at Warton, near Arnside, and Hapton. On the old road from Clitheroe to Chatburn, just beyond Pimlico, there are 'Fairy Banks' (Self Weeks 1920).

'Goblin builders' tales about disputed sites for churches are a common motif in folklore (ML7060 in the Aarne-Thompson Type Index). Lancashire has at least four such tales: Rochdale, Samlesbury, Winwick (now in Cheshire) and Leyland. The basis of the goblin builder tales is that fairies or goblins remove stones and building material, being used to build a church, and relocate them to a different site. Roby (1829) tells how the site of St Chad's church, Rochdale [896132] was altered from a site on the banks of the River Roch to one on the summit of a hill on the opposite bank, where it stands today.[8] Bowker (1883) records that the Leyland parish church of St Andrew [542216], which is located at the southern end of the modern town centre, was moved repeatedly from Whittle-le-Woods to Leyland. A young workman, guarding building material, attacked a huge cat 'with great unearthly-looking eyes' which sprang at him and attacked his throat. Next day, the cat, the foundations and building materials had vanished but the unfortunate young man was found lying dead. Halliwell (1849) says that the church was moved the night after it was completed. Next day, a marble tablet was found on which was written: 'Here thou shalt be, / And here thou shalt stand, / And thou shalt be called / The church at Ley-land'. Today, on the tower of St Andrew's, there appears to be a carving of a fat-looking cat. The font at St Ambrose's, Farington, which may be the ancient Leyland font, has a similar cat carving.

Hardwick (1872) repeats Wilkinson's and Baines's tales of goblin builders at Samlesbury and Winwick. A demon pig, or wild boar, is said to have determined the site of St Oswald's church at Winwick [604928]. There is a primitive carving of a pig, or boar, on the tower of St Oswald's, just above the western entrance. Burnley parish church also has a goblin legend, according to T.T. Wilkinson, 'confirmed' by a rude sculpture of a pig on the south side of the steeple.

Another common motif in fairytales is that of the changeling (Aarne-Thompson type ML5085). Silver considers the folklore of fairy changelings in which a human child is substituted, by fairies, with a changeling, an elfin creature often with an 'old, distorted face, a small or wizened body, and dark or sallow skin, and was often backward in learning to walk or speak' (1999: 60). Sometimes changelings were doll-like, immobile creatures called 'stocks'. Changelings were often strange, malicious and disturbing. Some children, allegedly changelings, were exhibited in street fairs. Martin Luther is said to have met, and attempted to exorcise, a changeling with a voracious appetite. (This, incidentally, would seem to indicate that the Protestant reformer believed in fairies.) [9] Belief in – and fear of – changelings was genuine and frightening. There were legal cases, especially in Ireland, of the killing or abandonment of changeling children, such as the tragic Cleary trial in Tipperary in 1895. Silver suggests that 'changelingism' may be a folk explanation of disabled children with congenital diseases. Disorders such as Hunter's, Hurler's and Williams's syndromes, phenylketonuria (PKU), progeria and homocystinuria may have physical symptoms similar to those reported for changelings. Susan Schoon Eberly's (1991) paper describes such cases. Changelings may also 'explain' 'failure to thrive' and other developmental deprivation. Giving birth to a disabled child today can be very upsetting for parents, but imagine in an age without modern medicine and more caring attitudes to disability, the dismay, shame and even horror of having a baby with a congenital disorder.

Lancashire has a changeling legend at High Halstead [881336]. A woman went to the well to fetch water, leaving her baby in the cot. When she returned, she found that the child had been replaced by a wizened old thing. She consulted a wise old man who advised her to attract the attention of the boggart. She returned home and poured water into an empty eggshell on the fire. The changeling watched the water boil in the egg shell and asked, in its shrill little voice, 'What are you going to do with that?' She replied, 'I'm going to brew'. The creature then said, 'Well, I'm three score and ten [70 years old] and I've never seen that done before'. The woman then took the changeling to the spring where she met a very old woman beating her own baby, with all her might. The two women exchanged children, without a word, and the woman returned to Halstead overjoyed at recovering her child (Nadin 1991).

Tales of capturing fairies by humans are common (Aarne-Thompson motif ML6010). Bowker (1883) tells that two poachers captured a fairy in a sack at Hoghton Brow. A similar tale is located at Barley Brow near Pendle [822405]. [10] Two poachers placed sacks over rabbit holes, but captured fairies rather than rabbits. As they were walking home with their sacks, they heard a voice call out from one of the sacks, 'Dick, where art thou?' Fairy Dick, in the other sack, replied, 'In a sack, on a back, riding up Barley Brow'. The poachers were so frightened they dropped their sacks, the fairies escaped, and they never poached again.

St Chad's church, Rochdale. Photograph by Karen Lawrinson

Not all boggart and fairy tales are benign or have happy endings. The terrifying Bee Hole Boggart of Brunshaw [858324] once seized a woman called 'Old Bet', leaving only her skin on a thorn bush (Bennett 1947). Bowker (1883) recounts the fearful tale of the headless boggart of Longridge. A Thornley man, Gabriel, was walking one night to the White Bull in Longridge when he met a woman carrying a large market basket covered with a cloth. The woman wore a deep-brimmed bonnet that obscured her face. He offered to carry the basket, which the woman passed to him, laughing and saying, 'You're very kind, I'm sure'. But Gabriel dropped the basket to the ground. The cloth slipped off revealing a human head with fixed eyes. The headless boggart turned to pick up her head, revealing an empty bonnet, and Gabriel fled in terror.

The Written Stone at Dilworth near Longridge [626379] is a massive stone, 9ft (3m) long, 2ft (0.61m) wide and 1ft (0.31cm) thick, set in a bank outside Written Stone Farm. It is inscribed 'Rauffe: Radcliffe: laid: this: stone: to lye: for ever A.D. 1655.' It is said that it was laid to pin down a troublesome boggart. Harland and Wilkinson (1873) recount that the farmer, who moved the stone into the house to use as a 'buttery stone', was plagued with poltergeist-style activity, by a restless spirit. The stone was replaced where it rests today. A holly hedge was planted along the lane for greater security to bind the boggart as long as there are green leaves on the tree.

Holly (*ilex aquifolium*) is well known in botanic folklore for its apotropaic power: it can ward away evil. It was planted as a protection against malevolent boggarts and evil spirits. Bringing holly indoors, during the Christmas season, helped to keep down house goblins, boggarts and other spirits. Pliny (*Natural History*, XXIV.71) said that holly planted by a house was protection against witch-craft. Lancashire holly was known as 'hollin', a name that occurs in place-names and may perhaps be an indication of apotropaic planting. However, holly-derived fairy sites may now be difficult to locate since many holly trees were chopped down to make bobbins for the cotton industry. Nicholls (1972) noted that, in 1802, as many as 150,000 trees were felled for bobbin manufacture.

Moston, a rather bleak, formerly rural district north of Manchester, had a rich 'faireen' folklore, according to Charles Roeder (1907). Moston Hall [878015] is the site of a 'fairy spade' tale. A fairy's little shovel, used for turning hearth cakes, was repaired by a kindly farmer. He was rewarded with good ale, which made him vigorous and healthy. A fairy spade legend also occurs in the Fylde (Bowker 1883). In this version, the farmer met a pretty 'little lass' fairy with a broken 'speet' or spade. He repaired it and was rewarded with 'a hanful o'brass'.

Sometimes boggart or fairy tales may have ulterior motives for their tell-ing. Can it be just coincidence that the noisy Clegg Hall boggart of Milnrow [922145] (Roby 1829; Eyre 1974) shared a house with coiners – counterfeiters using noisy presses in a secret chamber to make false money? The tale of the Heysham Head fairies, described by Elizabeth Hartley in 1938, was apparently published by the owners of Heysham Head, a pleasure garden close to the vil-lage of Heysham [409617]. It had a Rose Garden next to the Manor House, and this is where part of Hartley's story is located. The fairies grant Adam, a little boy, his wish to have a wishing well, a fairy glen and fairy steps. Naturally these wishes were granted and Adam eventually married a beautiful fairy princess named Mary de Overton. The Manor House was replaced by a café.

There are many more boggart legends in the county, often linked to halls and houses such as those at Rowley, Barcroft, Hackensall and Chamber, at Oldham. Tracing fairy and boggart sites can sometimes be helped using clues in place-names and on old maps. There are, for example, two Fairy Lanes near Manchester: one in Cheetham [834002] and the other near Sale Golf Course [SJ812914]. Fairy Street, Bury, connects the A58 Bolton Road with the B6196 Ainsworth Road. 'Fairywell' roads are in Brooklands, Sale and Timperley, originally in Cheshire. Different edi-tions of the Ordnance Survey maps can be revealing. Fairy Lane, Cheetham, was the site of a large brick works in 1931. The remains of a small stream and the exca-vated Barrow Hill are shown. On the 1842 1:50,000 map, Fairy Hill and Barrow Hill are shown clearly with a stream running from Fairy Hill to the Irwell. Clay from the reduced Fairy Hill was used to manufacture thousands of bricks that went to build houses and factories locally. All that is left now is the street name.

Above left: The Written Stone. Photograph by Karen Lawrinson

Above right: Fairy Lane, near Strangeways, Manchester. Photograph by Karen Lawrinson

What is the future of fairy lore in Lancashire? Despite the elimination of remote rural communities, it is likely that interest in fairies may still flourish. Local history and folklore studies are growing in popularity, perhaps reflecting an interesting 'local distinctiveness' promoted by groups such as Common Ground. There is a renewed interest in spiritual matters and paganism. Modern urban myths sometimes reflect motifs in fairy lore. Lancashire's newer citizens bring an awareness of spirits and fairies. Islam recognises 'djinns' and Hinduism is multi-theistic. Immigrants from Poland and Eastern Europe may be aware of the rich traditions of fairytales and folklore from their countries. The Internet has many sites concerned with folklore and local history, and blogs and social networking allow the exchange of tales and research. Perhaps the 'feeorin' will still be with us in the future.

AUTHOR'S NOTE

The Ordnance Survey grid references listed in this chapter are all in grid square SD, except for the sites at Sale and Greenfield, where full Grid references are provided. Some sites are difficult to locate now so the references are best approximations.

5

CHURCHES ON THE LANDSCAPE:
PARISH BOUNDARIES AND EARLY CHURCH SITES AS EVIDENCE OF CONTINUITY

LINDA SEVER

This chapter gives a general overview and discussion as to what extent it is possible to reconstruct the evidence for a pre-English and possible early Anglo-Saxon presence in the Lancashire landscape, in particular by using evidence of early Christian church sites, associated stone sculpture and parish boundaries as indicators of continuity. The second part of the chapter takes Bolton as a case study. It is followed by a list of stone sculpture sites in South East Lancashire, including Greater Manchester.

It is widely accepted amongst those who attempt to interpret the early medieval period in the northwest (and in particular the pre-Christian period) either through archaeology, anthropology, history, art history or other disciplines, that the greatest challenge is the lack of currently available evidence. As stated by N.J. Higham (1986: 242–3):

> ... the end of the artificial, Roman, economy has deprived the archaeologist of diagnostic, artefactual evidence on all but a small minority of sites, and has left us dangerously dependent on documentary sources, the interpretation of which is notoriously difficult.

He continues by stating that besides these few sources in the northwest area there are a handful of inscriptions and a very limited amount of archaeological evidence, much of which is of questionable value. The evidence is limited even further if one considers Lancashire alone, where all forms of evidence are scant.

However, Newman (2004) points out that our ideas about the period have been revolutionised, in particular through the linking of palaeoecological studies with archaeology on conventional archaeological sites, and also the realisation that the study of the vast resources of peat within the region can expand our understanding of the past, demonstrating that there was quite extensive early medieval activity which had previously simply not been recognised.

Another approach to the study of continuity has been the examination of land use and settlement. The work in this area is still largely predicted through place-name evidence (e.g. Ekwall 1922; Dodgson 1970, 1971, 1981; Fellows-Jensen 1983), acknowledged as not the most reliable form of evidence and often viewed as over-simplistic. However place-names remain an important tool for indicating particular types of settlement, such as those elements from British, Old English and Old Norse referring to church sites (*eccles church, kirk*; Kenyon 1991). Higham (2002) also points out that clusters of Old English names, particularly of the *-ham* and *-tun* type, have been recognised, usually in areas of better agricultural quality, suggesting early foci, perhaps permanently cleared in the Roman or even the later prehistoric periods. See Chapter 2 for further discussion of place-names. Other research has been through excavation of Roman forts, urban centres and rural settlements.

According to Newman, it is the fact that the dataset is so small that little analysis of the landscape and territories can be undertaken beyond the evidence that place-names can provide.

However, the tantalising prospect has been held out, particularly in the south of the region, of the continuity of boundaries as visible features in the landscape.

Newman 2004

Cramp (1994) has suggested that 'the conjunction of Roman or native fort, early place-name and later medieval estate centred on the same parcel of land, is one that can be noted again and again in the reconstruction of early settlement'. She points in particular to the juxtaposition of centres of lay and ecclesiastical power in this context. Examples can be seen in Cumbria and in Lancaster, and possibly also at Penwortham, near Preston, Lancashire.

It is in the area of Christian sites to which scholars have mostly been drawn when focusing on the early medieval period in the northwest. Thomas (1971) documented a small amount of material and documentary sources as evidence that a Christian population survived in sub-Roman Britain, but there is still hardly any concrete archaeological evidence and virtually none whatsoever for pre-Christian British heathen/pagan activity. One of the few exceptions seems to be a site from Ninekirks, east of Brougham in Cumbria, where nineteenth-century renovations to a church close to a Roman road uncovered a number of skeletons, one in a stone cist, accompanied by a silver-gilt cup mount dated to the eighth century (Bailey 1977). This demonstrates activity on the site in the early medieval period. Aerial photography of the area has shown an unusual ditched enclosure surrounding the present church. Loveluck (2002) has suggested that an early Christian focus at Ninekirks could possibly have supplanted a Celtic and Roman cult centre to Belatucadras at Brougham. In addition to this, the discovery of an extensive cemetery at Southworth Hall Farm, Winwick, in Northern Cheshire (Freke & Thacker 1987) seemed to focus on a Bronze Age burial mound. This feature was also noted by Williams (1997). At Winwick there were over 800 apparently Christian graves. The spatial distribution of the graves has led to the suggestion that there may once have been a building amongst them.

With regards to potentially pagan Anglian burials, very few have been recognised. Two urns that were presumed to be from pagan 'Anglo-Saxon burials' were found at Red Bank, Manchester (Holdsworth 1983). More recently, skeletons from Heronbridge in Cheshire were radiocarbon dated to AD 430–640 and AD 530–660. Three more sites have been identified in the region. A log coffin from the Quernmore area made from two pieces of oak from the same tree was dated to between the sixth and eleventh centuries (Edwards 1973). The North West Wetlands survey records what has seemed to have been the deliberate placing of heads and front feet of two, possibly more, cattle, which were found during peat cutting in Solway Moss (Hodgkinson et al 2000). They have been dated to the later seventh to eleventh centuries and, according to Newman (2004), seem to represent some survival of pagan tradition, perhaps offerings to a water deity. Material from the Roman and early medieval periods, as well as human remains, have been recovered from the Dog Hole, Haverbrack in Cumbria (Benson & Bland 1963).

Some evidence (albeit tentative) has been established for the re-use of earlier burial mounds, possibly from both the periods of conversion of the pagan peoples to Christianity in the sixth and ninth/tenth centuries. In the case of Lancashire and Cumbria, only in the east of the county, in the upper Eden Valley, is there evidence of the re-use of prehistoric burial mounds, for example around Crosby Garrett (O'Sullivan 1985; Loveluck 2002).

Lists of traditionally viewed pagan focal points offer a framework with which to explore topographical considerations (Morris 1989). In c.1005 Archbishop Wulfstan acknowledged the importance of sites such as springs, stones and forests to the pagans (reiterated in the later Cnut's code, c.1018, also attributed to Wulfstan). He called for every priest to 'entirely extinguish the heathen practice; and forbid worship of wells and necromancy... and in sanctuaries (on friðsplottum) and at elder trees' (Canons of Eadgar, c.16. See Blair 2006: 482). A generation later the Northumbrian Priest's Law, concerned mainly with the buying and selling of land amongst priests, included examination of evidence for sanctuaries that surrounded these sites, imposing a penalty 'if there is on anyone's land a sanctuary (friðgeard) round a stone or a tree or a well or any such nonsense.' (NPL c.54. See Blair 2006: 482n).

Certain Old English words that denote heathen shrines – hearg and wih or weoh (e.g. Harrow) – are also found in the landscape in and around Lancashire. Alongside these there are names linked to the heathen gods – Woden, Tiw, Thunor, Balder –

such as Grimsargh, Osbalderstone, Balderstone (all near Preston), demonstrating the later Scandinavian pagan influence within the area. There are also words such as *burh* denoting royal fortification and *halig* denoting holy (e.g. Halliwell in Bolton). Some holy well places, such as Fernyhalgh, Preston, were absorbed by the later Christian church, as were many pre-Christian sites, and this particaulr example is now in the grounds of a Catholic retreat house.

In his book *Churches in the Landscape*, Richard Morris (1989) stated that 'Christianity did not so much displace pagan religion as form a kind of crust upon the surface of popular culture.' The conversion of the pagan Anglo-Saxons to Christianity had begun by 620, but there is almost no pagan-period archaeological material from Lancashire, other than that already stated above. This could possibly indicate that their arrival did not take place until after the Northumbrian victory in 616 (Newman 2004). As also stated earlier in this chapter, certain types of place-names are now thought to indicate places of primary importance in the early phases of the Anglo-Saxon settlement: *-ham* (as in Kirkham and Heysham) and *-tun* (as in Bolton, Warrington and Preston). Places such as these have a known historical importance, for example as the centres of great estates or landholdings, with early churches that governed a wide surrounding area. It seems likely that the basic territorial structure of pre-Saxon Lancashire, which itself might have derived from pre-Roman divisions, was taken over by the newcomers. In this context, interpretations of place-name evidence relating to Christianity in post-Roman Lancashire are relevant (Higham 2004; Kenyon 1991). The word for 'church' in Celtic languages is derived from the Latin *ecclesia*, giving the British word *ecles* (Barrow 1969; Kenyon 1991; Higham 2004), which, in place-names, is usually held to indicate a place of worship dating from the pre-Saxon period. Lancashire has several such names, with Eccles in Manchester and three Ecclestons: one west of St Helen's documented by 1190 (Ekwall 1922: 108) in the Prescot parish, which by the Middle Ages meant 'priest's cot/manor' and may possibly be a late Anglo-Saxon replacement of the earlier church on a new site (Higham unpublished); another one west of Chorley astride the River Yarrow, which was of parochial status throughout the Middle Ages (Ekwall 1922: 108); and a third in the Fylde, where a small settlement, Little Eccleston, is in the medieval parish of Kirkham on the south of the River Wyre, adjacent to Great Eccleston, both of which were named holdings in Domesday. According to Higham (unpublished), this parish was already centred at St Michael's by 1086, but there seems a strong possibility that an earlier cult centre lay at one of these two sites. There is also Eccleshill outside of Blackburn parish, which in the mid-thirteenth century was documented as meaning 'church hill' (Ekwall 1922), and Ecclesriggs near Broughton-in-Furness. There was in fact an 'eccles' place in each of the post-Conquest hundreds of Lancashire, which suggests that these were perhaps units which survived relatively unaltered into later centuries. Higham (unpublished) calls for extensive research to be carried out, stating: 'If these place-names, as it generally believed, do offer the opportunity to localize post-Roman but pre-English Christian cult sites, then their research should be given a high priority and a systematic study take place of one at least of these concentrations.'

By the end of the seventh century Christianity was firmly established in the area and churches were being founded, although documentary evidence is negligible. The Domesday Book (1086) makes reference to only fifteen churches in the county and some are only noted implicitly – for example, at Childwall, where a priest is mentioned, or Preston to which three unnamed churches belonged.

Between the 660s and the 750s, many religious establishments were founded in England, often on sites enclosed by re-using prehistoric earthworks, with river and coastal situations being favoured (Muir 2000: 166). Blair states:

> It seems clear that the early West Saxons built their mother churches, where possible, near, but not adjacent to, Roman roads, often at the nearest permanent spring to the road ... When associated with Saxon *burhs* the West Saxon minsters appear to have been placed at the gates of the fortified townlet, near a river or stream and facing the market.

> Blair 1998: 58

In the northwest, once again, evidence for the supplanting of prehistoric or pre-Christian sites in order to found such religious establishments is sparse. It is, however, recognised elsewhere that some pagan sites were used for churches. We have, for example, accounts of what happened during the conversion period, such as Bede's account of Goodmanham in the 620s where he says that the site was remembered there, but not whether a church was built:

> [Cuifi] set out to destroy the idols... full of joy at his knowledge of the worship of the true God he told his companions to set fire to the shrine and its enclosures and destroy them. The site where these idols once stood is still shown, not far east of York, beyond the river Derwent, and is known today as Goodmanham.

> Bede 1990: 131

Returning to place-names, there has been much interest attached to the place-name element *kirk*, the Scandinavian equivalent of 'church' as in Kirkham and Kirkby (for instance, Kenyon 1991; Blair 2004). Although the alternative forms 'church' and 'kirk' were used interchangeably until the seventeenth century – so Ormskirk was often known as Ormschurch, and at Church near

Accrington the double form 'Church Kirk' survived until reasonably recently – these names possibly indicate places where the Viking settlers found existing churches in the tenth century (Blair 2004). In this context the hamlet of Bradkirk, northwest of Kirkham, is seen to be of special importance (Crosby 1998). No church is known here from documentary sources or from physical remains, but the name means 'board church', suggesting a wooden 'log cabin' church of the sort still found in northern Europe.

A high proportion of the twelve Kirkbys in Lancashire (including Cumberland and Westmorland) and Cheshire were important churches, with early sculpture or mother-parishes. For example, Kirkby Lonsdale, Kirkby Kendal, St Bees (Cherchebi *c.* 1125) and Kirkby Stephen have huge mother parishes, and the last retains both eighth- and tenth-century crosses.

It is the quality and the scale of early medieval Christian stone sculpture within the region that gives a strong indication of the pattern of churches in the early medieval landscape. The sculpture indicates the development of church sites and their continued use, particularly where certain Anglian sites also have Scandinavian examples (Blair 2005). Examples are to be found at Dacre and Workington in Cumbria and Halton and Whalley in Lancashire.

English stone sculpture arrived as an art form with Christianity, and it could be argued that sculptures were placed within the landscape to counterbalance the number of prehistoric standing stones already in place when they arrived. The earliest examples of Christian stone sculpture are in Northumberland and date back to the eighth century (e.g. Bewcastle Cross; Bailey & Cramp 1988).

There are many examples of pre-Conquest sculpture, although little to suggest early Anglo-Saxon origin. Examples of these are at Hornby and Gressingham in the Lune Valley, Burnley and Bolton. Heysham and Bolton-le-Sands have norse-type hogback stones and Whalley has ninth- or tenth-century crosses.

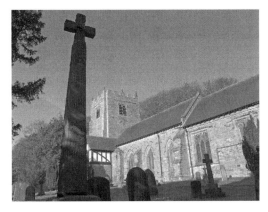

Whalley Churchyard. Photograph by Karen Lawrinson

Above left: Viking Age Cross A, Whalley church. Photograph by Karen Lawrinson

Above right: Viking Age Cross B, Whalley. Photograph by Karen Lawrinson

> The cross would have been a normal outward and visible sign of a site's Christian status, whether freestanding or carved or painted on an older holy stone or tree.

Blair 2005

Where there is no monastic or church presence, there is some evidence that stone crosses may have been set up on boundaries at crossroads and along routes in the eighth and ninth centuries as they were in the tenth and eleventh centuries. It is probable that none of these monuments date to earlier than the eighth century. The stone sculptures are prolific in the area and are worth noting. (For a full listing of stone sculptures in the southeast Lancashire area, see the end of this chapter.)

In the northwest as a whole, sixty-three per cent of sites with pre-Viking sculpture also have post-Viking sculpture (Fellows-Jensen 1985), and some with early pieces controlled large parishes. In terms of Viking-period carvings, these are more evenly distributed. An indication that there might have been some form of social disruption in the late ninth and early tenth centuries could possibly be why there is no evidence of sculptural continuity. The cultural assimilation of the settlers and Anglians north of the Lune has been represented in the iconography of the Gosforth cross, where pagan mythology and Christian teachings are found side by side (Bailey & Cramp 1988: 100–4). At Heysham there is also the linking of Christian and Scandinavian imagery on the hogback stone, which according to Cramp (unpublished) could indicate teaching or missionary activity.

Associated with the founding of churches was the development of the parish system, a process which was underway by the time of the Conquest and which, like elsewhere in northern England, produced a distinctive pattern of very large units. The medieval parish of Whalley was the second largest in the whole of England, embracing no fewer than forty-five townships and extending from Clitheroe to Haslingden, Accrington to Colne, while Ulverston parish extended from the Leven estuary to Langdale, and Prescot from the edge of Skelmersdale to the Mersey. Documentary and other evidence – notably analysis of their shape – shows that some of these big parishes had been created by the subdivision of even larger units in the early medieval period. This, together with information about the age and importance of early churches, makes it possible to reconstruct the system of minsters, or mother churches, which underpinned the organisation of the pre-Conquest church. Each administered a wide area and all of them show signs of antiquity, such as architectural and sculptural features and the payment into the sixteenth century or beyond of monetary tributes from former daughter churches (Blair 2005). Sometimes it is possible to see a link between these sites and those where British Christianity is postulated – Prescot is only a short distance from Eccleston, Manchester from Eccles, Blackburn from Eccleshill – and, as noted earlier, there are possible links between the territories which the churches governed and the ancient administrative and landholding units.

The ancient ecclesiastical parish was the basic unit of church organization before the nineteenth century (Winchester 1990:6). It can be defined as a community served by a priest in a parish church and supporting that priest by the payment of tithes and other dues. The practice of paying tithes had its origins in the Anglo-Saxon period and with this the parish acquired a 'territorial dimension' early, with its boundaries being those of the lands of the parish community from which its priest could claim tithes. There was a striking contrast between different counties. Winchester notes that eighty-five per cent of Gloucestershire's parishes contained just a single township, compared with only fifteen of Lancashire's sixty-eight parishes. Some of the northern parishes covered vast territories, with those stretching up into the moors and fells among the largest. For example, Whalley parish in Lancashire probably embraced more than forty-seven townships and over 105,000 acres (Winchester 1990: 7). But even lowland parishes could be extensive in the north – the parish of Kirkham in the Fylde in Lancashire contained seventeen townships and almost 44,000 acres. At the local level, however, large and small townships were often side by side; Bolton, Deane and Bury are examples of this.

It seems reasonable to contend that if the parochial pattern can be traced back largely unchanged to the later thirteenth century, then it could have been in the Anglo-Saxon period that the pattern of parishes began to be established or had already come into being. Late Saxon documents distinguish between minster churches or 'mother churches', ancient churches served by a group of clergy who ministered to a large area and 'field churches', which were lesser (and often more recent) churches which had their own graveyards. The minster churches were generally Royal or Episcopal foundations established in the seventh or eighth centuries, often close to important estate centres (Blair 2005).

Blair states that Cheshire and Lancashire show a strong correlation between mother-parishes and hundreds, each hundred usually comprising two or three interlocking parishes. Examples are:

Blackburn, Whalley
Leyland, Croston
Eccles, Manchester, Prestwich
Lancaster, Halton, Heysham, Melling
Preston, Kirkham, St Michael's
Warrington, Winwick, Wigan, Prescot

Some of the mother churches are older – Sandbach and Lancaster for example. Lancaster was an important minster in a Roman fort and with fragments of thirteen Anglian and Viking Age crosses, looks like the centre of a group, including Heysham, which is a twin-church coastal site with high-quality sculpture and painted plaster, and a series of churches up the Lune (Halton, Hornby and Gressingham) which have late Anglian crosses. They emerge in late sources as the heads of large mother parishes. Felicity Clark (see Chapter 6) has suggested that this could indicate that the Lune Valley group could be a trans-Pennine colony of a major centre such as Ripon.

PARISH BOUNDARIES

As Winchester (1997:3) states:

Anyone who has pored over one of the Ordnance Survey's old One Inch maps or the 2½ inch Pathfinder series is likely to have found their eyes following the dotted lines which mark the boundaries of civil parishes and other units of local administration. Snaking across the British countryside, following hedgerows, roads, footpaths, streams and rivers, or cutting across the landscape with no apparent reference to the lie of the land or to features of the human landscape, parish boundaries create a pattern of considerable complexity ... Why does a boundary which has been following a particular stream suddenly swing away to follow lanes and hedgerows for a couple of miles before rejoining the stream on its course to the sea? Why was a Roman road used to mark the limits of parishes in one area but totally ignored by the boundaries a few miles on?

One of the principal themes in the history of territorial units in Britain has been that a new unit of local administration is generally defined in terms of an existing one, and that new boundaries, either civil or ecclesiastical, replace or appropriate the older, already existing ones.

It has already been postulated that many parish boundaries include prehistoric elements. Boundaries commonly include prehistoric barrows or other ancient earthworks, stones and crosses at distinctive points along the boundary, reflecting the continuity of human involvement in the landscape and the continuing importance of 'landmarks' in creating a sense of place. It seems there is strong evidence elsewhere in Britain that parish boundaries were built on or follow very closely the territorial boundaries already in place.

In southern and midland England, many hundreds of Anglo-Saxon charters have survived, dating from the middle of the seventh century until the Norman Conquest in the mid-eleventh century. Farther north, few have survived, and only four charter boundaries are known for the whole of Yorkshire, and those are in the southern part of the county (Spratt 1991). The charters describe the boundaries often in terms of natural features, such as rivers or ridges, and frequently contain much detail, both natural, such as trees and pools, and artificial, such as barrows and roads, particularly Roman.

Stenton (1955) explains how the early charters usually have the simplest boundary descriptions, because the necessity for more sophisticated versions arose only when the boundaries later ran through more highly developed areas. Furthermore, the language of the charters often hints that the boundaries were old at the time the charters were written, features being described as 'well-known' or 'ancient'. Research carried out on territorial boundaries in Yorkshire concluded that many of the boundaries persist through medieval into modern times. 'In these remote areas, with comparatively little impact of the Roman period, one might postulate a continuity with the territorial system from the Bronze Age until the present time' (Spratt 1991: 463).

CASE STUDY: BOLTON

In order to try and see what evidence still exists in today's landscape of the old parish boundary system and thus, possibly, indicating earlier boundary markers or territorial or ritual sites, an attempt was made to map out some of the old boundary markers using earlier and contemporary Ordnance Survey maps and street maps, taking Bolton, Greater Manchester (erstwhile Lancashire), as a case study.

The Victoria History of the County of Lancaster (VCH 1908, Vol. 5:235) gives the following information about Bolton, on the borders of Greater Manchester and Lancashire:

The ancient parish of Bolton is 33,406 acres. Of the formation of the parish, nothing is known. The lands within it were in the 12th century held by three district tenures. Blackrod and Lostock go back to a 'remote period'.

Fixed in 1624, Bolton was divided into six portions, together with Wigan:

Bolton with its hamlets;
Turton with Longworth;
Edgeworth with its hamlets;
Blackrod with Aspull;
Rivington, Anglezarke and Lostock;
Harwood with its hamlets.

(VCH 1911: 235)

The old parish church in Bolton was erected in the fifteenth century. It was a low building and consisted of a chancel, nave with north and south aisles, a south porch and west tower. When it was taken down in 1866, several pre-Norman stones were found, including a cross in three pieces (now at the entrance to the current St Peter's parish church). There were also fragments of two other crosses, part of another cross shaft and two stones with carvings possibly dating to the eleventh century, together with fragments of twelfth- and thirteenth-century work, a sepulchral slab, a stone coffin and the remains of a recumbent female figure, apparently of fourteenth-century date, which, according to the editors of the VCH, showed that at least two stone churches had existed on the same site (VCH 1911: 236).

The Boundaries of Great Bolton (which contain the parish church) are given as follows:

Bounded north and east by the River Croal flowing East and South East to join the Irwell. Formerly the southwest part of the township was occupied by the moor, the first habitations sprang up along the course of the stream, the church standing above it at a point where its course changed from East to South. There are two noted wells – the memory preserved in Silverwell Street and Spa Road.

From the church, the road from Little Bolton leads westwards by Church Bank, Church Gate and Deansgate, from which the roads to Chorley and Deane branch off. The main street is crossed about 200 yards from the church, by the road from Manchester leading north by Bradshawgate and Bank Street into Little Bolton. At their crossing is the old Market place with its cross.

From Deansgate, Bridge St leads north across the Croal, in 1874–7 another road was further west – Marsden St.

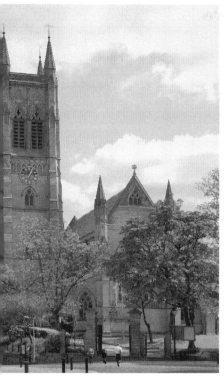

Far left: Bolton parish church. Photograph by Karen Lawrinson

Left: Tenth-century cross in Bolton parish church. Photograph by Karen Lawrinson

Below left: Remains of tenth- or eleventh-century cross in Bolton parish church. Photograph by Karen Lawrinson

Below right: Meeting of the Rivers Croal and Tonge. Photograph by Karen Lawrinson

From the west end of Deansgate, Moor Lane leads south and branches out west and to the west of Mor Lane and districts called Bullfield (now lost), Gilnow and Pocket.

From the junction of Moor Lane and Derby St, Weston St and Great Moor Street lead northeast to Bradshaw Gate, and Crook St and Trinity St.

(About this point was Sweet Green, said to have been named from the prevalence of wild camomile. Pilling Well is in the same district.)

Eastward across the railway station to the bridge over the Croal, leading into Haulgh. To the south of Crook Street were the Lecturers Closes. Rosehill lies to the south east of the town by the river.

As Bolton is now such a built-up area and there is no 1:25000 Ordnance Survey map available, some attempt was made to map the boundaries on an A–Z map. Many of the roads are still in existence, and some of the boundaries could be followed and mapped, although not a great deal of information or concrete evidence could be gleaned. Interesting points to note are that the boundaries are surrounded by and, at times follow the course of, the Rivers Croal and Tonge and Bradshaw Brook. Near to the church there is the field name of 'Round Field', suggesting (albeit tentatively) a prehistoric burial site with the Rivers Tonge and Croal forming natural boundaries. The Roman Road (Watling Street) lies to the east.

The church is also within extremely close proximity of the two well locations mentioned in the VCH. However, without further excavation of the church or the vicinity, it is extremely difficult to determine whether there are any significant earlier sites along the route of the boundary. Further study of street names or field names may possibly unlock some information.

Turning to the district mentioned as the largest in the VCH, Turton (Turton, 1212; Thurton, 1277; Terton, Torton, 1282), the area is given to have 4,614 acres and extends in a north and northwest direction for approximately five miles.

A large part of the centre is occupied by moorlands, known as Turton Height and Turton Moor, rising to 1,100 and 1,280 feet.

Along the N and E boundaries flows the Cadshaw or Bradshaw Brook, on the upper part formed two reservoirs. The village of Turton, called Chapeltown lies close to the brook about the centre of the valley, close to the junction of the boundaries of Turton, Edgeworth, Quarlton and Bradshaw.

Billy Brook bounds Chapeltown on the west and south; to the south of it the ground rises again, forming a spur on the greater hills mentioned. Here stands Turton Tower – at a height of 600 ft above sea. Still farther to the south, on the slope of the main elevation is the hamlet of Bromley Cross. Farther south on a tongue of land between Bradshaw and Eagley Brooks, lie the hamlets of Birtenshaw and Oaks. Eagley Brook forms the SW boundary of the township.

NW from Birtenshaw are villages and hamlets of Toppings, Dunscar, Coxgreen, Egerton or Walmsley and Dimple.

The principal road Bolton to Darwen, divides at the south end of the township so as to pass round each side of the central hill. The eastern branch goes through Turton Village to Edgworth and western through Egerton over Charters Moss to Blackburn.

On the summit of the hill to the northeast of Walmsley is a Druidical circle. It has been almost entirely destroyed by a farmer. Another circle has been found.

The hanging stone is near the extreme northwest boundary.

There are two ancient chapels – one at Turton (1523-4) close to the east boundary, the other at Walmsley (existed in 1531), near the west border.

VCH 1911:275

On the Pathfinder Ordnance Survey (Explorer 19) of the West Pennine moors, this route was easier to follow, though none of the original boundaries from the 1849 map of Turton were marked.

The 'ancient chapel' at Walmsley lies along the principal Bolton to Darwen Road, one of the original boundaries. The other chapel, also recorded as ancient, is close to the Roman Road and to Billy Brook, which is mentioned as being one of the boundaries to the west and south of Chapeltown. The most notable early site in this area is the enclosure and stone circle at Cheetham Close. Though not marked as lying on a boundary (possibly because of its height and remoteness) it is equidistant from the boundary to the west and to the east. It is also almost equal in distance from both the 'ancient' chapels. There are a number of springs and weirs lying on or close to what are described as the boundaries. The Roman road to the east of Turton seems to have been neglected with foots of hills, brooks and reservoirs having been chosen instead.

In examining the 1967 Ordnance Survey 1:10,560 of 1967 (SD 61 NE) of Turton Moor and Belmont and the 1975 Ordnance Survey (SD 61 NW) of Anglezarke moor and its environs, it is noted that the administrative, county borough, civil parish and county boundaries are clearly marked. In the case of Turton moor and Belmont, the administrative and parish boundaries seem to follow similar routes. However, on the Anglezarke map (1975), one parish boundary, to the west of Anglezarke is the same as administrative one, but there is another parish boundary alone just to the east of the administrative boundary, creating a different boundary enclosure. This parish boundary follows the course of various brooks, primarily Black Brook, for a number of miles, before joining the administrative boundary and sweeping downwards. It seems to fully encircle Anglezarke moor with its number of prehistoric monuments – Round Loaf tumulus and Pike Stones Long Cairn. It is also interesting to note that the parish boundary runs through Anglezarke reservoir and then along the course of Fill Brook, along Warth Brook, then Dean onto Black Brook. It also runs through Yarrow Reservoir, having followed the course of the River Yarrow. In this case, therefore, there is very close correlation between the parish boundary and the natural features of streams, brooks and rivers. The administrative boundary also runs over a number of springs and, at one point, alongside Black Brook. This accords with the work carried out by Hooke (1985: 68), where she noted that in northeast Worcestershire, 'the parish boundaries of Knighton, Lindridge and Pensax follow streams for much of their courses'.

Further archaeological research and investigation could possibly uncover more concrete evidence than the tentative and speculative work carried out above.

CONCLUSIONS

As expected, it remains very difficult to demonstrate continuity from Roman to British to English communities, particularly in Lancashire, where so much work still needs to be undertaken. It is even more difficult to show or prove the shift from pagan/heathen belief to Christianity, but a little easier to show the shift back to heathenism with the later Viking invasion, as they left many more imprints on the landscape, both in the form of artefacts, place-names and territorial organisation.

Recent archaeological work that has been carried out, such as that on the cemetery at Southworth Hall Farm in Winwick (Freke & Thacker 1987–88) where the Farm barrow was covered and surrounded by an extensive cemetery, drew some conclusions:

> The fact that it was cut around a pre-existing barrow strongly suggests Germanic influence; it was an especially common arrangement in early Anglo-Saxon times, whereas native British cemeteries, by contrast, tended to be more closely associated with existing settlements than with burial mounds.

> Freke & Thacker 1987–88: 33

They concluded that 'Winwick may have been a significant place in an area which long remained a British-speaking enclave and which had some special status' (Ibid: 36).

Returning to the case of the early Middle Ages, Higham notes (2001: 11): 'there is no alternative to the assumption that archaeology has so far failed to identify this community in the early Middle Ages'. He does point out, however, that it is possible that some British cult sites may eventually have metamorphosed into the 'Anglo-Saxon' monasteries or churches that are identified largely by their pre-Viking sculpture, or the occasional reference in Anglo-Saxon literature (Higham 2001: 12).

> What is needed is a model capable of explaining the flow of cultural influence from barbarian to British communities, and of resources from British communities to an Anglo-Saxon and/or Anglicising elite, across the mid to late fifth centuries.

> Higham 2004

Newman (2004) does state, however, that 'wherever and whenever radio-carbon dating has been undertaken, early medieval dates have been returned, even in the most unexpected places, such as from hillforts, or sites that typologically would seem to be classic Iron Age/Romano-British settlements.'

In landscape research and in scholars' continual search for evidence, there is the ongoing need to recognise how equally important were the wider landscapes of undeveloped or unmarked cult sites. Conceptions of sacred space would have had an added meaning for the inhabitants.

> Written (and thus clerical) sources stress the monumental and the architectural, emblematic of Roman civilisation and orthodoxy; our own intensively built-up environments encourage us to accept that emphasis and forget how many Anglo-Saxon communal activities must have taken place in the natural world and open air.

> Blair 2005

Further work could possibly be carried out following the model set out by Sahlqvist (2001), who used methods drawn from anthropology and archaeology to argue that the North European hundreds division could have its roots in Bronze Age (1700–500 BC) tribal territories, linked to barrows geographically interrelated in cardinal alignments and crosses on the landscape:

> Based on a hypothesis that the churches in the cross were built at earlier cult centres (e.g. barrows) it was investigated to see if barrows in the area are so geographically interrelated that they form cardinal alignments and crosses of this kind.

> Sahlqvist 2001: 88

With regards to territorial boundaries, he writes:

> Territorial boundaries in Bronze Age Scandinavia have probably been marked out only at certain points, cognitive nodes with intervisibility or perhaps communication

via fires or smoke signalling. The cross centres may have represented such nodes along boundaries. In fact these centres can be joined together into a schematic, boundary line, dividing the area surprisingly well in accordance with the territories indicated by the group of barrows as well as the hundreds.

This method and model would no doubt be dismissed outright by many scholars, but it is certainly worth at this point putting forward as a suggestion.

In early Christian England, landscape mattered more than architecture. We thus need to consider ritual landscapes along with physical remains – the various levels of religious expression, monastic and secular, and also take into consideration perceptions of sacred landscapes (Carmichael *et al*, 1994; Ashmore & Knapp 1999 and more recently Bradley, 2000, who explored the co-existence of monuments with unaltered spaces).

Harvey (2000) calls for research into and the examination of hagiographies and related saintly legends in order to place territorial and organisational development of ecclesiastical authority within contemporary experiences of landscape, linguistics and politics, and relationships with the past. He suggests how Bourdieu's notion of 'habitus' can be used to explain how aspects of continuity and deep memory may have been at the heart of these organisational developments. Along with Tilley (1994) he stresses the importance of looking at the features of the landscape which have provided a significant symbolic resource (rocks, rivers, trees etc.) (Harvey 2000: 202).

> The physical form of hills, rivers and objects were given symbolic meaning through the invocation of imagination and myth. Hagiographic stories could be moulded so as to reflect changing notions of social order and identity. They represent how medieval societies came to terms with the institutional developments that were occurring around them, reflecting a dialogue between the political manoeuvrings of an ecclesiastical elite and an existing communal ethos.

> Harvey 2000: 208

The application of this approach and the examination of the folklore, myths and legends of Lancashire and other parts of the northwest – for example where a church site and a nearby spring or well in which everyday experiences intersect with myth and legend – could 'explain the existence of a church in terms of it being part of a familiar landscape and in addition the physical landscape itself is explained as being inseparable from the religious experience, as set out by the ecclesiastical authorities' (Ibid: 207). Along with the attempt to locate and map church sites and parish boundaries, this could potentially widen the potential for research and provide new and interesting ways of viewing the historical landscape.

LIST OF STONE SCULPTURE SITES IN SOUTH-EAST LANCASHIRE AND GREATER MANCHESTER

This section will begin with the listing in alphabetical order of the extant stone sculptures and finds in the areas formerly known as the Blackburn Hundred, Salford Hundred and the Winwick site in the West Derby Hundred. It is to be assumed that all sculptures are ascribed to the Viking Age period, though some have previously been attributed (often wrongly) to the earlier Anglian period.

Accrington
Portion of a cross shaft found in 1847.

Anderton (near Chorley)
Portion of a cross shaft, which bears on one face the lower half of a human figure wearing a garment of above-knee length and shoes similar to those on the lost fragment from Slaidburn; on the other faces late pre-Conquest motifs (not specified). The upper half of the shaft was found some years later in Woodplumpton, near Preston. This bears the upper half of the human figure, very worn, but holding a cross in front of its chest. Decorative detail on the reverse side and on one of the narrow sides link the cross shaft closely with Bolton and Whalley.

Bolton-le-Moors
The church of St Peter stands on a steep promontory rising above the River Croal. An almost intact cross, as well as a number of fragments, was found in 1866 following the demolition of the old church. The cross is complete except for the upper arm of its head. It is ornamented with plaits and knots, etc. The closest parallel in design is that of Whalley. Also the head of a ring-headed cross was found, along with part of a shaft, rectangular at the base, changing to oval at the top.

One of the fragments (now housed in a small museum space in the corner of the church) is a carving in relief on what was upper surface of a stone or cross. This shows only the lower part of a body, four legs and part of tail of what, at various times, has been described as a dragon/serpent, horse or lion. It has a zigzag mane, long clawed feet and tail brought down between hind legs and in front of the body.

There is also the fragment of a stone from an originally rectangular base. Two figures are facing under a round arch. One figure has its hand removed, which floats between them, as does a spherical structure floating between their heads. This has been interpreted as Adam and Eve with the apple between them, though this is doubtful, as the cut-off hand cannot be linked to the Genesis story.

Burnley
(No longer exists). Complete expanded end cross, lacking horizontal arms, with raised bosses (like at Bolton and Whalley).

Cliviger
Cross has round shaft, expanded, and cross and central boss. Two roll mouldings separate the head from the shaft, and spaces between arms are completely removed.

Colne
The head survives and is of Saxon origin – one arm of a cross head with most of the centre boss attached. The arm is filled with regular and well-designed interlacing, with the strands continuing around the central boss to link with the other arms. A plain, square cross, raised up in relief, is now in Colne library.

Eccles
Part of an Anglo-Saxon cross-shaft (probably Viking age), with interlacing ropework ornament.

Eccleston
Very small fragment, too small and weathered to study or photograph.

Foulridge
Round-headed cross and shaft with depressions on the round head producing the effect of an expanded end cross.

Haslingden
Very small fragment of stone, described as a 'socket stone for double staff-rood'. This is the base of a Saxon cross consisting of a huge stone with two holes in it, similar to the three in Whalley churchyard. See Stretford for similar double-socket design and a suggested reason for the two holes.

Middleton, near Rochdale
Centre section of possible 'Celtic' cross (Iron Age, 800 BC–AD 42) with Celtic head carved on central boss, and the shaft and base of a Saxon cross from the early to middle Saxon-period (AD 410–850) found near St Leonard's church. Interlaced cross shaft with arms missing. The Saxon cross is badly weathered and barely discernible.

Pendleton
No information, but included in a list of sites in Lancashire by Wallis in 1932.

Prestwich

Fragment of decorated stone cross. The fragment, of millstone grit, is from a cross head, being a cusped arm terminal with simple interlace design created by the grooved technique dating from the eighth to tenth centuries. There is a possibility that the site of the churchyard had earlier Dark Age origins, due to its curvilinear shape and location on a promontory site (though, as already stated, this is disputed). Currently being recorded and researched by Greater Manchester Archaeology Unit.

Ribchester

The fragment of a Saxon cross with expanded ends to the arms and a fluted central boss (similar to Aughton), now recorded as lost, was found in Ribchester churchyard but subsequently moved to Salesbury. It was said to commemorate the preaching of Paulinus at Ribchester.

Stretford

Socket stone for double staff-rood, the same as at Haslingden. One possible suggestion for double crosses was that they acted as boundary markers. Double crosses may mark the meeting point of more than one ecclesiastical division. The cross originally stood on the south side of the Roman road from Manchester to Chester.

Tockholes

In the church graveyard there is a composite monument consisting of the socket stone and shaft fragment of a cross fixed to a large rectangular block, the whole set on a modern plinth. Attached is a legend, supposing that the upper part is a remnant of the churchyard cross, dating from AD 684. It is more widely believed, however, that the upper portion of the monument is a remnant of the old preaching cross, possibly dating from 984 and the lower part probably part of the ancient Toches Stone from which the parish gets its name and which, according to Taylor (1905), has its origins in *c.* 650.

Whalley

Originally considered to be either the cross of St Augustine or the cross of St Paulinus. Evidence for the former is often given as the article in the Harleian manuscript, but there is no evidence St Augustine ever came to Whalley, although a similar story is told around the lost Ribchester fragment.

Wallis lists fifteen fragments in 1921; by 1978 only ten were traceable. The only ones really able to be studied due to their larger size, or because they are almost complete crosses, are the three that stand in the churchyard of St Mary's church. Three virtually intact pre-Norman cross shafts, each constructed of local sandstone, are located in the churchyard.

Cross A

The Westernmost cross measures approximately 2.9m high and is of rectangular cross section, tapering towards the top. One freestanding cross carries a small but mutilated Anglo-Saxon crosshead, with expanded arms, rounded at the ends. The design on the east face is still discernible, whereas that on the west face and sides are much more weathered. On the east face the shaft is divided into six panels, the topmost and the lower two being filled with interlacing patterns, the two lowest being nearly square; the uppermost is elongated. Panel no. 2 from the top contains the figure of a bird, panel no. 3 has a figure of a person with upraised hands and a serpent on each side, and panel no. 4 is a beast of indiscernible nature. Romiley Allen (1894) describes the central panel as 'a nimbed saint with his hands upraised in the ancient attitude of prayer and having a serpent on either side of him'. The panel with the diagonal pattern on it, next but one to the bottom, is similar to a pattern visible at Winwick.

Cross B

Attributed to the late tenth/early eleventh century, both faces have a roll ending in a circular boss, below which two rolls curve out to the angles of the shaft; the ground is filled with spirals and the shaft is socketed into the base stone. The cross has a section of the shaft missing and the cross head is very mutilated.

Cross C

The shaft is very weathered and most of the decoration is obliterated, although some small sections of scrollwork are visible on the west face. The shaft is socketed into a base with holes at each end suitable for supporting other crosses or figures. The original cross head is missing.

There are a number of other fragments, most of which are built into the church walls. These include:

1. Another possible cross fragment, built into the back of the church with rows of pellets and traces of interlace.
2. A cross head with central boss on each side, with interlace joining arms round boss. Interlace on the end of at least one arm. Now in Blackburn museum.
3. Fragment of cross shaft.

Winwick

The cross head, now in the parish church at Winwick, has a transverse arm which is nearly 6ft across; the complete monument must have been one of the largest anywhere in Britain. The decoration is interlace and diagonal key on one side, with animals and spirals on the other and figure subjects on the ends of the arms. The underside of the arms has diagonal key decoration also. It has a large central boss, and round this boss are huge misshapen animals with abnormal heads. Their tails alternate under and over, as is common in interlacing patterns. The carving on the north end of the cross is a figure of a man in a long robe or smock, carrying in each hand the bucket of a handbell. A representation of what may be a church appears on the left of the man's head, and below it is either a sword or a cross. On the right-hand side of his head could be a long-shafted cross. The face of the stone is covered with an unbalanced series of fret patterns and knotwork. The reverse is no longer accessible but nineteenth- and early-twentieth century drawings show spiral work and animal ornament.

There is some sculpture just outside of the area under consideration, worth noting, primarily due to its proximity to the southeast Lancashire sites and also as some of this sculpture is already considered as part of another school or grouping.

In Cheadle, Cheshire, there are the remains of one, or possibly more than one stone cross. There was also another recent find in 2007 (information supplied by GMAU). Here, there are the remains of the upper part of a cross, which is almost certainly Anglo-Scandinavian. This is one of the school of monuments studied by Sidebottom, concentrated in the southwest Pennines; several others in eastern Cheshire are also of this 'school'. There is also an Anglo-Saxon cross in Stockport church, as in Mellor.

6

WILFRID'S LANDS?
THE LUNE VALLEY IN ITS ANGLIAN CONTEXT

FELICITY H. CLARK

The Lune Valley is certainly one of Lancashire's most beautiful landscapes, but it is also a fascinating historical landscape. This chapter will examine the various clues that suggest that in the Anglian period (*c.* 600–*c.* 850) there were a series of early Christian 'sacred sites' at intervals along the valley. These would have been monastic centres, known at the time as minsters. In addition, analyses of the stone sculptures from Heysham, Lancaster, Halton, Hornby and Gressingham will be used, alongside other evidence from those sites, to argue that this collection of minster sites indicates that the Lune Valley may well have formed one of the areas of land granted by the Northumbrian kings to Bishop Wilfrid at Ripon (North Yorkshire) in the mid 670s.

NORTHUMBRIA AND BISHOP WILFRID

In the seventh to mid-ninth centuries (i.e. prior to the Viking incursions), the Lune Valley was part of the Anglian kingdom of Northumbria – one of the Anglo-Saxon kingdoms that coalesced to form the kingdom of England in the tenth to eleventh centuries. The heartlands of Northumbria were east of the Pennines, but the influence of the Northumbrian kings gradually spread into the west in the seventh century. This westwards expansion is clearly seen in the *Ecclesiastical History of the English People* (*EH*), written by the monk Bede at the Northumbrian monastery of Monkwearmouth/Jarrow *c.* 731. In Book Two, Chapter Two of the *History*, Bede describes King Æthelfrith's victory over the British at Chester (Cheshire) in 616 (*EH*: 140), whilst in Book Two, Chapter Nine he refers to King Edwin's control over the islands of Man and Anglesey in the early seventh century (*EH*: 162). Bede goes on (in Book Three, Chapter

Four) to refer to the incorporation of the monastic site at Whithorn (Dumfries and Galloway) within the sub-kingdom of Bernicia and (in Book Five, Chapter Twenty-three) to the appointment of an Anglian bishop there by the time he was writing (*EH*: 222 & 558–560).

Wilfrid (d. 709/710) was a major figure in the Northumbrian church. Born in 634, he spent time in the monastery at Lindisfarne (Northumberland) in his teens, before journeying to Lyons and Rome. On his return to Northumbria he found favour at the royal court. Aldfrith granted him land and the monastery at Ripon (North Yorkshire). At the Synod of Whitby in 664 Wilfrid successfully spoke for those who wanted to see the Anglo-Saxon church calculate Easter according to the Roman, and not the Irish, tradition. In the same year Wilfrid was appointed Bishop of Northumbria. His bishopric was characterised by periods of exile due to political infighting. Nonetheless, Wilfrid was a notable figure in the early Northumbrian church and his building programme at Hexham – another royal donation – and Ripon was dynamic. Stephen, the author of *The Life of Wilfrid*, who, as a fellow monk at Ripon, probably knew Wilfrid personally, said of Wilfrid's church at Hexham that he had not 'heard of any other house on this side of the Alps built on such a scale' (*The Life of Wilfrid*, 47). The crypt of Wilfrid's church at Hexham, and that at Ripon, survives to this day, although the upper fabric of the church has long since been rebuilt in both cases (Bailey 1993).

So, Wilfrid was a prominent Northumbrian ecclesiastic and a great church builder. In terms of the Lune Valley, however, what matters most is that he was also the recipient of a number of important land grants. This is known from Stephen's account in Chapter 17 of *The Life of Wilfrid* of the dedication ceremony at Ripon. The most significant part of the account reads as follows:

> Then St Wilfrid the bishop stood in front of the altar, and, turning to the people, in the presence of the kings read out clearly a list of the lands which the kings, for the good of their souls, had previously, and on that very day as well, presented to him, with the agreement and over the subscriptions of the bishops and all the chief men, and also a list of the consecrated places in various parts which the British clergy had deserted when fleeing from the hostile sword wielded by the warriors of our own nation. It was truly a gift well pleasing to God that the pious kings had assigned so many lands to our bishop for the service of God; these are the names of the regions: round Ribble and Yeadon and the region of Dent and Catlow and other places.

> *Life of Wilfred*, 37

The location of the land grants, given in the original Latin as '*iuxta Rippel et Ingaedyne et in regione Dunutinga et Incaetlaevum in caeterisque locis*' and here translated as 'round Ribble and Yeadon and the region of Dent and Catlow and

131

other places' has been much debated. However, it is clear from the description of the places as 'regions' (*regionum* in the Latin) that the areas involved were quite sizeable. The current consensus identifies the named regions as, respectively: the district of Amounderness in south Lancashire, with a centre on the River Ribble at Preston, Ribchester or Ribbleton; an area equivalent to the Parish of Guiseley with Esholt, which includes modern-day Yeadon, in Yorkshire; the township of Dent in Sedburgh Parish (or possibly the whole Parish); and an area associated with the various places called Catlow in south Lancashire near Burnley – although at least one place-name specialist does not think Catlow derives from '*caetlaevum*' (Clark, forthcoming). What matters from all of this is that the Lune Valley is a prime candidate for the location of one of those as yet unidentified 'other places' granted to Wilfrid, precisely because it sits neatly between Dent (to the north) and the River Ribble and the Catlows (to the south).

At this point, it is important to question whether or not the valley could have been identified as a 'region' in the mid-670s. There is certainly an indication that the valley had an identity in the Roman period. Three Roman altars have been found in the valley, each dedicated to the god Contrebis. It has been suggested that this was the name given to the god of the river and that the region was named Contrebis after him (White 1978: 4). After the Roman withdrawal it is likely that the area continued to support a British community, as it is one of the few areas of good quality growing soil in Lancashire. If so, that community could have retained a collective identity. Kenyon (1991: 87) has gone so far as to suggest that the Lune Valley region may have been a small British kingdom, 'a successor to the Roman period *Contrebis*'. Thus far it seems quite plausible that the Lune Valley could have been one of those 'other places' granted to Wilfrid at Ripon in the mid-670s.

THE STONE SCULPTURE

To demonstrate that the valley probably *was* granted to Wilfrid, however, it is necessary to turn to the evidence of the eighth- and ninth-century stone sculptures from Heysham, Lancaster, Halton, Hornby and Gressingham. It will be seen that this sculpture is strongly indicative of two things: one, the presence of a group of linked minster sites in an 11-mile stretch of the lower Lune Valley, and two, the fact that this group of minster sites had an important relationship with Hexham and Ripon – the two centres most associated with Wilfrid. It was Bailey (1980: 81) who first argued that pre-Viking Age ecclesiastical stone sculpture (which almost always survives as fragments of stone cross shafts) all came from contexts that were 'in some sense monastic'. In other words, he saw sculpture such as that from the valley as produced at minster sites. His argument was based on the fact that the complexity of the Christian designs (or the iconography) of the monuments reveals that:

> [...] these carvings are the products of learned, literate communities fully conversant with the complexities of liturgical and patristic ideas, which contained men and women whose lives were adjusted to the prayerful contemplation necessary for a full understanding of the meanings of these monuments.

Bailey 1996a: 76

One of the examples that he discusses in relation to this is the 'loaves and fishes cross' from Hornby, which is dated to the ninth century by White (2004: 7). He observes that the five loaves and two fishes are clearly a reference to the miracle of the feeding of the 5,000. Furthermore, that miracle was interpreted in biblical commentaries of the period as a sign of God's fecundity and as a foreshadowing of the Last Supper, so it becomes possible to understand the other chief image on the shaft. Bailey argues that the depiction of the cruciform tree with fruit at the end of its branches is clearly a further reference to God's provision for man (Bailey 1996a: 60–64).

If the eighth- and ninth-century stone sculpture from the Lune Valley can thus be seen as indicative of the presence of minster sites, it is important to outline precisely how much sculpture there is from each of the five sites before analysing what it reveals about the links both between the sites, and between the valley and Hexham and Ripon. Edwards' (1978: 59–67) checklist of pre-Conquest sculpture from Lancashire, alongside more recent reports, reveals that the Lune Valley is home to much eighth- and ninth-century sculpture. Lancaster has produced by far the most material: fifteen fragments from probably thirteen pre-Viking crosses, and a capital from a column which is probably eighth or ninth century in date (Potts & Shirras 2001–02: 6–8). It should be noted that this proliferation of sculpture from Lancaster is mainly due to the reuse of broken-down crosses by the builders of the Norman precursor to the modern Priory church. No fewer than ten fragments were discovered in the north wall of the Priory when work began on the King's Own chapel in 1903 (White 2002–03: 7–8). The majority of the pieces are on public display at Lancaster City Museum. Heysham and Halton have both produced significant amounts of material. At Heysham there are five fragments from the Anglian period and several later pieces. At Halton there are twelve fragments from perhaps four crosses. The later period is again well represented in the Sigurd cross in the churchyard. Both Hornby and Gressingham are less well represented, providing three pieces each.

Above left: The Loaves and Fishes Cross, St Margaret's, Hornby. Photograph by J. Mountain

Above right: The Churchyard Cross, St Peter's, Heysham. Photograph by J. Mountain

Left: Part of the cross depicting the Apostles, St Wilfrid's, Halton. Photograph by J. Mountain

It is possible that all these pieces were sculpted at one centre and disseminated from there, but it is more likely that it was the sculptors who travelled and that the pieces were carved *in situ*.

It is the stylistic parallels between the Lune Valley pieces which reveal both the links between the five sites, and the relationship between them and the Wilfridian centres of Hexham and Ripon, and thus which make it possible to argue that the Lune Valley probably was one of those 'other places' donated to Wilfrid. There are three important parallels between the pieces that suggest that the minster sites of the Lune Valley were linked. Bailey (1996b: 30) has observed that the crosshead from Gressingham (Noble 1999: 23, fig. 34):

> was clearly produced by the same man who carved the small head fragment still surviving a few miles away at Hornby; he uses an identical ribbed motif on the side of the head and sets it out on an identical measurement unit.

Similarly Cramp (E&S, 112) has identified close parallels between the Heysham churchyard cross and a fragment from Halton. She writes that:

> [A] seated figure of Christ holding a book is relatively frequent on Northumbrian crosses of the period around the late eighth or early ninth centuries. The figure from Halton, although less finely carved is however nearest in type to Heysham because it also has the rather odd figure of the inward protruding block imposts as well as similar drapery.

A further parallel can be made between the cable edging (best described as the rope-like effect at the edge) on one of the Heysham pieces identified as a possible cross base, that on the Sigurd Cross from Halton, and that on the Lancaster fragment which depicts the crucifixion.

The evidence for thinking of the pieces as a group goes beyond a series of parallels however. There are two important motifs that occur on pieces from at least three of the five sites in the valley. The first can be termed the 'zigzag' motif; the second is best described as the use of 'pellets' or small raised bosses on the surface of the stone. The 'zigzag' motif has been found on a fragment of a cross head from Heysham (Collingwood 1927: 103, fig. 128), a fragment of a cross arm from Lancaster (Jones & Shotter 1988: 206) and the small fragment from Hornby. Given the latter piece's known association with Gressingham (see above), it is possible to trace a link between four of the five sites. On the reverse of the cross arm from Lancaster the shape is picked out by a series of pellets. Similar pellets are used on a portion of a cross head from Lancaster, which White (2002–03: 8) records was stolen from the Priory church in 1992. Fortunately, the piece was sketched by Collingwood (1927: 103, fig. 128). The figure just below the bosses on this piece has been interpreted as Christ, and the five bosses as representative of his wounds (Bailey 1980: 149). In addition to the two Lancaster pieces, both Heysham and Gressingham have produced fragments of crossheads with seven bosses in the centre.

These two motifs are not unique to the Lune Valley, however. The 'zigzag' motif is also found on pieces from Hexham, Ripon, Northallerton and Jarrow. Similarly, 'pellets' are used on Anglian pieces from Ripon, Northallerton and on later pieces from Bingham and Irton (E&S: 134 n.30). Northallerton is close to Ripon, and Monkwearmouth/Jarrow was another of early medieval Northumbria's major minsters, so it is reasonable to assume that both had contact with Hexham and Ripon. It is thus possible to argue that both the 'zigzag' and the pellet motifs can be identified with the artistic milieu of the two great Wilfridian minsters. Places that produce pieces showing this style might be said to be within the orbit of these two centres. In other words, the appearance of these two motifs on Lune Valley sculpture suggests that the Lune Valley sites had some relationship to – or at very least, contact with – Hexham and Ripon during the eighth and ninth centuries.

Above left: The Lancaster cross shaft with vine-scroll motif, on display in Lancaster City Museum. Photograph by F. Clark

Above right: The Churchyard Cross, St Margaret's, Hornby. Photograph by J. Mountain

The argument is further supported by the fact that a Hexham-inspired double vinescroll motif occurs at Lancaster. Vinescroll is a common motif on sculpture of the period, as it is a dual reference both to John 15:5, 'I am the vine and you are the branches', and to the Eucharist, as grapes are used to make the wine. Acca's cross at Hexham (Collingwood 1927: 31, fig. 39) has a beautiful and complex vinescroll motif. It has been dated to the mid-eighth century (Cramp 1984: 176). Collingwood (1927: 36) argues that the cross shaft from Lancaster that survives as two fragments and which has an equally complex vinescroll motif, should be seen as a 'reproduction' of Acca's cross. Cramp (1974: 131) has further noted that the way in which the trumpets open out is similar on the Hexham shaft and on the two Lancaster fragments. As before, it thus seems plausible to see Lancaster as within the orbit of a Wilfridian minster. It is possible to argue for one further stylistic link between Hexham and the Lune Valley series. The churchyard cross at Hornby and the doors at St Patrick's and St Peter's Heysham (E&S: 102, fig. 40) appear to use a similar three line motif, which is reminiscent of the architectural fragments from Hexham which are decorated with miniature balustrades (Cramp 1974: 117 & plate XIV). These pieces probably date to the late seventh century (Cramp 1974: 118). If Hexham really is the influence for this motif, we can see once again how the Lune Valley group should be considered as coming within the orbit of a centre known to have associations with Wilfrid. It is perfectly plausible that the reason for the relationship between the Lune Valley group and the orbits of Hexham and Ripon is that Wilfrid oversaw the foundation of a series of minster sites in the valley after the area was presented to him in the mid 670s. True, the sculpture itself is almost all likely to date from the period after Wilfrid's death, but it is nonetheless indicative of a continuing relationship between the valley and the great Wilfridian centres.

IDENTIFYING MINSTER SITES

If the sculptural evidence suggests that the Lune Valley was home to a series of minster sites in the eighth and ninth centuries, it is nonetheless worth examining any other evidence from the sites that supports the case for the presence of a minster. Before doing so, it is important to outline briefly those features that were common to, if not always pre-requisites of, early medieval minster sites. First, it is possible to define the kinds of places in which minsters were situated. Most minsters were established near to water and in places that may be described as 'prominent but not remote' (Blair 2005: 193). Common locations fitting this definition were peninsulas formed by converging rivers, headlands in river bends or coastal sites (Blair 2005: 193). Second, minster sites were usually enclosed. In some cases a boundary ditch would have been created, but sometimes containment would have been achieved by the 'natural topography of the site' (Blair 2005: 196) or by a hedge (Cramp 1976a: 204). For those minsters that were founded on Roman sites (the third common feature), be they forts, villas or walled towns, upstanding Roman remains would have formed a means of enclosing the site. One such example is Reculver in Kent (Blair 2005: 196). Enclosure offered stability, as did the fourth feature: the use of stone for buildings. With the exception of those from East Anglia, the minster sites so far excavated normally had stone buildings (Cramp 1976a: 249). The most common stone buildings found, unsurprisingly, are churches. Minsters very often seem to have had more than one church. Furthermore those churches were often aligned, as is the case at Jarrow, Whithorn and Hexham (Blair 2005: 199–201). A fifth feature, that of multiple aligned churches, can thus be identified. Sixth, and finally, the material culture found on minster sites is often diagnostic. Stone sculpture has already been discussed, but other items with Christian imagery and items that indicate a literate population, such as writing implements (known as *styli*) and lead plaques with writing on them, seem to be good indicators of the presence of a minster. Similarly, minsters appear to have been important trading centres (unsurprisingly given their static nature and prime locations), and as such excavation often reveals evidence of craft production and exchange (Cramp 1976b: 7). Additionally, coins of the period have also been recovered from minster sites.

Heysham

The first site to discuss then is Heysham, at the mouth of the River Lune. The sculptural evidence from Heysham has already been discussed, but there is plenty of other evidence that indicates the presence of a minster there. The windswept headland at Heysham is exactly the sort of place at which minsters were founded. It is 'prominent but not remote' and would have been an excellent point from which to control trade up and down the Lune Valley. Indeed Kenyon (1991: 98) has suggested that the coin hoard found at Attermire cave near to the Lancashire/ Yorkshire boundary, which included a Carolingian coin of Lothair I, may show trade, via Heysham, up the Lune Valley during the Anglian period.

However appropriate the location, it is the evidence for two eighth- or ninth-century churches at Heysham that really demonstrates the presence of an early medieval minster. St Patrick's chapel has been dated to the eighth century, although Cramp (E&S: 106) has suggested that the bird's head stone from the site (which could well be a finial from the roof or a chair arm and which is now kept in Lancaster City Museum), may date to as early as the late seventh century. Additionally, nearby St Peter's church has many sections which clearly date from the Anglian period: much of the Western wall, much of the wall over the chancel arch, parts of the wall over the arcades of the south nave and the now blocked south doorway. A reconstructed arch, which stands between the church and the chapel, has also been identified as the old north doorway removed during the nineteenth-century alterations to the church. This doorway 'closely resembles the doorway of St Patrick's chapel with jambs of through stones on either side of a rough arch formed from three further stones' (E&S: 87). It is not just the presence of two suitably early churches, but the fact that they are aligned with one another, which supports the case for Heysham being a minster site in the eighth and ninth centuries. Finally, there is one other major piece of evidence for a

St Patrick's chapel on the headland at Heysham. Photograph by J. Mountain

St Patrick's chapel (on the left behind the trees) and St Peter's church, Heysham. Photograph by J. Mountain

minster at Heysham. An excavation was carried out around St Patrick's chapel in 1977–78. This revealed that the chapel was plastered inside and out, making it a very prominent landmark from both land and sea (E&S: 117). Indeed the authors of the report go so far as to call it 'both conspicuous and architecturally effective' (E&S: 126). More importantly, though, one of the pieces of plaster had lettering on it, revealing the presence of a literate group on the site (E&S: 118). The plaster can be seen at Lancaster City Museum.

There is one problem, however – the authors of the report on the 1977–8 excavation do not think there was a minster at Heysham, concluding instead 'that St Patrick's was exclusively a centre for worship and burial' (E&S: 126). This conclusion is based on the absence of evidence for any timber precursor to the chapel, any hermit's cell or domestic refuse, or indeed an enclosing wall such as might be expected at a minster. However, it can be argued that absence of evidence ought not to be taken as proof of non-existence. The authors admit that evidence for an earlier timber church could be buried beneath the surviving stone foundations. Likewise they admit that there may have been a settlement around St Peter's church undetectable without excavation (E&S: 126). There may be no evidence for an enclosing wall, but the sea provided a means of demarcating part of the site and further seclusion could be gained just as easily, as at Oundle, by a hedge. Hedges rarely leave an archaeological trace and given the severe weathering to the site at Heysham, it is little wonder no such evidence was found. Of course none of this proves there was a hedge, but it does mean the possibility should not be ruled out. Likewise it is possible that there was a boundary ditch, but that the 1977–8 excavations simply were not wide enough to find it. Overall, the sculptural and architectural evidence seems to outweigh the concerns of the excavators and thus there seems to be very good reason to think that there was an early medieval minster at Heysham.

Lancaster

It is fair to say that the sculptural evidence from Lancaster is the strongest evidence for a minster at the site, but once again the topographical evidence and the material culture from the site support the case. Before discussing this evidence, however, two further points about the sculpture need to be observed. First, the lathe-turned stone capital found at Lancaster Castle (adjacent to the Priory) in 1995, is best paralleled by similar capitals from early medieval minsters at Reculver (built c.730) and the eighth-century crypt at Repton (Derbyshire) (Potts & Shirras 2001-02a: 6–7). Whilst it is relatively small to have topped a column that supported a nave arcade, it is (at 0.4m across) possible it topped a column that supported part of a triple arcade (Potts & Shirras 2001–02a: 8). Whatever its role, the stone is evidence of an important stone building (almost certainly a church) in eighth-century Lancaster.

Furthermore, Stephen of Ripon's description of Hexham includes a description of the 'various columns and many side aisles' of Wilfrid's church (*The Life of Wilfrid*, 47), and two large (1m) column bases – which may relate to Wilfrid's church – have been found at Ripon (Potts & Shirras 2001–02a: 7). Any arcaded minster church at Lancaster is thus likely to have had some relationship to those built by Wilfrid at Hexham and Ripon.

The second point to note about the sculptural evidence, which also adds to the probability that it was produced in a minster at Lancaster, is the fact that two of the cross fragments have Latin inscriptions (Okasha 1971: 89–90). It seems reasonable to assume that such crosses were set up at a site where there was a literate population. Also the fact that both inscriptions begin '*orate pro anima…*' (pray for the soul of …), seems to indicate that these were indeed monastic pieces as the formula is found only on pieces from other known minster sites. It occurs in full on pieces from Norham and York, and in part on pieces from Billinghan, Birtley, Hartlepool (Okasha 1971: 65–115) and Whitby (T. Pickles, *pers. comm.*).

A fragment of a cross with the inscription 'orate pro anima …', on display in Lancaster City Museum. Photograph by F. Clark

As has been mentioned above, much of the sculptural evidence from Lancaster was uncovered during building works at the Priory. The other pieces were all found in the surrounding area (White 2002–03: 8). It is thus likely that the Priory sits atop an earlier Anglian minster. Again the topographical evidence suggests this is likely. The Priory is situated within the Roman fort at Lancaster (White 2001: 33). The walls of the Roman fort were probably still standing at the time of any grant to Wilfrid – after all part of the Wery wall of the third phase fort stands to this day (White 2001: 25), and in 1094, when the Priory church's land was defined, part of one boundary was the 'old wall' (*vetus murus* in the Latin) (White 1978: 18). So any minster at Lancaster would have been in an appropriate enclosure. Additionally, it would have been situated in a commanding position on top of a hill over-looking the River Lune.

Finally, then, it is important to note that since 1914, three separate finds of Anglian coins known as *stycas* have been made near to the Priory. A group of about twenty *stycas* was found in the Vicarage garden in 1914, one coin was found during the 1975 excavations of the Old Vicarage site and a further single find was made in Vicarage field in 1978 (White 1983–84: 46). There is also one unprovenanced *styca* in Lancaster City Museum. It is dateable to Æthelred II of Northumbria's reign (841–4), as are three of the 1914 finds. The single 1978 find was struck for Archbishop Wigmund of York, giving it a possible date range of 837–54. White (1983–84: 46) has suggested that the coins may show 'the economic power of a monastic house'. He further argues that:

> … there seems to be no very good reason to believe that all the coins belong to a scattered hoard and one is left with the impression that perhaps something was going on here during the mid ninth century. The scatter of coins is not unlike that in and around the important Northumbrian monastery of Streanshalh at Whitby, and may be a pointer to unrecorded prosperity in the North at this period.
>
> White 1983–84: 48

The most obvious reason for such prosperity would be the existence of a minster at Lancaster, or indeed a string of minsters in the Lune Valley.

Halton

The church at Halton stands on a piece of raised ground in a bend in the River Lune. Like Heysham and Lancaster, it is exactly the sort of place where a minster might have been founded. Furthermore, Halton was clearly an important place in the medieval period: it formed the centre of the manor of King Harold's (d. 1066) brother Tostig. After the Norman Conquest, although Roger of Poitou moved the centre of the manor to Lancaster, Halton was still considered sufficiently important for a motte and bailey castle to be built there (Williamson 2001: 23). It is likely that this was, in part, due to the need to control the river crossing at Halton, and it is reasonable to infer that the crossing point was equally important in the pre-Viking Age, and thus that Halton was a prime candidate for a minster.

So the topographical and sculptural evidence points to a minster at Halton. In fact Lang (2000: 115) argues that the sculpture offers a clue to the specific function of the minster. One of the crosses, now in at least two fragments, has been identified by him as one of a series of monuments that might indicate baptismal centres. He links the cross to pieces found in Yorkshire at Otley, Dewsbury, Masham and Easby in terms of its size (all would have been comparatively large for the period), its style of carving (which is unusually classical) and its iconography (all of the pieces show the Apostles). Lang (2000: 118) argues that because of the association between the Apostles and baptism in early Italian churches this could well be a deliberate attempt to mark baptismal sites. He notes that the sixth-century mosaic from S. Cosma e Damiano in Rome shows the other Apostles as a flock of sheep beneath Saints Peter and Paul on the banks of the River Jordan, and that the Halton cross too shows a scene of a flock of sheep.

A further factor which, according to Lang (2000: 116–117), indicates that each of the sites could be baptismal centres, is their topography. He writes:

> [T]here are no surviving fonts from this period. The distribution of the Apostles pillars, however, is thought-provokingly centred on, or very near to, intersections in the main north-south Roman road routes and the westward river valley crossings of the Pennines. Easby's cross stood close to the shallows of the river Swale; Masham's stood on a low escarpment sloping down to the nearby Ure; Otley's ecclesiastical site lies by the Wharfe; Halton's by the Lune.

In the case of Halton, Lang's argument can be strengthened. The Viking-Age Sigurd cross in the churchyard can be seen as a teaching aid at a centre for conversion and baptism because of its parallel depictions of the Crucifixion and the Sigurd legend. Sigurd was a hero from Norse (Viking) mythology who killed a dragon named Fafnir with a special sword made for him by his foster-father. Sigurd cooked Fafnir's heart and in the process tasted the dragon's blood, which enabled him to understand the language of the birds and the beasts. Thompson (2004: 166–68) has discussed the reasons why it is likely that Sigurd was seen as a comparable figure to Christ. First, both men were the foster sons of a smith (Joseph was interpreted as a smith, rather than as a carpenter, in the early church), and second, Sigurd's tasting of Fafnir's blood may well have been seen as akin to Christ's tasting death, after which he defeated the devil and returned with more power than before.

The Sigurd Cross, St Wilfrid's, Halton. The Sigurd scenes are on the facing panel at the bottom of the shaft. Photograph by J. Mountain

If the probability of an Anglian minster at Halton is high, it is also worth noting that there is good reason to think that that minster may have had some form of relationship with Bishop Wilfrid. The church at Halton is dedicated to St Wilfrid, as is the holy well near to the church. This is not conclusive evidence of a relationship between Halton and the bishop in the seventh and eighth centuries. However, there is a reference to the church at Halton as dedicated to St Wilfrid in a Lancashire inquisition postmortem of 1252 (VCH Lancs: 8, 123, n. 63). This at least proves that the dedication goes back to the thirteenth century and is not a modern re-dedication.

Hornby and Gressingham

The final two probable minster sites in the Lune Valley can be considered together. The surviving eighth–ninth-century sculpture is clearly the strongest evidence for minsters at Hornby and Gressingham. Again it is worth noting that two of the Hornby pieces show evidence of (now sadly illegible) non-runic inscriptions (Okasha 1971: 81–82). This once again suggests the presence of a literate group at the site. Additionally the topography once more supports the likelihood of minsters on the sites. Hornby, at the confluence of the River

Lune and the River Wenning, and Gressingham, on raised ground above the first crossing of the Lune since Halton, were both key points in the valley. It is highly likely that, if there were as many as five minsters in the valley, such nodal points would have been attractive places at which to establish minsters.

Moving on to consider the dedicatory evidence it is possible to see a link to Bishop Wilfrid once more. The church at Hornby, outside which the church-yard cross stands and inside which the other fragments are housed, is dedicated to St Margaret. However, Hornby Priory, which on the evidence of the sur-viving Priory Farm was much closer to the River Lune than St Margaret's is today, was dedicated to St Wilfrid. The 'loaves and fishes cross' was found in the wall of a barn on the Priory site (Collingwood 1927: 57). So, although the Priory was founded in the twelfth century and dissolved in 1538 (VCH Lancs: 2, 160), and as such the dedication cannot be taken as evidence of a seventh- to mid-ninth-century link between Hornby and Wilfrid, there is a possibility that the dedication reflects an earlier link. It does, however, definitely show a late medieval interest in the saint in the valley. Finally, it is worth observing that the church at Melling, not far up the valley from Hornby and Gressingham, is referred to as St Wilfrid's in the 1540 will of Francis Morley (VCH Lancs: 8, 187 n.5). It is just possible that this late medieval interest in Wilfrid in the Lune Valley is the result of the area being one of those 'other places' granted to Wilfrid in the mid 670s.

WILFRID'S LANDS?

The Lune Valley was clearly an important place in the Anglian period. The fact that, beyond the valley, the only other sites in the whole of Lancashire and Cheshire to produce Anglian sculpture are Sandbach and Overchurch reflects this (Bailey 1996b: 23–24). Indeed Newman (1996: 101) has gone so far as to say that there was 'clearly something very unusual happening in the lower reaches of the Lune Valley' in the Dark Ages. This chapter has put forward the case that that 'something very unusual' was the granting of the valley to Bishop Wilfrid at Ripon in the mid 670s. Certainly the eighth- and ninth-century stone sculpture from the valley suggests that there were a series of important sacred monastic sites, known as minsters, at Heysham, Lancaster, Halton, Hornby and Gressingham. This is supported by the topographical location of those vari-ous centres and by the early medieval buildings on, and objects from, those sites. Furthermore, analysis of the sculpture suggests not only that the five sites were linked, but also that they had some relation to the great Wilfridian centres of Hexham and Ripon. The importance of Wilfrid to the valley in the later medieval period is also revealed through the dedication of churches to him at Halton, Hornby and Melling and in the dedication of a holy well to him at Halton. None of this amounts to conclusive proof that the Lune Valley was one of those 'other places' granted to Wilfrid, but it certainly makes such a suggestion eminently plausible.

WHERE TO GO

St Patrick's chapel and St Peter's church are just a short walk from the car park at the centre of Heysham Village. Lancaster Priory may be found atop Castle Hill adjacent to Lancaster Castle. In all cases the churches can be found following the brown signs for tourists. Likewise, Lancaster City Museum in Market Square, Lancaster, is well signposted. St Wilfrid's church is at the Lancaster side of Halton. The safest way to enter is by the drive and not through the gate, as this opens out onto a main road. The drive is easy to find close to the roundabout where High Road and Low Road meet. St Margaret's church in Hornby is on the main road and is a short walk from the car park by the River Wenning. Gressingham is reached by means of the (one car's width) Loyne Bridge. St John's church is easily visible on entering the village.

ACKNOWLEDGEMENTS

I gratefully acknowledge Lancaster City Museum for permission to photograph the Anglian sculpture kept there. My thanks go to the churchwardens of St Wilfrid's church at Halton for allowing me access to the Anglian sculpture inside the church, and to those who allowed me to look at the 'loaves and fishes' cross (currently kept safely locked away) in St Margaret's church, Hornby. Particular thanks go to Jeffrey Mountain for his photographic skills and to Glynn Mountain and Louise Mountain for accompanying us on our photographic adventure. Finally, I wish to thank John Blair, Paul Clark, Louise Mountain and Victoria Thompson for their comments on earlier drafts of this chapter. Any mistakes that remain are my own.

7

SACRED AND PROFANE:
CONTEXTUALISING MIXED MESSAGES ON
THE URSWICK CROSS

HEATHER RAWLIN-CUSHING

INTRODUCTION

It is generally held that the presence of sculpture is just as informative as docu-mentary or archaeological evidence when it comes to mapping and interpreting the ecclesiastical, and especially the monastic, landscape of pre-Viking, Anglo-Saxon England. The well-documented monastic sites of early Northumbria, for example, such as Lindisfarne, Jarrow and Monkwearmouth, Hartlepool, Whitby and York are not only brought vividly to life by Bede's descriptions and any archaeological evidence of their remains, but also, very strikingly, by the wealth of sculpture still surviving from these sites.[1] The sculptural evidence being so great in volume points towards the conclusion that the use of sculp-ture was a special preserve of the monastic hierarchy of Northumbria, or at least was used in such a way as to be particularly meaningful in the monastic context. A significant royal input for the sculpture at Whitby can be argued, but this also is seen within the context of members of the royal families of Northumbria occupying high ranking monastic positions and thereby utilising sculpture as a form of both religious and political power display.[2] That stone sculpture and wealth are seen to go hand in hand must be considered on the basis that sculptural production was a costly process, including sourcing, quarrying, trans-portation, carving (perhaps with both ornament and inscription), and possibly even painting of the finished piece, all requiring many men and hours. It was an option open, therefore, only to the higher echelons of Anglo-Saxon society.

Sculptural remains from the western reaches of the kingdom of Northumbria are fewer and while issues of survival rates will always raise the possibility that much has been irrevocably lost, archaeology and documentary sources suggest a more sparsely settled landscape than the east with fewer and more scattered ecclesiastical sites, meaning a more restricted environment for potential sculpture production.[3] It is within this context that a carved and inscribed cross shaft from the church of St Mary and St Michael, Great Urswick, can be studied for what it reveals of the ecclesiastical environment of western Northumbria during the pre-Viking, Anglo-Saxon period. Although now in Cumbria, the pre-1974 county boundaries placed Urswick firmly within the borders of Lancashire North-of-the-Sands, making this cross shaft an indisputable part of Lancashire's sacred history. Bearing runic inscriptions and enigmatic figurative imagery, the monument clearly has much to say about the people who designed and made it, the ways in which it was used and the messages it was intended to convey to its viewers, but it has proved difficult to fathom. This study offers a new analysis and interpretation of this challenging piece of pre-Viking sculpture and seeks to broaden our understanding of the uses and meanings of stone sculpture in the Anglo-Saxon northwest.

LOOKING AT THE URSWICK CROSS

We are fortunate in that, despite the incomplete and damaged condition of the shaft, parts of the carved surfaces of all four faces have survived, enabling a fairly comprehensive reconstruction of its overall design.[4] The two narrow sides, faces (b) and (d), seem to have been originally covered with two-strand interlace, only the very top of this design being visible on face (d). In his initial examination and interpretation of the shaft, shortly after its discovery in 1911, W. G. Collingwood drew comparisons between this interlace and that on other stones from the West Riding and Cumbria, namely those at Leeds (WR) and at Irton (Cu).[5] The main face appears to have been that carrying a panel of runic inscription in the centre. Above this is an interlace panel, which Collingwood compared to another West Riding piece, the Bertsuithe memorial from Thornhill, near Dewsbury. The inscription at Urswick, like Thornhill, is commemorative and reads:

> tunwini setæ æfter toroʒtredæ bekun æfter his bærnæ. gebidæs þer saule.
> Tunwini set up [this monument] in memory of Torhtred, a monument in memory of his lord/son. Pray for his soul.[6]

Some of the inscription continues onto the figure panel beneath, and this has generally been considered to show a level of incompetence on the part of the carver, assuming that he underestimated the amount of space the epitaph would require and failed to grid, chalk or etch the characters out in advance. From a technical perspective the space that the inscription occupies in the figure panel demonstrates that the latter was carved first; the runic characters fit between the

Urswick Cross, Parish church of St Mary & St Michael, Great Urswick, faces (a)–(c). Photograph: author's own

Above left: Cross commemorating Bertsuithe, parish church of St Michael & All Angels, Thornhill, West Riding. Photograph: author's own

Above right: Urswick Cross, Parish church of St Mary & St Michael, Great Urswick, figure panel, face (a). Photograph: author's own

heads of the two figures, rather than the figures being made to fit around the characters. The result of carelessness or not, this overspill of the epitaph can also be seen to act as a bridge linking the commemorative text to the imagery beneath it and forcing the viewer to acknowledge the faces of the two figures while reading the concluding part of the inscription, notably a request for prayers.

The figure panel is incomplete and it cannot be known precisely how much of the lower parts of the figures are missing, nor whether there was any further ornamentation beneath them. Collingwood surmised that when completed with a cross head, which he guessed could have been of similar form to that of the Irton cross, the Urswick cross would have stood easily over 6ft tall, by no means a colossal monument, but nevertheless impressively large.[7] The figure panel shows two, apparently male, figures facing each other and engaged in some form of conversation. The figure on the left reaches across to place his hand on the other's shoulder. They have either long hair or some form of headgear. The apparent high collar round each man's neck suggests secular dress, making less plausible any attempt to interpret the features around the heads as haloes. Between them is a cross staff, which despite the seemingly secular nature of the figures, lends the scene a distinctly Christian flavour and indicates some connection between this symbol and the men's 'conversation'. Collingwood compared these figures with representations of St John and the Virgin on stones from Burton-in-Kendal, Cumbria, and Kirkby Wharfe, West Riding, but also admitted the similarity of the collar features to that worn by a figure engaged in a similar form of 'conversation' on a shaft from St Mary Bishophill Junior, York.[8] The York figures certainly seem to wear secular dress, one carrying a knife or short sword at his waist, the other a horn, presumably either for drinking or hunting.

Some runes are inscribed across the chests of the two Urwick figures, forming an inscription distinct from that of the overflowing panel above and reading:

Lyl þis wo

It has been suggested that this equates almost to a maker's mark, the *wo* being an abbreviation of the word *wohrte*, meaning wrought, and effectively translating to 'Lyl made this'; such an inscription is rare on sculpture and difficult to interpret.[9] Should this Lyl be seen as the maker of the entire monument or merely the carver of the specific part he has highlighted, namely the figure scene? Why was it appropriate for the name of the carver to be so prominently displayed?

Collingwood assumed that the inscription on the figures was intended to identify or explain them in some way, but he misread the runes, translating the text as 'This was Lyl'.[10] Clearly this would provide a very specific interpretation of the figure scene, suggesting that one of the represented men was intended as a portrait depiction of the named Lyl. However, as the text stretches across

Shaft fragment, St Mary Bishophill
Junior, Yorkshire Museum, York.
Photograph: author's own

both figures, it would be difficult, especially using the correct transliteration of
the runes, to determine that Lyl was one or the other. Furthermore, it must be
remembered that there are two more names on this monument, Torhtred and
Tunwini, the deceased and his commemorator, respectively. The appearance of
the names of the three people most directly concerned with the production
and erection of this monument, combined with a depiction of two men in
secular dress engaged in some form of conversation or interaction, must form
the crux of any interpretation of this face of the cross.

The imagery of the corresponding face (c) should be seen to be no less significant for the overall message and meaning of the monument. It has been
established in the case of other monuments that reading in the round was
intended, and that opposing faces of cross shafts could hold complementary
messages for viewers.[11] In this respect, it should be considered that the imagery
of face (c) of the Urswick cross may be directly related to the concepts and
issues addressed by the text and imagery of face (a), and that the one may have
been intended to be read as an extension of or complement to the other.

What remains of this face, portions from the top and bottom having been broken away, contains an inhabited tree scroll. In and of itself, the concept of an inhabited scroll in early Northumbrian sculpture is not unusual.[12] However, this scroll is not merely inhabited by birds and beasts, but includes two figures within its boughs. These figures are relatively central when imagined in the context of the completed cross, corresponding to the position of the commemorative inscription on face (a), and it is possible that centrality was intended to indicate importance, in other words, to be a key feature for interpretation of the iconography. The right-hand figure faces forwards, the left-hand figure to the right. It may have been intended that the figure on the right should appear to be seated in the branches, although this is by no means clear. These figures are given the same moulded feature around their heads as those on face (a), which seems to indicate hair rather than a halo, and there are indications of the same kind of collar feature on the right-hand figure. The sex of these figures is not clear, but they bear a decided similarity to the figures on the opposing face. It is significant, when all other figures on the cross interact with one another, that on face (c), one of the figures looks directly out towards the viewer. This device acts to draw the viewer into the imagery and to encourage connection and participation.

Urswick Cross, parish church of St Mary & St Michael, Great Urswick, figures in tree scroll, face (c). Photograph: author's own

Beneath the figures, the plant stem becomes a scroll that encloses at least two curled quadrupeds. The precise nature of these beasts is unclear, but they appear to be nested in the scroll, rather than active within it picking fruit or gnawing branches. In the branches above the human couple two birds perch; again they are not active. In 1911, Collingwood tentatively suggested that this imagery may have been intended as a depiction of Adam and Eve in the Garden of Eden, but the apparent clothing worn by each figure speaks against this, as does the absence of an obvious serpent.[13] Alternatively, Richard Bailey has suggested that the scene represented the ascent of the 'cosmic tree' to Heaven.[14] As the inscription on face (a) clearly indicates the commemorative nature of this monument, it would be appropriate to consider that the imagery of face (c) may also hold a commemorative message, in this case perhaps a symbolic representation of souls making the journey to Heaven.

As the above discussion demonstrates, however, it is in the figurative carvings of the Urswick cross that most uncertainty as to its interpretation may be found. The figures seem to be secular in terms of dress, but are accompanied by symbols – the cross and the animal-inhabited scroll – that suggest an emphatically Christian message. It is difficult on this basis to adequately identify these figures, or even to determine whether the figures on face (a) and those on face (c) are in fact intended to represent the same people. However, one aspect of this monument can be adjudged with some certainty: this cross holds a commemorative inscription and, therefore, acted as a memorial to the deceased man, Torhtred. Furthermore, the inscriptions reveal that the monument was erected by a kinsman or close associate of the deceased, Tunwini, and that the figure carving, or perhaps the monument in its entirety, was produced by Lyl. It is also apparent that whereas the 'maker's mark' inscription format is not commonly encountered on sculpture, the epitaph type that is used at Urswick is found elsewhere, as Collingwood compared it with an inscription from Dewsbury. As it is in this inscription that we find the most solid information about the circumstances of this monument's erection and use, it is helpful to consider other monuments that utilise a similar text.

THE 'BECUN' EPITAPH GROUP

The existence of a group of pre-Viking stone monuments all using the same basic formula of *X sette þis becun æfter Y*, 'X set up this monument in memory of Y', for their commemorative inscriptions is a fact worthy of note. This epitaph is invariably constructed in Old English. The word used to denote the term 'monument' is *becun*, which can be taken in this specific context to mean 'monument' or 'memorial', or in more general usage 'sign' or 'token'.[15] The epitaph form is most frequently found on freestanding crosses, of which there are eight extant survivals, although the group also contains a slab fragment and a small coped monument, making a total of ten extant sculptured stone monuments displaying evidence of the use of this epitaph form. What sets this epitaph formula apart from others, such as 'pray for X' or 'here lies X', is the fact that both the commemorator and the commemorated are named, which is significant as it provides us with a rare opportunity to learn something about the people erecting and using commemorative monuments, as well as those they memorialise.

There is no apparent geographical pattern to the usage of the *becun* type of epitaph; it appears four times at Thornhill and once at Dewsbury in the West Riding; at Yarm and Wycliffe in the North Riding; at Falston in Northumberland; at Carlisle and Bewcastle in Cumbria, and, of course, at Urswick. However, it would be fair to say that this distribution is interesting when compared with the distribution of the majority of pre-Viking sculpture produced throughout the Anglo-Saxon kingdom of Northumbria. The *becun* monuments fall distinctly west of the main concentrations of sculpture production for the period, are in general not accompanied by the same volume of sculpture at their respective sites as may be found at the monasteries of the northeast, and, furthermore, these sites are not known as large and socially or politically important monastic foundations.

Thornhill is the most interesting of the sites because it has four clear examples of the use of this commemorative motif among the remains of at least half a dozen individual monuments. The first, being the lower part of a freestanding cross, with the inscription in runes at the base and a plant scroll panel above, the three other sides left plain, was set up by one Ethelbert in remembrance of Ethelwini:

   + *eþelbert sete æfter eþelwini.*[16]

It uses an abbreviated form of the epitaph, which omits the word *becun*, but the overall meaning of the inscription is not altered. This abbreviated form is used again on the second Thornhill example, another shaft with the inscription in runes at the base and a panel of animated interlace above.[17] Again the other three faces are plain. In this case, Eadred remembers Eadthegn:

   + *eadred sete æfter eateȝnne.*

A third Thornhill shaft follows much the same basic pattern, but this time the ornamented panel contains interlace and this theme is continued around the whole shaft.[18] The runic inscription here is longer and takes a more developed form:

   + *gilsuith arærde æft berhtsuithe becun bergi. gebiddath thær saule.*

Above left: Cross commemorating Ethelwini, parish church of St Michael & All Angels, Thornhill, West Riding. Photograph: author's own

Above right: Cross commemorating Eadthegn, parish church of St Michael & All Angels, Thornhill, West Riding. Photograph: author's own

This translates literally as 'Gilsuith raised in memory of Berhtsuithe this monument on this mound [grave?], pray for her soul.' This is noteworthy because it gives a clear indication of the use of this particular monument as a gravestone. Furthermore, this shaft stands out among the group as the only one in which either the commemorator or the commemorated is identifiably female, signalling that this level of funerary commemoration was not reserved only for men, although they do seem to be the primary recipients of such treatment.

The fourth Thornhill fragment also suggests a function as a grave stone, comprising two jointing pieces of a slab.[19] Although there is little text left on the surviving stones to deal with, there is enough to easily make out in Latin the letters AEFT of *æfter*, OSBER, presumably the beginning of a name such as Osbert, and BEC from *becun*.

Just a few miles up the road from Thornhill at Dewsbury was discovered a fragment of a cross head, one face of which carries an inscription, the other some plant scroll ornament.[20] This is the piece that Collingwood compared with the Urswick cross. The inscription is incomplete and missing the names of both the commemorator and the deceased, but like Urswick, has the added dimension of revealing information about the relationship between the two:

> … becun aefter beornae. gibiddað ðaer saule.

This is a feature that occurs again at Wycliffe in the North Riding, on a shaft fragment on which it appears that the entire main face held an inscription while the other faces were left blank.[21] Again, the inscription is incomplete:

> bada sette æfter berehtwini becun æfter …

It provides the names of the commemorator and the commemorated individual, apparently Bada and Berhtwini, in the standard abbreviated form of the epitaph, but then continues *becun æfter*, 'a monument in memory of …', and presumably here would continue to reveal the relationship between the two named individuals. Indeed, Urswick offers the only complete example of this form of the epitaph, providing both the names of the commemorator and deceased and their relationship to one another.

The alignment of commemorative inscription and figure carving witnessed at Urswick is echoed in only one of the other *becun* monuments, the massive cross from Bewcastle in Cumbria, where the runic inscription panel is positioned above the carved figure of a falconer, sometimes interpreted as John the Evangelist, but more convincingly identified, especially by Catherine Karkov, as a portrait of the commemorated man, displaying the trappings of his aristocratic status.[22] The runic inscription is badly worn and may have been tampered with in the past:

> þis sigbecn … setton hwætred, -þgær, … æft   -lcfri-
> This victory monument was set up by Hwætred, -þgær and … in memory of -lcfri-

The fact that the cross is described specifically as a victory monument suggests that its commemorative function is more complex than a simple gravestone. There has been, and doubtless will continue to be, much speculation as to the full meaning of this monument, taking into account all of its ornament and its similarity to the Ruthwell cross.[23] For the present discussion, however, it will suffice to say that this appears to be another example of the *becun* epitaph form, and there are convincing arguments in favour of the falconer depiction being a representation of a secular figure commemorated by this cross.

Above left: Inscribed grave-cover fragment, parish church of St Michael & All Angels, Thornhill, West Riding. Photograph: author's own

Above right: Bewcastle Cross, church of St Cuthbert, Bewcastle, Cumbria. Photograph: author's own

South of Bewcastle at Carlisle is an inscribed fragment, constituting the lateral arms of a cross head, with an inscription on both sides.[24] Although the text is very fragmentary, Collingwood reconstructed it to read: 'Sigred set up this monument in memory of Suithbert'.

Much further north, at Falston in Northumberland, survives a small coped monument, which is particularly remarkable within the group because this stone carries the same inscription written out twice, once in runes, on the right, and once in Latin letters, on the left.[25] The two texts are virtually identically transcribed. The name of the commemorator is unclear in each case, but the rest of the epitaph can be made out:

eo[…]ta æftær hrœthberht becun æftær eomæ gibidæd þer saule
… in memory of Hrœthberht, a monument in memory of his uncle, pray for his soul

Again this is the extended form of the motif, which signals a relationship between the commemorator and the deceased; in this case, a familial connection is clear.

Taken as a group, these monuments seem to be demonstrating a very particular and easily recognisable form of lay commemoration. This is supported most strongly by those inscriptions which include a description of the relationship between the commemorator and the deceased – at Falston, a nephew commemorates his uncle; at Dewsbury and Urswick the words *beornae* and *baeurnae* are used to indicate either fathers commemorating sons or retainers remembering their lords. At Wycliffe also a relation between the two named individuals was probably originally stated, although unfortunately that part of the inscription is now lost. Further, the evidence of the names themselves hints at familial ties – at Thornhill, Ethelbert remembers Ethelwini, and Eadred remembers Eadthegn. The repetition of the first name element in each case suggests that the individuals were close family members. Alliteration at Wycliffe and Urswick suggests the same thing, where Bada remembers Berhtwini and Tunwini remembers Torhtred, respectively.

Inscribed cross-slab (reconstruction), Bede's World, The Museum of Early Medieval Northumbria, Jarrow, County Durham. Photograph: author's own

Another aspect of the inscriptions to take into consideration is the use of language and script. It is significant that this is an Old English construction and it stands out against the other epitaph forms of pre-Viking Northumbria, which favour the Latin language, for example *orate pro X* or *hic requiescit X*. It is important when considering the use of text on Anglo-Saxon sculptural monuments to consider the role of the written word in early English society, as well as the use of language. As commemorative monuments are invariably found in connection with ecclesiastical sites, it might be argued that the evidence of literacy that they provide speaks only of ecclesiastical literacy. Yet, if it can be accepted that the *becun* group of monuments does demonstrate the commemoration of high status members of the lay society, then it should follow that the choice to use a textual form of remembrance was also something meaningful and useful for the laity.

TEXTS AND MONUMENTS

The Church returned Latin to post-Roman England as its own official language, distinct from the pre-existent vernacular Old English.[26] Latin was a specifically Christian and ecclesiastical language, therefore, which makes the choice of Old English for the *becun* epitaph form significant; it distances it from the ecclesiastical world and places it firmly within the grasp of the rest of society. At the same time, however, in a society that was largely illiterate, a written message was also a status symbol, as it implied wealth and education.

When arguing that the *becun* epitaph formula represents a lay commemorative expression because of the language it is invariably constructed in, there is one final example of its use that provides the exception that proves the rule. This is found on a shaft fragment from Yarm in the North Riding.[27] The inscription panel is broken away at the top, so the text is incomplete and a little confusing in consequence of this:

> ... berehct + sāc + alla + signum æfter his breodera s setæ +
> ... berehct + the priest + Alla + set up this sign in memory of his brother(s) +

Immediately striking is the fact that the word *becun* has been transplanted by the Latin word *signum*, meaning sign. *Signum* also occurs at Jarrow, County Durham, on an incomplete inscribed cross slab, the Latin inscription of which has been reconstructed to read: 'In this unique sign, life is given back to the world'.[28] The sign referred to, of course, is the cross as the symbol of Christianity and redemption. It seems, then, at Yarm a straightforward translation has been made from the Old English word *becun*, meaning monument, token or sign, to the Latin word *signum*. The reason, it would seem, was to make this epitaph form more appropriate to ecclesiastical, rather than lay usage. The abbreviation *sāc* for the Latin *sacerd* or *sacerdos* indicates that one of the named individuals was a priest. If we had the rest of the inscription its context would be clearer, but there is another clue in the use of the term *breodera(s)*, meaning brother(s). Is Alla commemorating his brother(s) in a biological sense or in a monastic sense? A precedent for the commemoration of brothers in a monastic sense may be found at Billingham, County Durham, in the form of a fragment of a small slab, of name stone type, bearing a fragmentary Latin inscription that has been recreated to read: 'Pray for our brothers and for all Christian men'.[29] The Yarm inscription seems, therefore, to be a deliberate adaptation of the *becun* epitaph format to make it more suitable for ecclesiastical commemoration, which implies, of course, that its normal usage was for the commemoration of the laity.

We should also take into consideration when examining the *becun* group of monuments the choice between the use of runic futhorc or Latin alphabet. Raymond Page has stated that 'for much of the Anglo-Saxon age runes and Roman served the same ends and there is no need to draw distinctions between them and no justification for deducing the nature of a text from the type of lettering it is written in'.[30] However, the Yarm example has shown that language was certainly considered significant, as Latin words can be transposed into Old English sentences for the purpose of making a specific point. It could not be argued that the composer of the Yarm epitaph did not know the word *becun*, for example. Similarly, the significance of having a choice of scripts to work with is demonstrated by the Falston piece, where futhorc and alphabet are employed literally side by side for the expression of the same message. What was the purpose of this? Were some people literate in runic characters and others in Roman letters, so that this monument catered for anyone who could read Old English? Or did each script hold specific connotations, meaning that by choosing to use either or both, a patron could reveal something about himself that may even have been recognisable to people who could not read, on the basis that they may still be able to recognise the different scripts.

Exactly half of the *becun* monuments, including the Yarm piece, use Roman letters and half use runes. Runes are practical because they are more compact than any other form of script and can allow for a long text to be fitted into a confined or awkward space, but that does not seem to be a primary motivation for their use on many of these monuments, the main function of which seems to have been the display of the commemorative text. Runes have sometimes been considered a cryptic script, decipherable only by initiated clerics and used on monuments such as the Ruthwell and Bewcastle crosses to inspire meditation and contemplation.[31] For Ruthwell this interpretation may stand up, but in the case of these commemorative inscriptions, surely not. Furthermore, Page has argued for the possibility of widespread secular literacy in runes and one of the specific ways he proposes they may have been useful was for monumental inscriptions.[32] Ó Carragáin has also recently commented that 'runes seem to have been valued as an archaic script of historical interest'.[33] So, through the use of runes it is possible that a pre-Christian heritage could be remembered, and could be useful, therefore, in the commemorative context for indicating heritage and rank among the ruling classes. By making reference to the past, those using runes establish themselves as part of a history, and in the naming of specific individuals, especially in a family context, this reference becomes an implication of their belonging to a well-established dynastic line.

On the other hand, the Roman alphabet can be viewed as a more modern, day-to-day script. Unlike runes, it can be used not only for Old English texts, but also for Latin, the language of the educated clergy. It is also the script of books, objects so intrinsically and symbolically valuable that wealthy laymen were desirous of acquiring them, even if they were not able to read themselves.[34] If runes imply all that is significant of the past, the Roman script represents all that is potent in the present. To a contemporary audience, for whom the ability to read and write signified privilege rather than right, and piety, wealth and social standing rather than basic necessity, the use of both scripts, whether they could actually be understood by viewers or not, held a superfluity of meaning, looking backwards and forwards at once, and demonstrating rank and power at every turn.

INTERPRETING THE URSWICK CROSS

The inscription at Urswick places this cross shaft firmly within the *becun* group of monuments. The text indicates a kin-group connection between the commemorator and the deceased both through the alliteration of their names and the description of their relationship to one another. The ambiguity over the word *bærnæ*, which might translate as either lord or son, is, of course, a modern one; contemporary viewers of this monument would have laboured under no such confusion. But perhaps modern viewers need not labour either. Perhaps, in fact, we are provided with the tools to understand the full message of the inscription in the figure carving beneath. It has already been stated that the overflow of text into the pictorial panel encourages the viewer to 'read' the two panels together and draw a connection between them. A connection between the inscription panel at Bewcastle and the figure carving beneath it has also been convincingly argued by Farr.[35] If the Bewcastle falconer can be seen as a 'portrait' depiction of the man commemorated in the inscription above, it is reasonable to consider that one of the Urswick figures may represent the commemorated Torhtred.

However, this line of argument has obvious initial problems, not least the fact that the figure representation at Urswick is not, like that at Bewcastle, a posed representation of an individual displaying characteristic traits. It does not, therefore, seem immediately appropriate as a form of commemorative image. Yet, it should be recognised that the commemorative inscription itself is multi-faceted. It is not simply an invitation to readers to pray for a particular individual, or a reminder that the person's physical remains lie buried beneath it. It is a declaration of responsibility on the part of the erector of the monument and a clarification of why that responsibility fell to them. Tunwini shouldered the responsibility, and presumably also the expense, of erecting Torhtred's memorial; he did it because Torhtred was his lord or son. Consequently, it is important to recognise that the *becun* epitaph provides readers with just as much, if not more, information about the commemorator as it does about the deceased. Take into account also the foregoing discussion of the significance of text and it becomes clear that this group of monuments is heavily weighted with social information.

Knowing that specific individuals took up the responsibility of erecting monuments for deceased members of their family, and found it necessary to advertise this fact in text on the monuments, leads to more questions. To whom did this responsibility commonly fall and why? Or, to put a different slant on this question, who might usually take it upon themselves to erect a memorial, and why? If the texts of these monuments can be argued to be loaded with a subtext of socially relevant information, what are the implications of this?

On the monuments in the *becun* epitaph group that provide information as to the relationship between the commemorator and the deceased, there are two examples of the commemoration of a son or lord (Urswick and Dewsbury) and one example of the commemoration of an uncle (Falston). There is also the case of Yarm, where Alla commemorates his brother(s). It is possible that in these cases the relationship between the commemorator and deceased is specifically mentioned because the commemorators wished to make an explicit point about why they, rather than anyone else closely associated with the deceased, had erected the monument. These relationships are clearly a significant factor in the overall message of the monuments.

At Urswick the text is accompanied by a figure scene of two men conversing. One places his hand on the other's shoulder. This gesture is an integral and significant part of the composition. It is not a gesture with direct parallels in Anglo-Saxon sculpture and is, therefore, open to interpretation. A similar gesture on the St Mary Bishophill Junior shaft, where the left-hand figure places his hand on or near the hilt of the other's knife, seems to be a staying action. However, both men in this scene look out at the viewer; the impression is that their private discussion has been interrupted. At Urswick, in contrast, the viewer does not attract the attention of the two men, but observes their interaction unnoticed and from a distance.

The cross shaft behind the two figures is certainly a symbol of Christianity, but taken within the context of the men's probable secular attire and the social connotations of the inscription, it may hold a more pertinent meaning. Something is undoubtedly being communicated between these two men, to which the viewer becomes a witness. The cross in the background can be seen to legitimise this event in the eyes of the Church and the Christian community of Urswick, ecclesiastical and secular alike. In the light of the foregoing interpretation of the *becun* inscription formula, and its close relation to the figure scene at Urswick, it is possible to suggest that this scene encapsulates a particular and significant event involving Tunwini and Tohrtred and effectively constitutes 'portrait' representations of both men. In this context, the hand gesture of the figure on the left could be seen as symbolic of Torhtred's official appointment of Tunwini as his heir and successor, thereby providing Tunwini with the motivation and responsibility of erecting the monument and choosing the particular epitaph form that he did.

Richard Bailey has suggested that the image on the reverse of the cross, of two figures within an inhabited scroll, may be symbolic of the ascent of the 'cosmic tree' into Heaven.[36] There is no reason to dispute this interpretation, although some attempt must be made at clarifying the identities of the two figures. Based on their apparent similarity to the figures on face (a), here interpreted as the named deceased and his commemorator, it is tempting to identify them as the same men. However, clearly only one of these men was in a position to make such an ascent at the time that the monument was erected. But in this respect, perhaps, the significance of the outward-looking figure can be recognised. After all, it is fair to argue that as a symbol, the 'cosmic tree' as the route to eternal life is appropriate to all Christians, living or dead. Indeed, it may be seen as a message of more pertinence to a living audience for the fact that it extols adherence to Christianity as the means of every man's salvation. Therefore, the figure engaging the stare of the viewer in this image can be interpreted as the still-living Tunwini, at once anticipating his own future path to Heaven, along which he will follow Torhtred, and at the same time encouraging viewers to contemplate their own route to salvation.

CONCLUSION

The modern viewer may consider the Urswick Cross to be a rather primitive or clumsy piece of carving, with poorly planned out inscriptions that exceed their panels and human and animal representations that seem crudely proportioned and lacking in detail and accuracy. Alternatively, though, and looking beyond the stone's surface, it should be considered that this monument is highly sophisticated in its message and mode of expression and provides the viewer with all the tools needed for a full and informative reading. The epitaph was specifically formulated to reveal socially important information about both the deceased and the commemorator. The figure scene beneath reaffirms the connection between the two men and serves to both identify them as Christian and offer legitimisation of their interaction; if anyone doubted Tunwini's right to succeed Torhtred, their concerns are here visually refuted and laid to rest. The opposing face of the shaft engages more fully in the religious beliefs and hopes of the commemorator. He assumes Torhtred will achieve salvation and maintains hopes of the same fate for himself, whilst encouraging the viewer to understand and share these beliefs in Christianity.

This monument is a testament to the power of the Church in secular life in pre-Viking Northumbria. The church at Urswick offered the physical backdrop to the monument, its most potent symbol, the Cross, forms the 'canvas' upon which these messages are carved, this symbol is used again to legitimate the social assertions made in the epitaph and its accompanying figure carving, while the shaft of the cross, decorated with the limbs of a giant tree, is symbolically climbed by both the deceased and his commemorator signalling the pathway to salvation.

Such a reading leads us away from the general conception of pre-Viking sculpture as a monastic preserve, communicating only ecclesiastically significant messages. At Urswick, in contrast, secular individuals can be seen to express messages of secular importance to the local community as a whole, infused with the authority of the Church. It should be remembered, of course, that the probable cost of producing stone monuments, coupled with the relative scarcity of extant examples, indicates that this method of monumental commemoration was available only to the higher echelons of either ecclesiastical or lay communities. It is likely, therefore, that both Torhtred and Tunwini, as high-ranking members of the Urswick community, were patrons of the church, but this does not lessen the secular significances of this monument. Rather, it seems to speak of a healthy interaction between the Church and lay communities at Urswick and a good level of pastoral care. For the messages of the monument to be effective to their intended, that is secular, audience, it must be assumed that members of the laity were able to see and approach it. This in turn suggests that they visited the church and that it formed a part of their everyday landscape. Furthermore, the scattered, yet consistent, appearance of the *becun* epitaph formula across Northumbria and particularly in its more western reaches, away from the heavily monastically influenced east coast, suggests that in this part of the region at least, such a situation was common.

8

NORSE MYTHS WRITTEN IN STONE

DEREK BERRYMAN

This chapter will identify sites and artefacts relating to and depicting Norse mythology and deities in the Lancashire area and just over the border into neighbouring Cumbria. Some sites and stone crosses have already been discussed in detail earlier in this book. Most have been studied in depth by archaeologists, art historians and linguists. Here, an overview will be given and places of interest indicated for the general reader. For the benefit of seeing the details of the carvings, the author has chosen to use line drawings as well as photographs of many of the images.

Many of the earliest identified 'Celtic' Crosses that have been dated from the fifth, sixth and seventh centuries CE, are to be found as cross slabs, which are plain slabs of stone, not sculpted into crosses. They are an expression of Christianisation and they depict the work of the early saints such as St Patrick (fifth century) and St David (sixth century). In his seminal work *Celtic Crosses of Britain and Ireland*, Malcolm Seaborne gives an insight into the development of the stone crosses in Celtic areas of Britain (and Brittany). It could be argued that the later Anglo-Saxon and Viking stone crosses of the north of England were possibly a development from these, and further evidence of this could be the fact that there is a concentration of both Celtic cross slabs and Norse Crosses on the Isle of Man. Furthermore, R.I. Page traced the Scandinavian settlers of the west coast of Cumbria and Lancashire as coming via the Orkneys and western Scotland.

Over the centuries, with county boundaries changing, the artefacts were never confined to one specific area, but were subject to patterns of settlement. The areas cannot, however, be viewed in isolation, as communication took place between the various groupings, such as in the area north of the Mersey where there was communication between York and Dublin (the last king of Dublin and York, Eric Bloodaxe, was killed in 954) (Bailey 1996). Routes of communication also possibly had the effect of bringing both Anglian and Norse crosses to the area, with the distribution being affected by the topography; the region was boggy and consequently not conducive to close habitation.

The Norse style of carving on the stone Hogbacks, the enigmatic carved stone bears at Dacre and the myths shown on the stone crosses all indicate the presence of Scandinavian settlers; this group probably came via the north of Scotland and down the west coast. Most crosses have ornamentation in a braided or knot-work fashion, and Norse crosses are distinguished from the Anglian crosses by the cutout wheelhead. (The north of England was also settled by the Angles from the east and it was in Anglo-Saxon England that stone crosses apparently originated.) The Norse Vikings would have been settled in the Isle of Man from the eighth century and it is on the Isle of Man where there is a concentration of carved stone crosses with Scandinavian-style animal ornaments and runes. From there it is likely that settlers came to what is now Lancashire and Cumbria to develop a style peculiar to those areas.

The evidence is circumstantial rather than documentary, although according to an information board on the footpath on the route of the old railway track from Keswick to Threlkeld, sheep are still counted using Norse numbers! Some place-names are undoubtedly Norse, such as Aspatria (the ash tree of St Patrick), Ormskirk (church of a man called Ormr) and Silloth (barn by the sea) (A.D. Mills 2003). In addition, the largest single hoard of Viking treasure was found in Cuerdale in the Ribble valley, near Preston, weighing about 40kg, and contained penannular brooches and arm rings similar to those from Ireland that date it to *c*. 905 (James Graham Campbell 1991).

The Norse myths are, like the Greek myths, part of the tradition of folklore that has been inherited and absorbed by English culture. Some, like the Viking discovery of America, described in *Grænlending Saga* and *Erik's Saga* (translated by Magnus Magnusson in *The Vineland Sagas* (Penguin 1965) are now believed to contain an element of truth; other traditions, such as the creation, are stories told to satisfy innate curiosity.

Richard N. Bailey in his book *England's Earliest Sculptors* (Bailey 1996) makes the point that the art of the period is not limited to the crosses, but is manifest in illuminated manuscripts, metalwork, ivories and embroideries. Lines from the Anglo-Saxon poem *The Dream of the Rood* (Vercelli CXII) is on the cross at Ruthwell. It is written in Anglo-Saxon runes, and some of the inscription was lost when iconoclasts broke the cross after the Act passed in 1642 by the Assembly of the Church of Scotland. A translation into modern English of the poem is to be found in *Anglo-Saxon Poetry* (Bradley 1982).

One only has to look to Tolkien's *Lord of the Rings* and Wagner's *Ring Cycle* to find modern approximations to Teutonic literature that gives the feel of lost Norse stories. The Teutonic influence is widespread; Odenswald, near Heidelburg means Odin's wood and Wednesbury in the West Midlands is the stronghold of

Woden. These and many other place-names, together with stories such as that of Wayland the Smith, testify to the extent of Germanic culture (Page 1990).

There is evidence that some at least of the crosses were originally painted in a variety of gaudy colours. Fragments of gesso (a plaster-like covering) have been found on some crosses and on others layers of red paint (that the author believes could be red lead) and seem to have been used as a base or primer for the final colour. There is evidence in the form of holes with which to fasten metal embellishments or decorative jewels (Bailey 1996). Unfortunately the ravages of weather and enthusiastic cleaning have left little or no evidence of the original finish. Iconoclasts have broken many crosses, sometimes intent on destroying papal or pagan motifs, and bits have been reused in the walls or foundations of later buildings and so are irrecoverable.

There are few crosses depicting the Norse myths. Only one, that at Halton, is in Lancashire, and therefore for the purposes of the theme of this chapter, it is necessary to venture a little further north into Cumbria, where the cross at Gosforth completes the scene. There are other crosses or sculptures depicting the Sigurð story at York, Ripon and Kirby Hill. Struggles with serpents are shown at Ovingham, Penrith and Great Clifton. At Kirklevington a figure with two birds appears. Could it be Odin with his ravens Huginn and Munnin (Bailey 1996)? At Halton, near Lancaster, Sigurð (whose story is discussed below) is shown in different scenes of his story, rather like a comic strip. The crosses at Gosforth and Aspatria show Odin and Viðar. Interestingly enough, if one examines the myths as they appear on the crosses, beginning with the stories of the characters and finishing with Ragnarök on the Gosforth cross, some narrative coherency may be seen across them.

Examining the background to the story of Sigurð, it can be seen that it is based on an account in one of the Eddic poems, *Reginsmal*. R.I. Page (1990) summarised the tale thus:

A rich farmer had three sons, two were shape changers, Fafnir and Otr, the third a dwarf, Regin. Like all dwarves he was an accomplished craftsman, a smith. Otr could change into an otter and was killed one day by the god Loki who threw a stone at it and then, with his companions, Odin and Hoenir carried on to the farmer's house. When the farmer recognised his son's otter skin he and his sons demanded blood money in the form of sufficient gold to fill the otter skin and cover it. Loki went to get the gold which he took from Andvari, a dwarf, who cursed the treasure, including a ring. When the gold was being handed over there was a whisker showing and so Odin had to reluctantly give the ring that he had kept on one side. The two brothers demanded their share, and when their father refused Fafnir killed him. He took the gold and hoarded it in the wilderness. He then became a dragon.

The next part of the story relates how King Volsung had ten sons and one daughter, Signy, who was to be married to King Siggeir of Götaland, Sweden (Signy is not to be confused with Sigyn, more of whom later).

At the wedding feast an old man (who was actually Odin) thrust a sword into a tree and said that whoever could remove it should have it. Signy's brother Sigmund was the only one who succeeded but then when he refused to sell it to his host it created ill will between the two families.

There was eventually a fight between the two families in which King Volsung was killed and the ten sons made captive. They were chained to a log in the middle of the woods and left there. Each night a wolf came and ate one until only Sigmund was left. Signy came and smeared honey over Sigmund's face and into his mouth. When the wolf came that night she licked the honey off Sigmund's face and put her tongue in his mouth. Sigmund bit hard and the wolf pulled back, her tongue was torn out and so she died.

Sigmund was later killed in battle and his son, Sigurð, was born later. Sigurð was fostered into the king of Denmark's court, and had as tutor the smith Regin, the disaffected brother of Fafnir, now a dragon guarding his stolen wealth. Regin made Sigurð want a horse. The king gave him the freedom to choose from his stud. He met a bearded old man (Odin) who advised him how to choose and he chose one sired by Sleipnir, Odin's eight-legged horse, and he called it Grani.

Now Regin put into Sigurð's mind the desire for money. He told Sigurð that there was treasure for the taking guarded by the dragon Fafnir. Regin forged a sword but it shattered when Sigurð tried it on the anvil so a second sword was made. This also shattered. Sigurð went to his mother and asked for the bits of his father's sword that she had kept. Although the new sword sliced through the anvil, it was so sharp that it could cut a strand of wool floating down the river.

Sigurð went to a spot that Fafnir passed daily and dug a pit, he was then advised by Odin to dig more holes to catch the dragon's poisonous blood. Sigurð waited in the pit, sword drawn, until Fafnir passed overhead. He struck upwards and killed the dragon. He then cut out the dragon's heart and roasted it. In doing so he put his finger in his mouth and, tasting the blood, found that he could understand the language of the birds who warned him that Regin was planning to kill him. So he killed Regin and went off to collect the dragon's gold. [Dragons always guard a treasure hoard of gold.] This much is depicted on the surviving sculptures, the rest of the tale is told by Snorri Sturlusson.

The story continues with Sigurð meeting the Valkyrie Brunhild, who he released from armour in which she lay in an enchanted sleep. They fell in love and Sigurð gave her a ring – *the* ring. There is confusion in the tale at this point. Sigurð married Gudrun after being given an enchanted drink and he agreed to help his friend Gunnar court Brunhild. She had declared that she would only marry the man who could ride through the flames surrounding her hall. Gunnar tried but his horse shied away. He borrowed Grani, but Grani also shied so Sigurð and Gunnar changed appearances and this time Sigurð was able to ride through the flames in the guise of Gunnar. Gunnar married Brunhild. Eventually Sigurð regained his memory and when Gudrun eventually told what had happened Brunhild was livid and plotted vengeance on Sigurð and Gudrun. She persuaded Gunnar that he should kill Sigurð, but as the two were bloodbrothers he could not do the deed himself. A younger brother, Guttorm, was enlisted to do the murder which he did while Sigurð was asleep with Gudrun. Sigurð, awakened by the fatal blow, threw his sword at Guttorm, slicing him in two. Gudrun woke, covered in blood and was inconsolable. Sigurð died, accusing Brunhild of the responsibility for the preordained fate. As the funeral pyre was prepared Brunhild killed herself and was cremated with her lover, with the sword between them as it had been when they first met.

Snorri tells us that the treasure was thrown into the River Rhine and has never been seen since. Part of the treasure included the cursed ring and of course lends itself to the plot of Tolkien's *Lord of the Rings*.

The pagan myths of the Norse were an oral tradition and were not written down until the thirteenth century, well after the establishment of Christianity in Scandinavia (although that was relatively late; the year 1,000 for Iceland). There are therefore gaps in the knowledge of these stories, the only contemporary evidence being that illustrated in stone carvings in the British Isles and, in Scandinavia, wood and metalwork.

The major sources of the myths are the *Poetic Edda*, to be found in the *Codex Regius*, the *Prose Edda* written by the Icelandic farmer Snorri Sturlusson, both written in the thirteenth century, and Skaldic Verse composed from the ninth century into the Middle Ages. R.I. Page in *Norse Myths* makes the point that the slightly different versions that have come down makes the story difficult to put together, with the added problems of translating from old languages with subtle variations of meanings, and kennings (a reference to something that the audience would already know or understand as told by previous wandering storytellers) that are not necessarily understood by a wider audience. A typical kenning was the 'whale road', meaning the sea, or 'the otter's blood money' for gold – the start of Sigurð's story makes this kenning clear. Unfortunately, the meanings of some kennings may not be understood in this modern age if the original story has been lost.

HALTON

The 'Sigurð' shaft at Halton in Lonsdale has been dated to the eleventh century (Collingwood 1927) and depicts part of the story of Sigurð (Wagner's Siegfried).

Far left: The Sigurd Panel on the cross at St Wilfred's Churchyard, Halton. (Photograph by Karen Lawrinson)

Left: Sigurd Panel line drawing (Derek Berryman)

The cross is to be found in St Wilfred's churchyard (grid reference SD 499657). When approaching from the M6 motorway leave the M6 at junction 34, turning left onto the A683 towards Caton. The first turning on the left is signed for Halton and is a minor road that crosses the River Lune into Halton. The first left turn leads to the church, directly through a junction of four minor roads. The church is on the right-hand side and there is a car park by a redundant pub immediately before it. As it is on a blind bend it is advisable to cross the road to the pavement to walk up to the churchyard entrance.

GOSFORTH

The church at Gosforth is further north towards Whitehaven on the A595, about 10 miles south of Egremont [grid reference NY 072035].

The village is on the right-hand side when coming from the south. As the main car park is passed on the left with a café and the Wheatsheaf pub nearby it is better to continue to the fork in the road. Take the left-hand fork and continue to the edge of the village and park near the school and rectory. The cross is in the churchyard and the 'fishing stone' is in the church together with two Hogsbacks and other carved stones from earlier church buildings.

The stone stands nearly 5m tall and is set in its original socket to the south of the church and is carved from one piece of stone. The impetus for interpreting the figures on the cross came in 1881 when Professor George Stephens identified a figure on a stone at Kirby Stephen as coming from Norse mythology. Two local men deciphered the recognition of the characters and myths that they represented in 1888. These were Dr C. Parker, a local GP in Gosforth, and the Revd W.S. Calverley, rector of Aspatria and Dearham successively (Bailey 1996). They detected a pattern to the images and realised they could be traced to the Norse sagas and myths.

> The order of these events may be followed if we start at the south side at the foot of the shaft, go round with the sun and up and down the sides alternately we get a remarkable parallel to the chief events in the Völuspó in the Edda.

> Cumberland and Westmoreland Antiquities Society N.S. xvii, 99f.

The south side starts with chaos. The gods Odin on a horse and Eikthymnir, the hart from whose antlers flow twelve rivers, allude to the creation.

The next side (west) shows Loki, Odin and Heimdal Loki was mischievous and as the stories progress he develops into a vicious and evil character. He contrived the death of Balder and was ejected from Asgard by the gods as punishment. He was bound and shackled to a rock and condemned to lie under

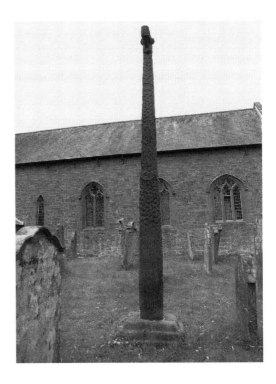

Gosforth Cross.
(Photograph by Karen Lawrinson)

a drip of poison from a serpent. His faithful wife Sigyn knelt beside him and caught the poison in a bowl. When she took the bowl away to empty it the movement of the agonised Loki caused earthquakes.

Odin has many names and Wodan, Woden and Wotan are the most common. He is also known as Grim. He is the father of Thor, Balder, Hohe, Tyr Brigi, Heimdal Ull, Vidar Hernod and Vali. Udin's wives were Fjorgyn, Frigga and Rind. Odin was the chief god and was a shape changer. He had one eye, having exchanged the other for wisdom. He seems to have spent much of his time roaming the earth seducing women. He was then known as Grim. He had an eight-legged horse called Sleipner, although he is shown here on a four-legged horse. Odin had two ravens, Hugin and Munin, who flew across the earth gathering news for him.

Heimdall is shown next holding a horn and holding off two beasts. He is the guardian of the gods and will blow the Gjallerhorn when there is danger to Asgard, the home of the gods. He stands at the end of the Bifrost Bridge; we see it as the rainbow. The bridge connects Asgard with earth. Heimdall has very acute hearing; he can hear grass grow and a leaf fall. As you would expect of a watchman, he can see to the end of the earth and does not need sleep. At Ragnarok, Heimdal and Loki kill each other.

The third face, the north, is the attack on the gods; a winged dragon attacks two horsemen and Odin. The dragon is presumably a representation of the World Serpent.

The fourth face shows Vidar, son of Odin and the giantess Grid, slaying the Fenris wolf. Fenris was the son of Loki and the goddess Argbada. The gods were suspicious of Fenris and he was seen as a threat. It was decided to bind him and he was tricked into being bound to see if he could break the bonds. The first two were easily broken, but the third was too strong and when he was securely bound a sword was placed in his mouth with the point up to the palate.

Baldr was a handsome, good-natured god, well loved by the other gods. He had been given protection from harm by all other plants and creatures who promised never to hurt him, except for a small sprig of mistletoe that was considered too small to be a threat. The gods soon found a new sport: they would throw missiles at him and know that they would cause no harm. Now the god Hermod was blind and could not join in the fun. Loki plucked the mistletoe and placed it in Hermod's hand and then guided him so that he could throw. Baldr was killed and the distraught Hermod volunteered to go to Hel, the goddess in charge of Niflheim, to try to persuade her to allow Baldr to return. The request was agreed to on condition that everything in the world wept for him. An old woman in a cave refused to shed tears for him (it is suggested that it is Loki) so Baldr had to wait before he was resurrected.

Ragnarok, the story of the end of the world, is depicted on the cross at Gosforth as the giant and violent battle as described in the Eddas. Also known as Gotterdammerung, it is the death of many of the gods and the beginning of

Left: Panel from the Gosforth Cross. (Photograph by Karen Lawrinson)

Right: Details of Norse myths on Gosforth Cross. (Photograph by Karen Lawrinson)

the new world, and is generally known to us as the 'Twilight of the gods' – the concluding part of Wagner's *Ring Cycle*.

> Ragnarok will be preceded by three winters without any summer in between. There will be conflicts and feuds, morality will disappear and this will be the beginning of the end.

The east side, more clearly described by Bailey, has a crucifixion scene, incorporating the figure of Christ with blood flowing from the side and beneath that panel is Longinus, the soldier who pierced Christ, holding a spear. The figure with him is wearing a trailing dress; traditionally it should be Stephaton, the soldier who offered vinegar on a sponge. The two-headed serpent below is presumed to represent evil. Above the panel with Christ is Viðar avenging the death of his father Odin by tearing Fenris asunder.

Thor fights the World Serpent and kills it and then perishes from the venom that drips onto him. Loki and Heimdall kill each other. Odin is swallowed by Fenris, who in turn is killed by Viðar. The figure shown with arms outstretched has also been interpreted as Baldr, whose rebirth was equated with the resurrection of Christ. The end of the gods at Ragnarok was to be followed by a new god.

Inside the church, the stone known as the 'Fishing Stone' depicts the story of Thor fishing. According to the mythology, however, this was no ordinary fishing trip.

Thor visited the giant Hymir in the hope that he would have the chance to seize his great cauldron so that the gods could brew beer in it. He stayed the night and next morning Hymir said that he was going fishing. Thor wanted to join him but Hymir goaded Thor, saying that he was too feeble to withstand the cold of the open sea. Thor was angry and insisted, but was told to find his own bait. He went to Hymir's herd of cattle and tore the head off the largest. The two started to row and Hymir warned that they might meet the World Serpent. Thor carried on rowing and then threw the baited line over board. The World Serpent took the bait and so the two tussled. Thor heaved so hard that his feet went through the bottom of the boat and stuck to the ocean floor. The Serpent was face to face with Thor and spitting venom. Thor was about to kill it with his hammer when Hymir chopped through the fishing line and the monster escaped. Thor threw his hammer after the Serpent, knocked Hymir overboard and waded ashore.

Thor 'Fishing Stone'. (Photograph by Karen Lawrinson)

Page 1990

There are many stories about Thor, the warrior god, and his hammer (used as a talisman and occurring frequently in archaeology). His hammer (also called Mjollnir) flashing through the sky was seen as lightning and heard on land as thunder. He also had a belt that doubled his strength when he wore it, and iron gloves, worn when he swung his hammer. Thor had many encounters with the World Serpent and other enemies of the gods, giants, monsters and primeval forces.

These stones at Gosforth, together with the 'Sigurð' panels at Halton and other sites, to my knowledge, summarise the extent of the Norse myths carved in stone in mainland Britain.

The theological message of the cross at Gosforth has had many interpretations. The juxtaposition of pagan and Christian symbols could suggest that the advice given by Pope Gregory (Sherley-Price 1955) to be tolerant of the heathen traditions was being followed 300 years later.

The crosses at both Halton and Gosforth have been dated to the eleventh century (Collingwood *op cit*) and indicate that the stories were still well known at the time of carving. Both bear witness to the slow assimilation of the old religion into the Christian tradition and indicate that the Norse myths were well remembered and retold right up to the end of Anglo-Saxon England and beyond.

NOTES

CHAPTER 2

1 Cameron, K. (1988), *English Place-Names*, London.
2 Ekwall, E. (1922), *The Place-Names of Lancashire*, Manchester.
3 Gelling, M. & Cole, A. (2000), *The Landscape of Place-Names*, Stamford. See also Gelling, M. (2005), *Signpost to the Past*, Chichester.
4 Mills, A.D. (2003), *Oxford English Dictionary – British Place-names*, Oxford.
5 Mills, D. (1986), *The Place-names of Lancashire*, London.
6 Cameron (1988), p. 141.
7 Ibid, p. 146.
8 Ibid.
9 Kenyon, D. (1991), *The Origins of Lancashire*, Manchester.
10 Ibid, p. 82.
11 Ibid, p. 84. The studied Lancashire hām-named sites are Aldingham, Bispham (West Derby), Heysham, Cockerham, Penwortham, Padiham, Higham, Habergham, Rochdale formerly Recedham, Thornham, Gressingham and Tatham.
12 Kenyon (1991), p. 84.
13 Crosby, A.A. (2007), *Of Names and Places: Selected Writing of Mary Higham*, English Place-name Society and the Society of Name Studies in Britain and Ireland, p. 75. The studied hām pre-Conquest names are Aldingham, Altham, Bispham [Amounderness], Bispham [West Derby], Cockerham, Gressingham, Heysham, Kirkham, Penwortham, Rochdale formerly Recedham and Tatham. The post-Conquest hām-names are Abram, Cheetham and Irlam.
14 The twenty-nine pre-Conquest names with personal prefixes denoting earlier settlements are Huncoat, Little Woolton, Much Woolton, Knowsley, Melling, Harleton, Ainsdale, North Meols, Amounderness, Grimsargh, Whittingham, Goosnargh, Hambleton, Elswick, Swainshead, Aldcliffe, Torrisholme, Caton, Melling, Hornby, Farleton, Wennington, Tatham, Cantsfiled, Whittingham, Thirnby, Aldingham, Staining, and Ulverston. See Ekwall (1922).
15 Mills, A.D. (2003), p. 141.
16 Ibid, pp. 281–2.
17 Ekwall (1922), p. 116.
18 Mills, A.D. (2003), p.282.
19 Kenyon (1991), p. 102.
20 Mills, A.D. (2003), p. 240.
21 For a full listing of Viking antiquities unearthed at Heysham consult Edwards, B. (1998), *Vikings in North West England – The Artifacts*.
22 Rawlinson, J. (1969), *About Rivington – A Description of One of the Prettiest Villages in Lancashire*.
23 Ibid.
24 Ibid.
25 The Anderton Cross (Headless Cross) upper stone is now housed at the Harris Museum and Art Gallery, Preston, Lancashire. Edwards (1998), p. 82.
26 Edwards (1998), pp. 81–4.
27 Ibid, p. 83.
28 Mills, D. (1986), p. 58 and Kenyon (1991), p. 102.
29 In etymology terms 'Croal' simply means 'winding' for instance the Croal Valley translates to 'the winding valley'.
30 Mills, A.D. (2003), p. 87.
31 Kenyon (1991), p. 102.
32 Ibid.
33 Ibid.
34 Mills A.D. (2003), p. 127.
35 Kenyon (1991), p. 102.

36 Mills, D. (1986), p. 53.
37 Ibid, p. 81.
38 Ibid, p. 122.
39 Ibid, p. 123.
40 Ibid, p. 527.
41 Ibid, p. 129.
42 Ibid, p. 133.
43 Ekwall (1922), p. 208.
44 Ibid, p.133.
45 Ibid, p. 93.
46 Ibid, p. 212.
47 Ibid, p. 257.
48 Ibid, p. 130.
49 Ibid, p. 101.
50 Ibid, p. 76.
51 Ibid, p. 109.
52 Ibid, p. 115.
53 Ibid, p. 113.
54 Ibid, p. 182.
55 Ibid, p. 85.
56 Ibid, p. 170.
57 Ibid, p. 77.
58 Ibid, p. 48.
59 Mills, D. (1986), p. 63.
60 Dyer (1981), p. 81.
61 Edwards (1998), pp. 18–19.
62 Dyer (1981), p. 186.
63 Mills, D. (1986), pp. 65 and 104.
64 Dyer (1981), p. 187.
65 Ekwall (1922), p. 85.
66 Dyer (1981), p. 89.
67 Ekwall (1922), pp. 98 and 99.
68 Ibid, pp. 93 and 94.
69 Ibid, p. 110.
70 Ibid p. 221.
71 Ibid p. 89.
72 Ibid, p. 152.
73 Ibid, p. 213.
74 Dyer (1981), p. 186.
75 Ibid, p. 90.
76 Ibid p. 93.
77 Ekwall (1922), p. 152.

CHAPTER 3

1 Rivet, A.L.F., & Smith, C. (1981), *The Place-Names of Roman Britain*, Cambridge: Cambridge University Press, pp. 267–8. But for the interpretation of strength as well as brilliance, see also Delamarre, X. (2003) (2nd edn), *Dictionnaire de la Langue Gauloise: une approche linguistique du vieux-celtique continental*, Paris: Editions Errance, pp. 71–2.
2 Ibid, p. 277.
3 Wacher, J. (1981), *The Towns of Roman Britain*, London, Batsford, p. 406.
4 Cassius Dio, *Historiarum Romanorum quae Supersunt*, LXXI.xvi.2.
5 An interesting reconstruction by Peter Taylor, originally made for Channel 4's TV archaeology programme *Time Team,* is at www.fectio.org.uk/articles/makedraco3.htm.

6 Makkay, J. (1995), 'The Treasures of Decebalus', *Oxford Journal of Archaeology*, 14:3, pp. 333–43.
7 Morris, J. (1989), *The Age of Arthur: A History of the British Isles from 350 to 650 AD*, London: Weidenfeld & Nicholson, pp. 48–54.
8 Kenney, E.J. (trans.) (1998), *Apuleius: The Golden Ass*, London: Penguin Classics.
9 Whitaker, T.D. (1818) (3rd edn), *An History of the Original Parish of Whalley, and Honor of Clitheroe*, London: Routledge (commented on by Thornber, W. (1852) *Historic Society of Lancashire and Cheshire: Proceedings and Papers, Session IV, 1851–52*, Liverpool: Brakell, p. 108).
10 Henig, M. (1984), *Roman Religion in Britain*, London: Routledge, p. 120.
11 De La Bédoyère, G. (2002), *Gods With Thunderbolts: Religion in Roman Britain*, Stroud: Tempus, pp. 146–7.
12 Green, M.J. (2003), *The Gods of Roman Britain*, Princes Risborough: Shire Archaeology, p. 26.

CHAPTER 4

1 The Aarne-Thompson Type Index, compiled by Antti Aarne and Stith Thompson in *The types of the folktale* (1961), classifies motifs and assigns type numbers to tales. Changeling stories, for example, are type ML5085.
2 Blake's account of a fairy funeral was quoted by Allan Cunningham (1829) in the *Lives of the eminent British painters*, according to Gilchrist (1863).
3 Euhemerism is the theory which explains mythology as growing out of real history, its deities as merely larger-than-life people. Euemeros was a fourth-century BC Sicilian philosopher.
4 A practice which survived into the twentieth century in the Roof Gardens of Blackpool Tower where, from 1927–1930, 'Midget Town' was populated by people with restricted growth.
5 Christina Rossetti's poem *Goblin market* (1859; published in 1862), with its repressed eroticism, uses words like 'sly', 'evil' and 'rat-like' to describe goblins.
6 See Joseph Bradbury (1871), *Saddleworth sketches*.
7 Katherine Briggs (1898–1980), the doyenne of twentieth-century English folklorists, describes Roby's style as 'in almost unreadable diction' (Briggs 1967).
8 St Chad's parish church stands on Sparrow Hill, Rochdale, overlooking the Esplanade, under which the River Roch flows. There are 122 steps from the Esplanade to the church.
9 Quoted in E. S. Hartland (1891), *The science of fairy tales*, p. 109.
10 Recorded by an anonymous correspondent in *Notes and queries*, February 1853.
11 For fairy botanical folklore see Grigson (1987), Mabey (1996) and Pickering (1995).

CHAPTER 7

1 Bede, *Historia Ecclesiastica*, B. Colgrave & R.A.B. Mynors (eds), Oxford (1969). For discussions of the archaeology of the sites, see R. Cramp, *Wearmouth and Jarrow Monastic Sites*, 2 vols, Swindon (2005-6); R. Cramp, 'A reconsideration of the monastic site of Whitby', in R.M. Spearman & J. Higgitt (eds), *The Age of Migrating Ideas: early medieval art in northern Britain and Ireland*, Edinburgh (1993), 64-74; R. Cramp & R. Daniels, 'New finds from the Anglo-Saxon monastery at Hartlepool, Cleveland', *Antiquity* 61 (1987), 424-32; D. O'Sullivan & R. Young, *Lindisfarne Holy Island*, London (1995); A.D. Phillips & B. Heywood (ed.), *Excavations at York Minster, Vol I: From Roman Fortress to Norman Cathedral*, London (1995). For sculpture from these sites, see *Corpus of Anglo-Saxon Stone Sculpture*, vols. 1 and 3.
2 J. Hawkes, 'Statements in stone: Anglo-Saxon sculpture, Whitby and the Christianization of the North', in C.E. Karkov (ed.), *The Archaeology of Anglo-Saxon England: basic readings*, New York (1999), 403-21.
3 See R. Cramp, 'Anglo-Saxon settlement', in J.C. Chapman & H.C. Mytum (eds), *Settlement in North Britain 100 BC–AD 1000*, British Archaeological Reports, British Series 118 (1983), 263-97.
4 W.G. Collingwood, 'A rune-inscribed Anglian cross shaft at Urswick church', *Transactions of the Cumberland and Westmorland Antiquarian and Archaeological Society*, 11 (1911). R.N. Bailey & R. Cramp, *Corpus of Anglo-Saxon Stone Sculpture, Vol II: Cumberland, Westmorland and Lancashire North-of-the-Sands*, Oxford (1988), 148-50.
5 W.G. Collingwood, 'A rune-inscribed Anglian cross', 465. On the Irton and Leeds crosses, see *Corpus of Anglo-Saxon Stone Sculpture*, vols. 2 and 8, respectively.
6 R.I. Page, *An Introduction to English Runes*, London (1973), 153-6.
7 W.G. Collingwood, 'A rune-inscribed Anglian cross', 465.

8 W.G. Collingwood, 'A rune-inscribed Anglian cross', 466. On Burton-in-Kendal see, On Kirkby Wharfe, see, On St Mary Bishophill Junior, see.

9 R.N. Bailey, *England's Earliest Sculptors*, Toronto (1996), 105f.

10 W.G. Collingwood, 'A rune-inscribed Anglian cross', 467.

11 See for example R.N. Bailey's discussion of the 'riddle' layout of the Ruthwell Cross, *England's Earliest Sculptors*, 61-5.

12 W.G. Collingwood, *Northumbrian Crosses of the pre-Norman Age*, London (1927), 39-55.

13 W.G. Collingwood, 'A rune-inscribed Anglian cross', 466.

14 R.N. Bailey, 'The sculpture of Cumberland, Westmorland and Lancashire-north-of-the-Sands in the Viking period', Vol. I, Unpublished Ph.D. thesis (University of Durham), 1974, 45-6.

15 *Bēcun* is the Northumbrian form of the OE *bēacen*, see J.R. Clark Hall, *A Concise Anglo-Saxon Dictionary*, 4th edition, Toronto (1960).

16 R.I. Page, *Introduction to English Runes*, 149-50; E. Coatsworth, *Corpus of Anglo-Saxon Stone Sculpture*, vol 8, Oxford (2008).

17 W.G. Collingwood, *Northumbrian Crosses*, 126; R. I. Page, *Introduction to English Runes*, 149; E. Coatsworth, *Corpus of Anglo-Saxon Stone Sculpture*, vol 8, Oxford (2008).

18 R.I. Page, *Introduction to English Runes*, 141-2; E. Coatsworth, *Corpus of Anglo-Saxon Stone Sculpture*, vol 8, Oxford (2008).

19 E. Okasha, *Hand-List of Anglo-Saxon Non-Runic Inscriptions*, Cambridge (1971), 118; E. Coatsworth, *Corpus of Anglo-Saxon Stone Sculpture*, vol 8, Oxford (2008).

20 W.G. Collingwood, *Northumbrian Crosses*, 59; E. Coatsworth, *Corpus of Anglo-Saxon Stone Sculpture*, vol 8, Oxford (2008).

21 E. Okasha, *Hand-List*, 129-30; J. Lang, *Corpus of Anglo-Saxon Stone Sculpture*, vol. 6, Oxford (2001), 266-9.

22 C.E. Karkov, 'The Bewcastle Cross: some iconographic problems', in C.E. Karkov, R.T. Farrell & M. Ryan (eds), *The Insular Tradition*, Albany (1997), 9-26.

23 See for example R.I. Page, 'The Bewcastle Cross', *Nottingham Medieval Studies* 4, 36-57; É. Ó Carragáin, 'Christ over the beasts and the Agnus Dei: two multivalent panels on the Ruthwell and Bewcastle crosses', in P. Szarmach & V.D. Oggins (eds), *Sources of Anglo-Saxon Culture*, Kalamazoo (1986), 37-43; É. Ó Carragáin 'A liturgical interpretation of the Bewcastle cross', in M. Stokes & T.L. Burton (eds), *Medieval Literature and Antiquities*, Cambridge (1987), 15-42; F. Orton, 'Northumbrian sculpture (the Ruthwell and Bewcastle monuments): questions of difference', in J. Hawkes & S. Mills (eds), *Northumbria's Golden Age*, Stroud (1999), 216-26.

24 W.G. Collingwood, *Northumbrian Crosses*, 58.

25 E. Okasha, *Hand-List*, 71-2; R. I. Page, *Introduction to English Runes*, 154; R. Cramp, *Corpus of Anglo-Saxon Stone Sculpture*, vol. 1, Oxford (1984), 172-3.

26 See C.P. Wormald, 'The uses of literacy in Anglo-Saxon England and its neighbours', *Transactions of the Royal Historical Society*, 27 (1977), 95-114; R. McKitterick, *The Carolingians and the Written Word*, Cambridge (1989), 4.

27 E. Okasha, *Hand-List*, 130; J. Lang, *Corpus of Anglo-Saxon Stone Sculpture*, vol. 6, Oxford (2001), 274-6.

28 W. Levison, 'The inscription on the Jarrow cross', *Archaeologia Aeliana*, 21 (1943), 121-6; R. Cramp, *Corpus*, vol. 1, 112-3; R. Bailey, *England's Earliest Sculptors*, Toronto (1996), 49-50.

29 E. Okasha, *Hand-List*, 52-3; R. Cramp, *Corpus*, vol. 1, 51-2.

30 R.I. Page, *Introduction to English Runes*, 117.

31 É. Ó Carragáin, 'A liturgical interpretation of the Bewcastle cross', 38; R. Bailey, *England's Earliest Sculptors*, 61-2.

32 R.I. Page, *Introduction to English Runes*, 98-118.

33 É. Ó Carragáin, *Ritual and the Rood: liturgical images and the Old English poems of the Dream of the Rood tradition*, London & Toronto (2005), 44.

34 P. Wormald, 'The uses of literacy in Anglo-Saxon England and its neighbours', *Transactions of the Royal Historical Society*, 27, 96. On the value of books and book ownership, see R. McKitterick, *The Carolingians and the Written Word*, Cambridge (1989), 135-64.

35 C. Farr, 'Questioning the monuments: approaches to Anglo-Saxon sculpture through gender studies', in C. Karkov (ed.), *The Archaeology of Anglo-Saxon England: basic readings*, New York (1999), 375-402.

36 R.N. Bailey, R.N. Bailey, 'The sculpture of Cumberland, Westmorland and Lancashire-north-of-the-Sands in the Viking period', Vol. I, Unpublished Ph.D. thesis (University of Durham), 1974, 45-6.

BIBLIOGRAPHY

BOOKS AND ARTICLES

Alcock, S. & Osborne, R. (eds) (1994), *Placing the Gods, Sanctuaries and sacred space in ancient Greece*, Clarendon

Alexander, M. (2002), *A companion to the folklore, myths and customs of Britain*, Sutton

Allen, J.R. (1892–95), 'The Early Christian Monuments of Cheshire and Lancashire', *Journal of Architectural and Archaeological Historical Society*, 5, Chester, pp. 133–74

Andrews, E. (1913), *Ulster folklore*, Elliot Stock

Andrews, E. (2006), *Faeries and folklore of the British Isles*, Arris

Arnold, J., Davies, K. & Ditchfield, S. (1998), *History and Heritage: Consuming the past in contemporary culture*, Donhead

Ashmore, W. & Knapp, A.B. (1999), *Archaeologies of Landscape: Contemporary Perspectives*, Oxford

Bailey, R.N. (1981), 'Scandinavian Myth of Viking Period Stone Sculpture in England', 11th International Saga Conference

Bailey, R.N. (1974), 'The sculpture of Cumberland, Westmorland and Lancashire-north-of-the-Sands in the Viking period', vol. I, unpublished PhD thesis, University of Durham

Bailey, R.N. (1977), 'A Cup Mount from Brougham, Cumbria', *Medieval Archaeology*, 21, pp. 176–180

Bailey, R.N. (1980), *Viking Age Sculpture in Northern England*, London

Bailey, R.N. (1989), 'What Mean These Stones? Aspects of Pre-Norman Sculpture in Cheshire and Lancashire', Bulletin of the John Rylands Library, pp. 21–46

Bailey, R.N (1993), *Saint Wilfrid's crypts at Ripon and Hexham, Newcastle-upon-Tyne: Society of Antiquaries*, Newcastle-Upon-Tyne

Bailey, R.N. (1996), *England's Earliest Sculptors*, Toronto: Pontifical Institute of Medieval Studies

Bailey, R.N. & Cramp, R. (1988), *Corpus of Anglo-Saxon Sculpture, II: Cumberland, Westmoreland and Lancashire North of the Sands*, Oxford

Beaumont, B. (trans.) (1985), *Flaubert and Turgenev: The complete correspondence*, Athlone Press

Bede (1969), *Historia Ecclesiastica, B.* Colgrave & R.A.B. Mynors (eds), Oxford

Bell, T. (1998), 'Churches on Roman Buildings: Christian Associations with Roman Masonry in Anglo-Saxon England', *Medieval Archaeology*, 42, p. 7

Bennett, W. (1947), *The History of Burnley*, Burnley Corporation

Benson, D. & Bland, K. (1963), 'The Dog Hole, Haverbrack', *Transactions of the Cumberland and Westmorland Antiquarian and Archaeological Society*, 63, pp. 61–76

Biddick, K. (1993), 'Decolonising the English Past: Readings in Medieval Archaeology and History', *Journal of British Studies*, 32:1, pp. 1–23

Blackshaw, P. (2001), *Healey Dell: a hidden history*, self-published

Blair, J. (1998), 'Minster Churches and Settlement formation in Anglo-Saxon England. A paper given to International Medieval Congress, Leeds', in R. Muir (2000) *The New Reading the Landscape,* Exeter

Blair, J. (1995), 'Debate: Ecclesiastical organization and pastoral care in Anglo-Saxon England', *Early Medieval Europe*, 4:2, pp. 193–212

Blair, J. (2005) The *Church in Anglo-Saxon Society*, Oxford

Blair, J. & Pyrah, C. (eds) (1996), *Church Archaeology: Research Directions for the Future*, CBA Research Report, 104

Blair, J. & Sharpe, R. (eds) (1992), *Pastoral Care Before the Parish*, Leicester: Leicester University Press

Bonner, G. (ed.) (1976), *Famulus Christi: studies in commemoration of the thirteenth centenary of the birth of the Venerable Bede.* London: SPCK

Bowker, J. (1883), *Goblin tales of Lancashire*, Sonnenschein. Available as an e-book from www.archive.org/details/goblintalesoflanoobowkiala

Bradley, J. (1990), 'Sorcerer or Symbol? Weland the Smith in Anglo-Saxon Sculpture and Verse' *Pacific Coast Philology*, 25:1/2, pp. 39–48

Bradley, R. (1993), *Altering the Earth*, Scotland: Society of Antiquaries

Bradley, R. (2000), *An Archaeology of Natural Places*, London: Routledge

Bradley, R. (2003), 'A life less ordinary: the ritualization of the domestic sphere in later prehistoric Europe', *Cambridge Archaeological Journal*, 13, pp. 3–23

Bradley, R. (2006), *Rock Art and the Prehistory of Atlantic Europe*, London & New York: Routledge

Bradley, R. & Williams, H. (eds) (1988), 'The Past in the Past: The Reuse of Ancient Monuments', *World Archaeology*, 30, London: Routledge

Branston, B. (1993), *The Lost Gods of England*, London: Constable

Brewer, T. (1995), *The Marketing of Tradition: Perspectives on tourism and the heritage industry*, Hisarlik

Briggs, K. (1967), *The Fairies in Tradition and Literature*, London: Routledge

Briggs, K. (1976), *A Dictionary of Fairies*, London: Penguin

Brooks, D. A. (1986), 'A Review of the Evidence for Continuity in British Towns in the 5th and 6th Centuries', *Oxford Journal of Archaeology*, 7, pp. 99–114

Brooks, D.A. (1988), 'The Case for Continuity in Fifth-Century Canterbury Re-examined', *Oxford Journal of Archaeology*, 7, pp. 99–114

Brown, I. (2002), 'More Seahenge', *3rd Stone*, 44, p. 65

Burl, Aubrey (1976, 2005), *The Stone Circles of Britain, Ireland and Brittany*, New York: Yale

Buxton, K. & Howard-Davis, C. (2000), 'Bremetenacum: Excavations at Roman Ribchester 1980, 1989–1990', *Lancaster imprints*, 9, Lancaster University Archaeological Unit

Calvert, J. (1984), 'The Iconography of the St Andrew Auckland Cross', *Art Bulletin*, 66:4, pp. 543–555

Cambridge, E. & Rollason, D. (1995), 'Debate: The pastoral organization of the Anglo-Saxon Church: a review of the 'Minster Hypothesis', *Early Medieval Europe*, vol iv 4:2, pp. 87–104

Cambridge, E. (1984), 'The early church in county Durham: a reassessment', *Jour Brit. Arch.. Assoc.* CXXXVII, pp. 65–85

Cameron, K. (1968), 'Eccles in English Place-names' in M.W. Bailey & R.P.C. Hanson (eds) *Christianity in Roman Britain*, Leicester, pp. 87–92

Cameron, K (ed.) (1977), *Place-name Evidence for the Anglo-Saxon Invasion and Scandinavian Settlements*, English Place-names Society

Cameron, K. (1988), *English Place-Names*, London

Campbell, J. (ed.) (1991), *The Anglo-Saxons*, London: Penguin

Carmichael, D.L., Hubert, J., Reeves, B. & Schanche, A. (eds) (1994), *Sacred Sites, Sacred Places*, London

Carr, J. L. (1977), *Lancashire, the County Palatine, Map*, Quince Tree Press

Carruthers, M. (1990), *The Book of Memory: A Study of Memory in Medieval Culture*, Cambridge: Cambridge University Press

Carver, M (ed.) (2003), *The Cross Goes North: Processes of Conversion in Northern Europe, AD 300–1300*, York: University of York

Cassidy, B. (ed.) (1992), *The Ruthwell Cross, Index of Christian Art: Occasional Papers 1*, Princeton University Press

Cassidy, B. (1996), 'The dream of St Joseph on the Anglo-Saxon Cross From Rothbury', *Gesta*, 35:2, pp. 149–155

Casson, S. (1932), 'Byzantium and Anglo-Saxon Sculpture I', *The Burlington Magazine for Connoisseurs*, 61:357, pp. 265–269 and 272–274

Clark, F. (2003), 'Wilfrid's Lands? The Lune Valley in its Anglian Context', paper delivered at Medieval Conference, Leeds University

Clark, F. (forthcoming), 'Thinking about Western Northumbria' in S. Turner & D. Petts (eds), *Early medieval Northumbria: current work and future directions*, Turnhout: Brepols

Clark Hall, J.R. (1960), *A Concise Anglo-Saxon Dictionary* (4th edn), Toronto

Coatsworth, E. (2008), *Corpus of Anglo-Saxon Stone Sculpture*, vol. 8, Oxford

Colgrave, B. (ed.) (1927), *The Life of Bishop Wilfrid by Eddius Stephanus*, Cambridge: Cambridge University Press

Colgrave, B. & Mynors, R.A.B. (eds) (1969), *Bede: Ecclesiastical History of the English People*, Oxford: Oxford University Press

Collingwood, R.G., & Wright, R.P (1995), *The Roman Inscriptions of Britain: I, Inscriptions on Stone; Epigraphic Indexes (Roman Inscriptions of Britain)*, Vol.1 (2nd edn), Stroud

Collingwood, W.G. (1911), 'A rune-inscribed Anglian cross shaft at Urswick church', *Transactions of the Cumberland and Westmorland Antiquarian and Archaeological Society*, 11

Collingwood, W.G. (1927), *Northumbrian Crosses of the pre-Norman Age*, London: Faber & Gwyer

Coombes, P.M.V. (2003), *The palaeoecology of Recent Human Impact in the Lake District*, PhD thesis. University of Southampton

Cope, Julian (1998), *The Modern Antiquarian: A Pre-Millenial Odyssey through Megalithic Britain*, London: Thorsons

Cowell, R.W. & Innes, J.B. (1996), *The Wetlands of Merseyside*, Lancaster: Lancaster Imprints 2

Cramp, R. (1966), 'The decoration', in B. Edwards, *A portion of an inscribed Pre-Conquest cross shaft from Lancaster. Medieval Archaeology*, 10, pp. 146–149

Cramp, R. (1977), 'The Mercian School of Sculpture', in A. Dornier (ed.), *Mercian Studies*, pp. 191–233

Cramp, R. (1983), 'Anglo-Saxon settlement', in J. C. Chapman & H. C. Mytum (eds), *Settlement in North Britain 100 BC–AD 1000, BAR British Series*, 118, pp. 263–297

Cramp, R. (1986), 'Anglo-Saxon and Italian Sculpture', *Settimane*, 32, pp. 125–40

Cramp, R. (1992) Studies in Anglo-Saxon Sculpture, Pindar: London

Cramp, R. (1999), *Grammar of Anglo-Saxon Ornament: Corpus of Anglo-Saxon Stone Sculpture*, London: British Academy Publications

Cramp, R. (2004), 'Whithorn and the Northumbrian Expansion westwards. Stranraer; Third Whithorn Lecture', North West Region Archaeological Research Framework Early Medieval Resource Assessment Draft

Cramp, R. (2005–6), *Wearmouth and Jarrow Monastic Sites*, 2 vols, Swindon

Cramp, R. & Daniels, R. (1987), 'New finds from the Anglo-Saxon monastery at Hartlepool, Cleveland', *Antiquity*, 61, pp. 424–432

Crawford, B. (ed.) (1996), *Scotland in Dark Age Europe*, Scotland: St Andrews

Crosby, A. (1998), *A History of Lancashire*, Chichester: Phillimore

Crosby, Alan A. (2007), *Of Names and Places: Selected Writing of Mary Higham*, English Place-name Society and the Society of Name Studies in Britain and Ireland

Crosby, A. (2000), *The Lancashire Dictionary of Dialect, Tradition and Folklore*, Smith Settle

De la Bédoyère, G. (2002), *Gods With Thunderbolts: Religion in Roman Britain*, Stroud: Tempus

Deshman, R. (1997), 'Another look at the Disappearing Christ: Corporeal and Spiritual Vision in Early Medieval Images', *Art Bulletin*, 79:3, pp. 518–546

Diebold, W. J. (2000), *Word and Image: An Introduction to Early Medieval Art*, Oxford: Westview

Dixon, J. & Jarvinen, J. (2004), *Journeys through Brigantia: Vol. 11. Circular walks in the East Lancashire Pennines*, Aussteiger

Dodgson, J. McN. (1970, 1971, 1981), *The Place-names of Cheshire, Various Volumes*, Cambridge: Cambridge University Press

Dodwell, C.R. (1982), *Anglo-Saxon Art: A New Perspective*, Manchester: Manchester University Press

Doyle, R. (1870), *In Fairyland: A Series of Pictures from the Elf-World*, Longmans: Green, Reader & Dyer

Dumville, D.N. (1997), *The Churches of North Britain in the First Viking Age*, Fifth Whithorn Lecture, Whithorn

Eberly, S.S. (1991), 'Fairies and the Folklore of Disability: Changelings, Hybrids and the Solitary Fairy', in P. Narváez Garland (ed.), *The good people: new fairylore essays*, New York: Garland

Eco, U. (1986), *Travels in Hyper-reality*, Picador

Edwards, B.J.N. (1973), 'A Canoe Burial near Lancaster', *Antiquity*, 47, pp. 298–301

Edwards, B.J.N. (1978), 'An Annotated Checklist of Pre-Conquest Sculpture in the Ancient County of Lancaster', *Lancashire Archaeological Journal*, 1, pp. 53–81

Edwards, B.J.N. (1999), 'Viking Influenced Sculpture in North Wales: its ornament and context', *Church archaeology*, 3, pp. 5–16

Edwards, B.J.N (1998), *Vikings in North West England: The Artefacts*, Lancaster: Lancaster University Press

Edwards, B.J.N. (2000), *The Romans in Ribchester, Discovery and Excavation*, Lancaster: Centre for North-West Regional Studies, University of Lancaster

Ekwall, E. (1922), *The Place-names of Lancashire*, Manchester: Chetham Society Series 81

Eyre, Kathleen (1974), *Lancashire Legends*, Dalesman

Farmer, D.H. (ed.) (1985), *The Age of Bede*, London: Penguin Classics

Farrell, R.T. & Ryan, M. (eds) (1997), *The Insular Tradition*, Albany

Farrer, W. & Brownbill, J. (1914), *The Victoria history of the counties of England, Lancashire*, London: Archibald Constable

Fellows-Jensen, G. (1985), *Scandinavian Settlements in the North West*, Copenhagen

Fields, K. (1998), *Lancashire Magic and Mystery*, Sigma Leisure

Fleming, A. (1983), 'The Prehistoric Landscape of Dartmoor. Part 2', *Proceedings of the Prehistoric Society*, 49, pp. 195–241

Fleming, A. (1978), 'The Prehistoric Landscape of Dartmoor. Part 1', *Proceedings of the Prehistoric Society*, 44, pp. 97–123

Foote, S. (2006), *Monastic Life in Anglo-Saxon England, c.600–900*, Cambridge: Cambridge University Press

Foote, P.G. & Wilson, D.M. (1980), *The Viking Achievement: The Society & Culture of Early Medieval Scandinavia*, London: Sidgwick & Jackson

Freke, D.J. & Thacker, A.T. (1987), 'Excavations at the inhumation cemetery at Southworth Hall Farm, Winwick

Cheshire in 1980', *Journal of the Chester Archaeological Society*, 70, pp. 31–38

Geake, H. & Kenny, J. (eds), *Early Deira: archaeological studies of the East Riding in the fourth to ninth centuries AD*, Oxford: Oxbow

Gelling, M. & Cole, A. (2000), *The Landscape of Place-Names*, Stamford

Gelling, M. (1978), *Signposts to the Past: Place-Names and the History of England*, London: JM Dent & Sons

Gem, R. (1993), 'Architecture of the Anglo-Saxon Church 735 to 870: From Archbishop Ecgberht to Archbishop Ceolnoth', *Journal of the British Archaeological Association*, 146, pp. 29–66

Gilchrist, A. (1863), *Life of William Blake Pictor Ignotus*, Cambridge: Cambridge University Press

Gilks, J.A. (1985), 'A note on the collared urn from Fairy Holes Cave, Whitewell, Lancashire', *Trans Lancs Cheshire Antiq Soc*, 83, pp. 188–193

Green, M.J. (2003), *The Gods of Roman Britain*, Princes Risborough: Shire Archaeology

Griffiths, A (1993), *Lancashire Folklore*, Leigh Local History Society

Grigson, G. (1987), *The Englishman's Flora*, Phoenix House, Dent

Grimm, J. & Grimm, W. (1948), *Complete Fairy Tales*. Routledge: reprinted 2002 (originally published in 1812–1822 in 3 vols as Kinder- und Haus Märchen)

Glasgow University Archaeological Division (2001), *An archaeological Excavation of Behalf of Historic Scotland, the National Museum of Scotland*, Highland Council and Ross and Cromarty Enterprise, Glasgow

Gurevich, A. (1988), *Medieval Popular Culture: Problems of Belief and Perception*, Cambridge: Cambridge University Press

Hadley, D. & Richards, J. (eds) (2000), *Cultures in Contact: Scandinavian Settlement in England in the 9th and 10th Centuries*, London: Turnout

Hall, R.A. (2000), 'Scandinavian Settlement in England – The Archaeological Evidence', *Acta Archaeologica*, 71, pp. 147–157

Hallam, J. (1970), 'The Prehistory of Lancashire', *Archaeological Journal*, 77, pp. 232–237

Halliwell, J.O. (1849), *Popular Rhymes and Nursery Tales of England*, Warne

Hamerow, H. & Macgregor A., (2001), *Image and Power in the Archaeology of Early Medieval Britain: Essays in Honour of Rosemary Cramp*, London: Oxbow

Hardwick, C. (1872), *Tradition Superstitions and Folklore: Chiefly Lancashire and the North of England*, Manchester: A. Ireland; Reprinted E.J. Morten 1973

Harland, J. & Wilkinson, T.T. (1867), *Lancashire Folk-lore*, Warne

Harland, J. & Wilkinson, T.T. (1873), *Lancashire Legends*, London: Routledge

Hartley, E. (1938), Heysham Head Fairy story: the Fairy Folk of Hessam, self-published

Harvey, D.C. (2000), 'Landscape Organisation, Identity and Change: Territoriality and Hagiography in Medieval West Cornwall', *Landscape Research*, 25:2, pp. 201–212

Harvey, D.C. & Jones, R. (1999), 'Custom and Habit(us): The meaning of Traditions and Legends in Early Medieval Western Britain', *Geografiska Annaler: Series B, Human Geography*, 81:4, pp. 223–233

Hauser, A (1959), *The Philosophy of Art History*, London: Routledge & Kegan Paul Ltd

Hauser, A. (1968), *The Social History of Art: Vol 1: From Prehistoric Times to the Middle Ages*, London: Routledge & Kegan Paul Ltd

Hawkes, J. (1996), 'The Rothbury Cross: An Iconographic Bricolage', *Gesta*, 35:1, pp. 77–94

Hawkes, J. (2002), *The Sandbach Crosses: An Iconographic Study*, Dublin

Hawkes, J. & Mills, S. (eds), *Northumbria's Golden Age*, Stroud

Henderson, G. (1972), *Early Medieval*, London: Harmondsworth

Henderson, G. (1985), 'The John the Baptist Panel on the Ruthwell Cross', *Gesta*, 24:1, pp. 3–12

Henig, M. (1984), *Roman Religion in Britain*, London: Routledge

Hewison, R. (1987), *The Heritage Industry*, Methuen

Higgit, J. (1986), Early *Medieval Sculpture in Britain and Ireland*, Oxford: Oxford University Press

Higham , N.J. (1979), *The Changing Past: Some Recent Work in the Archaeology of Northern England*, Manchester

Higham, N.J. (1986), *The Northern Counties to AD 1000*, London

Higham, N.J. (2001), 'Briton in Northern England in the Early Middle Ages: Through a Thick Glass Darkly', *Northern History*, XXXVIII:1

Higham, N.J. (2004), 'From Sub-Roman to Anglo-Saxon England: Debating the Insular Dark Ages', *History Compass*, 2 BI 085, pp. 1–29*

Higham, N.J. (2004), *A Frontier Landscape: The North West in the Middle Ages*, Windgather

Higham, N.J. (unpub), *Eccles Place-Names in the North West: Opportunities for Research*

Hill, P. (1996), *Whithorn and St Ninian: The Excavation of a Monastic Town 1984–91*, London: Sutton

Hird, F. (1911), *Old Lancashire Tales*, reprinted Book Clearance Centre, 2000

Hodgkinson D., Huckerby, E, Middleton, R. H. & Well, C. E. (2000), 'The Lowland Wetlands of Cumbria', *North West Wetlands Survey*, 6, Lancaster Imprints 8

Holm, J. & Bowker, J. (eds) (1994), *Sacred Place*, Pinter

Hooke, D. (1981), *The Anglo-Saxon Landscape of the West Midlands: The Charter Evidence, BAR British Series*, 95, Oxford

Hooke, D. (1985), *The Anglo-Saxon Landscape: The Kingdom of the Hwicce*, Manchester

Hooke, D. (1988), *Anglo-Saxon Settlements*, Oxford: Oxford University Press

Hunter, M. (1996), *Preserving the Past: The rise of heritage in modern Britain*, Alan Sutton

Hutton, R. (1999), *The Triumph of the Moon: A history of modern pagan witchcraft*, Oxford: Oxford University Press

Hutton, R. (2006), *The Pagan Religions of the Ancient British Isles: Their Nature and Legacy*, London: Blackwell

Ivakhiv, A.J. (2001), *Claiming Sacred Ground*, Indiana: Indiana University Press

Jakob Benediktson (ed.) (1986), *Islendingabok Landnamabok* (Penguin translation), Reykjavik

Jones, G. & Shotter, D. (1988), *Roman Lancaster: rescue archaeology in an historic city*, Manchester: University of Manchester

Kantorowicz, E.H. (1960), 'The Archer in the Ruthwell Cross', *Art Bulletin*, 42:1, pp. 57–59

Karkov, C, Larrat, S. & Jolly, K. (2006), *The Place of the Cross in Anglo-Saxon England*, Manchester: DS Brewer

Karkov, C. & Orton, F. (eds) (2005), *Theorising Anglo-Saxon Sculpture*, West Virginia University Press

Karkov, C. & Hardin Brown, G. (eds) (2003), *Anglo-Saxon Styles*, New York: State University of New York Press

Karkov, C.E. (ed.) (1999), *The Archaeology of Anglo-Saxon England*, New York

Karkov, C., Ryan, M. & Farrell, R.T. (eds) (1997), *The Insular Tradition*, New York

Kenyon, D. (1991), *The Origins of Lancashire*, Manchester: Manchester University Press

Kermode, P.M.C. (1907), *Introduction to Manx Crosses*, London: Bemrose & Sons Ltd

Kirby, D.P. (ed.) (1974), *Saint Wilfrid at Hexham*, Newcastle-upon-Tyne: Oriel Press

Kurth, B. (1945), 'The Iconography of the Wirksworth Slab', *The Burlington Magazine for Connoisseurs*, 86:506, pp. 114 and 116–121

Lachman, G.V. (2003), *A Secret History of Consciousness*, Lindisfarne

Lancashire County Council Environment Directorate (2007), *Lancashire Sites and Monuments Record*. List of SDM Monuments: Full Report

Lang, A. (1911), 'Fairy' in *Encyclopaedia Britannica* (11th edn), Cambridge: Cambridge University Press

Lang, J.T. (ed.) (1978), *Anglo-Saxon and Viking Age Sculpture and its Context*, Oxford: Oxford University Press

Lang, J.T. (1976), 'Sigurd and Weland in Pre-Conquest Carving from Northern England', *Yorks Arch Journal*, 48, pp. 83–94

Lang, J.T. (1984), 'The Hogback: A Viking Colonial Monument', *Anglo-Saxon Studies in Archaeology and History*, 3, pp. 85–176

Lang, J.T. (2001), *Corpus of Anglo-Saxon Stone Sculpture*, vol. 6, Oxford

Leclerq, J. (1974), *The Love of Learning and the Desire for God: A Study of Monastic Culture*, translated by C. Mishrahi, Fordham University Press

Levison, W. (1943), 'The inscription on the Jarrow cross', *Archaeologia Aeliana*, 21, pp. 121–126

Lofthouse, J. (1948), *Three rivers*, Hale

Lofthouse, J. (1976), *North-country Folklore in Lancashire, Cumbria and the Pennine Dales*, Hale

Loveluck, C. (2002), in Brooks, C., Daniels, R. & Harding, A., 'Past, Present and Future: The Archaeology of Northern England', *Durham Architectural and Archaeological Society of Durham and Northumberland Research Report*, 5, pp. 155–162

Lowenthal, D. (1985), *The Past is a Foreign Country*, Cambridge: Cambridge University Press

Lowenthal, D. (1996), *The Heritage Crusade*, Free Press

Mabey, R. (1996), *Flora Britannica*, Sinclair-Stevenson

Mackay, A.W. & Tallis, J.H. (1994), 'The Recent Vegetational History of the Forest of Bowland, Lancashire, UK', *New Phytologist*, 128, pp. 571–584

Magnusson, Magnus (transl) (1965), The Vinland Sagas Penguin

Makkay, J. (1995), 'The Treasures of Decebalus', *Oxford Journal of Archaeology*, 14:3, pp. 333–343

Mandler, P. (1997), 'Against "Englishness": English culture and the limits to rural nostalgia 1850–1940', *Transactions of the Royal Historical Society*, 6th series, vol vii pp. 155–175

March, H.C. (1891), 'The Pagan Christian Overlap in the North', *Trans Lancs Cheshire Antiq Soc*, 9, pp. 49–89

Marsh, J. (1982), *Back to the Land: The pastoral impulse in England, from 1880 to 1914*, Quartet

Marshall, A. (1976), *Healey Dell*, Lancashire Naturalists Trust

Mayr-Harting, H. (1991), *The Coming of Christianity to Anglo-Saxon England*, London

McKitterick, R. (1989), *The Carolingians and the Written Word*, Cambridge

Mills, A.D. (2003), *Oxford English Dictionary – British Place-names*, Oxford

Moreland, J. (1999), 'The World(s) of the Cross', *World Arch*, 31:2, pp. 194–213

Morris, C.D. (1977), 'Northumbria and the Viking Settlement. The evidence for land-holding', *Archaeologia Aeliana*, 5th series, 5, pp. 81–103

Morris, J. (1989), *The Age of Arthur: A History of the British Isles from 350 to 650 AD*, London: Weidenfeld & Nicholson

Morris, M. (ed.) (1983), *The Archaeology of Greater Manchester 1*, Manchester

Morris, R. (1989), *Churches in the Landscape*, London: Orion

Muir, B.J. & Turner A.J. (1998), *The Life of Saint Wilfrid by Edmer*, Exeter: University of Exeter Press

Muir, R. (2000), *The New Reading the Landscape: Fieldwork in Landscape History*, Exeter

Musson, R.C. (1947), 'A Bronze Age cave site in the Little Bolland area of Lancashire', *Trans Lancs Cheshire Antiq Soc*, 59, pp. 161–170

Nadin, J. (1991), 'Ghouls, demons and fairies in East Lancashire', *Burnley Express* article

Nevell, M. (1997), *The Archaeology of Trafford: a study of the origins of Community in North West England before 1900*, Manchester

Neuman de Vegvar, C. (1990), 'The Origin of the Genoels-Elderen Ivories', *Gesta*, 29:1, pp. 8–24

Newman, R. (ed.) (1996), *The archaeology of Lancashire: present state and future priorities*, Lancaster: Lancaster University Archaeological Unit

Newman, R. (ed.) (2004), *North West Archaeological Research Framework: Early Medieval Resource Assessment Draft*

Nicholls, P.H. (1972), 'On the evolution of a forest landscape', *Transactions of the Institute of British Geographers*, 56, No. 56 (July 1972) pp. 57–76

North, R. (1997), *Heathen Gods in Old English Literature*, Cambridge: Cambridge University Press

Ó Carragain, É. (2005), *Ritual and the Rood: liturgical images and the Old English poems of the Dream of the Rood tradition*, London & Toronto

Okasha, E. (1971), *Hand-List of Anglo-Saxon Non-Runic Inscriptions*, Cambridge

Orton, F. (2004), 'Northumbrian Identity in the 8th century: The Ruthwell and Bewcastle Monuments; Style, Classification, Class and the Form of Ideology', *Journal of Medieval and early Modern Studies*, 34.1, pp. 95–145

Orton, F. & Wood, I. (2007), *Fragments of History, Rethinking the Ruthwell and Bewcastle Monuments*, Manchester: Manchester University Press

O'Sullivan, D. & Young, R. (1995), *Lindisfarne Holy Island*, London

O'Sullivan, D. (1985), 'Cumbria Before the Vikings: a Review of Some "Dark Age" problems in north-west England', in J.R. Baldwin & I.D. Whyte (eds), *The Scandinavians in Cumbria*, Edinburgh, pp. 17–35

Owen, G. (1981), *Rites and Religions of the Anglo-Saxons*, Newton Abbott: David & Charles

Owen-Crocker, G. & Graham, T. (1998), *Medieval Art: Recent Perspectives*, Manchester: Manchester University Press

Page, R.I. (1960), 'The Bewcastle Cross', *Nottingham Medieval Studies*, 4, pp. 36–57

Page, R.I. (1973), *An Introduction to English Runes*, London

Parker, C.A. (1986), *The Ancient Crosses at Gosforth, Cumberland*, London

Parsons, D. (1975), *Tenth-Century Studies*, Chichester: Phillimore

Phillips, A.D.M. & Heywood, B. (ed.) (1995), *Excavations at York Minster, Vol I: From Roman Fortress to Norman Cathedral*, London

Phillips, A.D.M. & Phillips, C.B. (eds) (2002), *A New Historical Atlas of Cheshire*, Chester

Phillips, C.W. (1937), 'Some Stone Monuments', *Antiquity*, 11:43, pp. 294–299

Pickering, D. (1995), *Cassell's Dictionary of Superstitions*, Cassell

Padel, O. (1987), *The Parish Boundary*, London: Common Ground

Philpott, R.A. & Adams, M.H. (forthcoming), *Irby, Wirral: Excavations on a Late Prehistoric Romano-British and Medieval Site, 1987–96*

Philpott, R.A. & Cowell, R.W. (1992), *An Archaeological Assessment of land east of Telegraph Road Irby*, Liverpool Museums Archaeological Report

Pluskowski, A. (2002), 'Mapping neo-medieval forests in the popular Western imagination', *3rd Stone*, 44, pp. 22–27

Potter T. & Andrews, R. (1994), 'Excavation and survey at St Patrick's Chapel and St Peter's Church, Heysham', *The Antiquaries Journal*, 74, pp. 55–134

Potts, W.T.W. & Shirras, A.D. (2001–2), 'An Anglo-Saxon capital from Lancaster', *Contrebis* 26, pp. 6–8

Potts, W.T.W. & Shirras, A.D. (2001–2), 'An Anglo-Saxon stone from Halton', *Contrebis* 26, p. 9

Potts, W.T.W. (1994), 'Brettaroum, Bolton-le-Sands and the Late Survival of Welsh in Lancashire', *Contrebis* 26, p.19

Price, W.F. (1899), 'Notes on some of the places, traditions, and folk-lore of the Douglas Valley', *Trans of the Historic Soc of Lancs & Cheshire*, 51:15, pp. 181–220

Raw, B.C. (1967), 'The Archer, the Eagle and the Lamb', *Journal of the Warburg and Courtauld Institutes*, 30, pp. 391–394

Rawlinson, J. (1972), *About Rivington – A Description of One of the Prettiest Villages in Lancashire*, Chorley, Lancashire: Nelson Bros

Richardson, R.C. (2004), 'William Camden and the re-discovery of England', *Transactions of the Leicestershire Archaeological and Historical Society*, 78, pp. 108–123

Richmond, I.A. (1945), 'The Sarmatae, Bremetennacvm Veteranorvm and the Regio Bremetennacensis', *The Journal of Roman Studies*, 35:1&2, pp. 15–29

Rivet, A.L.F. & Smith, C. (1981), *The Place-Names of Roman Britain*, Cambridge: Cambridge University Press

Roby, J. (1829), *Traditions of Lancashire. Longman 2 vol. selection.* Reprinted *as Lancashire myths and legends*, by Book Clearance Centre, 2002

Roeder, C. (1907), 'Some Moston Folk-lore', *Trans Lancs & Cheshire Antiq Soc*, 25, pp. 65–78

Rosenthal, J.T. (1979), 'Bede's Ecclesiastical History and the material Conditions of Anglo-Saxon Life', *Journal of British Studies*, 19:1, vol 19, No.1 pp. 1–17

Russell, J.C. (1994), *The Germanization of Early Medieval Christianity: A Sociological Approach to Religious Transformation*, Open University Press

Salisbury, J.E. (ed.) (1993), *The Medieval World of Nature*, Garland Medieval Casebooks

Sahlqvist, L. (2001), 'Territorial Behaviour and Communication in a Ritual Landscape', *Geografiska Annaler, Series B, Human Geography*, 83:2, pp. 79–102

Samuel, R. (1984), *Theatres of Memory: Past and present in contemporary culture*, Verso

Sawyer, P.H. (1971), *The Age of the Vikings*, Oxford: Oxford University Press

Schama, S. (1996), *Landscape and Memory*, Harper Collins

Schapiro, M. (1944), 'The Religious Meaning of the Ruthwell Cross', *Art Bulletin*, 26, pp. 232–245

Schapiro, M. (1963), 'The Bowman and the Bird on the Ruthwell Cross and Other Works: The Interpretation of Secular Themes in Early Medieval Religious Art', *Art Bulletin*, 45:4, pp. 351–355

Schapiro, M. (1979), *Late Antique, Early Christian and Medieval Art*, US: George Brazillier

Schapiro, M. (1993), *Romanesque Art*, US: George Brazillier

Schapiro, M. (1998), *Theory and Philosophy of Art: Style, Artist & Society*, US: George Brazillier

Scragg, D. (ed.) (2003), *Textual and Material Culture in Anglo Saxon England*, Manchester: DS Brewer

Self Weeks, W. (1920), 'Further Legendary Stories and Folklore of Clitheroe District', *Lancashire & Cheshire Antiquarian Society Transactions*, 38, pp. 35–86

Semple, S. (1998), 'A Fear of the Past: The Place of the Prehistoric Burial Mound in the Ideology of Middle and Later Anglo-Saxon England', *World Arch*, 30:1, pp. 109–126

Shanks, M. (1991), *Experiencing the Past: On the character of archaeology*, London: Routledge

Sidebottom, P. (1997), 'Monuments that mark out Viking land', *British Archaeology*, 23, http://www.britisharch.co.uk

Silver, Carole G. (1999), *Strange and Secret Peoples: Fairies and Victorian Consciousness*, Oxford: Oxford University Press

Skeates, R. (2000), *Debating the Archaeological Heritage*, Duckworth

Smith, T.C. & Shortt, J. (1890), *The history of the parish of Ribchester, in the county of Lancaster*, London: Bemrose & Sons

Speake, G. (1980), *Anglo-Saxon Art and Its Germanic Background*, Oxford: Clarendon Press

Spearman, R.M. & Higgit, J. (eds) (1998), *The Age of Migrating Ideas: Early Medieval Art in Northern Britain and Ireland*, Edinburgh: National Museums Scotland

Spratt, D.A. (1991), 'Recent British Research on Prehistoric Territorial Boundaries', *Journal of World Prehistory*, 5:4, pp. 439–480

Standring, Robert (1882), *Healey Dell or, the history of fairies: meetings of the Fairy Queen and Healey Dwarf in the Fairy Chapel*, Rochdale: James Clegg

Stanley, E.G. (2000), *Imagining the Anglo-Saxon Past: The Search for Anglo-Saxon Paganism & Anglo-Saxon Trial by Jury*, Cambridge: DS Brewer

Steane, J.M. & Dix, B.F. (1978), *Peopling Past Landscapes, Council for British Archaeology*, London

Stenton, F.M. (1955), *The Latin Charters of the Anglo-Saxon Period*, Oxford

Stenton, F.M. (2001), *Anglo-Saxon England*, Oxford: Oxford University Press

Stokes, M. & Burton, T.L. (eds) (1987), *Medieval Literature and Antiquities*, Cambridge

Stone, A. (1999), 'Hogbacks: Christian and Pagan Imagery on Viking Age Monuments', *3rd Stone*, 33★

Stone, L. (1955), *Sculpture in Britain: The Middle Ages*, London: Penguin

Strong, R. (1996), *Country Life: 1897–1997: The English arcadia*, Boxtree

Swanton, M. (ed.) (1987), *The Dream of the Rood*, Exeter

Swanton, M. (trans. & ed.) (2000), *The Anglo-Saxon Chronicles: New Edition*, London: JM Dent

Szarmach, P. & Oggins, V.D. (eds) (1986), *Sources of Anglo-Saxon Culture*, Kalamazoo

Szarmach, P.E. & Rosenthal, J.T. (1997), *The Preservation and Transmission of Anglo-Saxon Culture*, Western Michigan: Medieval Institute Publications

Taylor, H. (1906), *Ancient Crosses and Holy Wells of Lancashire*, Manchester: Sherratt & Hughes

Thomas, C. (1971), *The Early Christian Archaeology of Northern Britain*, London

Thomas, J. (1999), *Rethinking the Neolithic*, Cambridge: Cambridge University Press

Thomas, K. (1983), *Man and the Natural World: Changing attitudes in England 1500–1800*, Allen Lane

Thompson, V. (2004), *Dying and death in later Anglo-Saxon England*, Woodbridge: The Boydell Press

Thornber, W. (1851–52), *Historic Society of Lancashire and Cheshire: Proceedings and Papers, Session IV*, Liverpool: Brakell

Tilley, C. (1994), *A Phenomenology of Landscape: Places, Paths & Monuments*, Oxford: Oxford University Press

Trench-Jellicoe, R. (1998), 'The Skeith Stone, Upper Kilrenny, Fife, in its context', *Proc Soc Antiq Scot*, 128, pp. 495–513

Trubshaw, B. (2005), *Sacred Places: Prehistory and popular imagination*, Heart of Albion Press

Tupling, G.H. (1949), 'The Pre-Conquest and Norman Churches of Lancashire', *Trans of the Lancs & Cheshire Antiq Soc*, 60, pp. 1–28

Wacher, J. (1981), *The Towns of Roman Britain*, London: Batsford

Wallis, J. (1921), 'Whalley Crosses', *Trans of the Lancs & Cheshire Antiq Soc*, vol 24, pp. 11–13

Webster, L. & Backhouse, J. (1991), *Anglo-Saxon Art & Culture, AD 600–900*, London: British Museum Press

Werner, M. (1990), 'The Cross Carpet page in the Book of Durrow: The Cult of the True Cross, Adomnan and Iona', *Art Bulletin*, 72:2, pp. 174–223

Westwood, J. (1985), *Albion: a Guide to Legendary Britain*, Granada

Westwood, J. & Simpson, J. (2005), *The Lore of the Land: a Guide to England's Legends, from Spring-Heeled Jack to the Witches of Warboys*, Penguin

Whitaker, T.D. (1872) (4th edn), *An History of the Original Parish of Whalley, and Honor of Clitheroe*, London: Routledge

Whitaker, T.W. (1980), *Lancashire Ghosts and Legends*, Hale

White, A. (1978) (4th edn), *Roman Lancaster*, Lancaster: Lancaster Museum

White, A. (1983–4), 'Anglo-Saxon coins from Lancaster', *Contrebis*, 11, pp. 46–49

White, A. (2001), 'Continuity, charter, castle and county town 400–1500', in White, A. (ed.), *A History of Lancaster*, Edinburgh: Edinburgh University Press

White, A. (2002–3), 'A previously unrecorded Anglo-Saxon stone fragment from Lancaster', *Contrebis*, 27, pp. 7–8

White, A. (2004), *A short history of St Margaret's church Hornby*, Arkholme: Contact

Whitelock, D. (1941), 'The Conversion of the Eastern Danelaw', *Saga Book*, 12/3, pp. 159–176

Williams, H. (1997a), 'Ancient Attitudes of Ancient Monuments', *British Archaeology*, No.29, p. 6

Williams, H. (1997b), 'Ancient Landscapes and the Dead: the reuse of Prehistoric and Roman monuments as early Anglo-Saxon burial sites', *Medieval Archaeology*, 41, pp. 1–32

Williams, J. (2003), 'Meyer Schapiro In Silos: Pursuing an Iconography of Style', *Art Bulletin*, 85:3, pp. 442–468

Williams, R. (1985), *The Country and the City*, Hogarth Press

Williamson, I.A. (1957), 'Extwistle Hall. Man saw Goblins carrying a Coffin bearing his own name', *Northern Daily Telegraph*

Williamson, P. (2001), *From source to sea: a brief history of the Lune Valley*, Upper Denby: Peter R. Williamson

Wilson, D.M. (1968), 'Archaeological Evidence for the Viking settlements and Raids in England', *Journal of the British Archaeological Association*, XXX, pp. 37–46

Wilson, D.M. (ed.) (1981), *The archaeology of Anglo-Saxon England*, London: Methuen

Wilson, D.M. (1984), *Anglo-Saxon Art from 7th Century to the Norman Conquest*, London: Thames & Hudson

Winchester, A. (1990), *Discovering Parish Boundaries*, Shire

Winterbottom, M. (1978), *Gildas, The Ruin of Britain and Other Works*, Chichester

Wittkower, R. (1971), *Sculpture: Processes and Principles,* London: Allen Lane

Wood, C. (2002), 'The meaning of Seahenge', *3rd Stone*, 43, pp. 49–54

Wood, I. (1987), 'Anglo-Saxon Otley: An Archiepiscopal Estate and its Crosses in a Northumbrian Context', *Northern History*, 23, p. 20

Wormald, C.P. (1977), 'The uses of literacy in Anglo-Saxon England and its neighbours', *Transactions of the Royal Historical Society,* 27, pp. 95–114

Worthington, A. (2004), *Stonehenge: Celebration and subversion,* Alternative Albion

Wright, P. (1985), *On Living in an Old Country,* Verso

WEBSITES

www.,britarch.ac.uk

www.healeydell.org.uk/fairies_chapel.html

www.jacknadin2.50megs.com/index.html

www.megalithic.co.uk

www.northernearth.co.uk

www.westlancsdc.gov.uk/countryside/index.cfm?ccs=125&cs=269

PROJECTS

Investigation of the Setting and Context of the Hilton of Cadboll Cross-Slab, Recovery of the Stump and Fragments of Sculpture. PROJECT 1078. D. Murray & G. Ewart, 2001 'GUARD'. Sponsors: (The Royal Commission on The Ancient and Historical Monnuments of Scotland) National Museum of Scotland, Highland Council

INDEX